The Illuminati Manifesto

The Illuminati Manifesto

Solomon Tulbure

Writers Club Press
San Jose New York Lincoln Shanghai

The Illuminati Manifesto

Writers Club Press
an imprint of iUniverse, Inc.

For information address:
iUniverse, Inc.
5220 S. 16th St., Suite 200
Lincoln, NE 68512
www.iuniverse.com

Under the authority of The Order of The Illuminati Council

ISBN: 0-595-21055-4

Printed in the United States of America

This book is dedicated to the men and women of the mind, to every enlightened human being, to all those who thirst and hunger for justice and freedom.

Contents

Foreword

For time immemorial various forms of evils and injustices have plagued human history. As time went by man has sought to find answers to questions, which were beyond his grasp. In the search for answers man has ignored the most important issues of life; those of justice, freedom and happiness. The wise amongst them sought to introduce various ideas as probable answers to the questions they knew they could not find answers to. Out of such fantastic ideas mankind gave birth to various forms of myths, which seemed good enough to be accepted as fact. But the results of such myths did not solve the problems of objective reality, the myths turned man against man, it gave rise to wars, which brought all forms of devastation upon the face of the earth.

Hidden within the depths of a savage human race were men and women of the mind, men and women who would later have to resolve to secret societies in order to protect themselves from the tyranny of the savage rulers of the times. Amongst the countless secret societies were the Illuminists, those who were courageous enough to challenge all accepted knowledge and seek the truth, not in myths but in the facts of reality. The Illuminati is once such group of people who survived the harsh hurricanes of human mindlessness and the tyrannies of those who sought to maintain absolute power of the human race.

Our vision and goals are clearly spelled out in this abridged version of our Manifesto, the core principles of what we represent. We had hoped to publish an unabridged version of our Manifesto, however, due to recent events and other reasons we have decided it is not yet the proper time to publish all of our protocols and perspectives. Perhaps in 50-100 years the rest of our protocols will find a more fertile ground and at such a time we will publish an unabridged Manifesto. Nevertheless, in order to squash the many lies that have been written about our organization we thought it necessary to put forth our imprint on the world scene once more.

It is the proper time, a perfect time to bring to light the truth of things with regards to our nature and our true intentions. This Manifesto is to be found in Part Two of this book. Part One contains essential reading materials written by Solomon Tulbure, a noble Master of the Light. Part Two is the abridged Illuminati Manifesto, which has been composed by Solomon, her majesty Osiris and Lady Diane of York. It is our hope that by publishing this book we will encourage others to join us, to see that perfect equality can be brought to our planet, that humanity can be united into a perfect union. It is our hope and vision that through enlightenment we can establish a universal love of humanity in the hearts and minds of each individual; that there is indeed an absolute moral standard. To establish a Golden Age and to save humanity from self-destruction we introduce this Manifesto to the masses as part of a phase with the sole purpose being the political transformation of the world. In time, humanity will know that we are the friends of truth, the sole saviors of the world, the only messiah mankind will ever have. It is our hope and aspiration it is our desire that this Manifesto will light the fire of reason in the minds of mankind; that men and women of the mind will join us in this most noble endeavor.

Acknowledgements

We would like to thank the Unseen Head and the Illuminati Council for entrusting us to be the chosen holders of the lamp, the ones to light the fire in the minds of men.

We also wish to thank the Circle of Light for its moral support.

Las but not least a special THANK YOU to our most treasured friends of the Orion System.

Introduction

In light of our success and with the growing number of worthless books written about us and our Freemason friends, we have decided that time is ripe for us to emerge to the forefront, at least in part, and in doing so we need to set the record straight once and for all.

First, a little brief insight into the origins of the Illuminati Order. This is not intended to be a concise history of the Order of The Illuminati but merely a snapshot of the truth of things with regards to important events in the history of our secret society. Pharaoh Sesostri the First had a son named Lidus, whom learned the ways of architecture and built many fabulous structures. He became very famous and many of the wealthy had paid him large fortunes to teach their sons the arts of Geometry and of architecture, how to build fabulous temples and homes for the wealthy. Lidius became very rich and famous and his school became renowned worldwide. Lidius had a love for exotic animals and birds and he used his wealth to establish for himself a little private zoo where he would spend much of his time, playing with various animals. It was during this time that he discovered he could transmit his thoughts and feelings to some of the animals, especially tigers, cattle, horses and many others.

He then told his servant Yaber, who he trusted with his life, about his new discovery and asked him if he could test his ability on him. As time went on the two discovered what is now known as "telepathy." Yaber, who ran Lidius' school of Masonry passed on this ability to those whom, took an oath to secrecy. As time went by they discovered that if they formed a triad they can induce thoughts and emotions into others whom were unaware they were being subjected to a psychological experiment. They visited temples where they would find sincere subjects whom were ripe for exploitation. The Telepathic Craft worked well, so well in fact that they were able to extract more money for their work from their clients. As they traveled, they spent many years working on major construction projects and the Masons sought to expand their brotherhood and establish powerful friends wherever they went. They decided to teach the craft to all that were wealthy and were in high positions. Priests and priestesses were prime candidates, as well as political leaders, kings and governors.

It was in Rome that the craft found fertile grounds, as well as in Greece. The pagan priests whom were initiated into the craft united into another secret society, which would take over the Roman government through religion. They formed regular triads in every temple, where the unsuspecting subjects were being brainwashed literally, with thoughts and emotion transmitted by the triads; the worshipers were feeling what they thought were spiritual or mystic experiences, when this in fact was nothing more than a trap. And so, the Church prospered. Kings became victims of triads, as well as any ruler in authority. This is how the Church obtained its power. The Craft found its way in many secret societies in just about every religion throughout the world, as time went by.

By the late 1600s Masonic lodges were abandoning the rules of the masters and all forms of infighting took place. The Masonic Brotherhood was to remain a secular institution, but renegades started their own Masonic Lodges, invented initiation rituals, and permitted just about anyone whom wished and had wealth or position of power to join their Lodges. The Church, even though it banished and denounced the Masonic Order, sent agents (Jesuit priests) to infiltrate the organization, which until the 1700 was comprised of secularists, philosophers and the educated elite and men of influence. In 1701 a group of friends gathered together at the house of a host whom had invited them to his birth day party. It is during this occasion, while the 13 of them were in the host' cellar admiring the fine wine collection and relaxing in the cool of the chamber that the issue of politics and religion was brought up. These wealthy friends decided then and there to seek out all the Masons whom were atheists, deists, agnostics and freethinkers and initiate them into "a circle of friends" with the goal to eradicate religion and seek to free man kind from the chains of superstition. The new initiates were taught the art of the Craft and learned to master it and use it to find potential new recruits.

Adam Weishaupt was soon called before the council and asked if he would be the "Initiator of the Order" later to be known as The Illuminati Order. Weishaupt was very successful, as he had deep and far-reaching connections as well as close friendship with the Enlightened Masons of Europe. He set up many Illuminati Lodges within the European Lodges, and charged a group of loyal friends to start Lodges in America and recruit every liberal minded person of notoriety. The Circle of Friends already had special friends in America and the founding fathers of the US constitution were among the strongest Illuminists, having recruited many industrialists and bought many others with funds provided by the Circle of Friends. John Adams had established many institutions in France, Germany, and England, after which the Illuminati were ordered to operate from deep underground cover.

When the Church flexed its muscles and ordered the Jesuits to seek the destruction of the Illuminati throughout Europe, the Illuminati Council had ordered Weishaupt to seek out and provide shelter for all our European agents. As time went on, the Masonic brotherhood became more and more of a social club and even today, it is nothing more than that. During the 1950s many of the Jesuits had begun to teach the craft to other religious leaders and just about anyone whom had lots of money. While we were in a state of absolute war with the Church and the socialists, the order shared a common secret, the craft of telepathy. Both sides has thousands of Telepathic Masters and no matter how much we were seeking each other's destruction, we were unwilling to teach the craft to irresponsible persons, especially religious persons. What alarmed us is the discovery that many preachers have acquired the craft and many others whom used it to practice what is now known as "psychic" powers. None of the psychics have any mysterious powers other than telepathy, which is quite normal, and all humans posses the ability. We discovered later on that the Jesuits were teaching even ordinary people the craft, in order to use them as servants and do other dirty work or to seduce children for sexual exploitation.

When the Vatican decided to have the VIA (Vatican Intelligence Agency) ordered the liquidation of one of our dear friends, John F. Kennedy, because he was preparing to expose the Church and the Jesuits, we declared an all out war against the Vatican. Many people in the world have no idea how powerful the Catholic Church actually is. If Catholics knew how few of the Catholics priests actually believe in god, they would be shocked.

In 1971 the Council decided to separate the men from the boys, so to speak, within the Masonic brotherhood and to put to real tests those whom came to our side. All Enlightened Freemasons were asked to start other secret organizations and to recruit the Mossad, MI5 and other Intelligence services to form triads with our other Intelligence agencies. It was during this time that the Jesuits set up shop in the Middle East and began to train Muslim clerics in the craft, whom in turn use the craft to turn loyal subjects into complete robots, to carry out suicide attacks against our Jewish friends and the western world.

With the birth of the Internet we have finally discovered the medium to initiate the Illuminati Order recruitment efforts publicly and with fewer secrets, now that we have achieved much of what we had worked so hard for; the spreading of the gospel of reason. Time has come to initiate the second (and third) phase of our struggle, the struggle for freedom from religion and superstition, freedom from tyrannical governments, theocracies and dictatorship. We have fashioned the US and many other nations and prepared the world for what is to come in the next 50-100 years. It is during this time that much of our vision will become reality, and prepare the way for the final phase, which shall remain secret for the time being.

This is the great secret of the Church and the mystics and all the looters and tyrants who sought to extinguish the atheists and Illuminists. The Church' dress has been raised, we have uncovered her nakedness. Now people are to know what is the power behind the power of the Church. If you are a Catholic, or religionists of any kind, now you know why you feel "spiritual" connection or experience during religious services and especially during songs in church etc.

There are triads in large churches transmitting telepathic messages to all the unsuspecting subjects and individual preachers doing the same in their small churches and the same in Synagogues and Mosques, especially when they need money. Here is a test for you. Walk into any Catholic Church 15 minutes before Mass, or before regular Sunday services and we bet you will feel a sense of gentle fear mixed in with a sense of mystery. This is because telepathic messages can be recorded and played back as you can any other recording. Telepathy works at the quantum level, utilizing all forms of quantum waves. Telepathic transmissions piggybacks onto just about any form of artificial energy.

Soon our scientists will have measuring devices, which can measure quantum waves with extreme precision and then you all will have your so much desired scientific evidence. But, to the skeptics, we have provided you with basic instructions for learning how to develop and use your telepathic ability. Try it and see for yourself.

We have decided to make this public as a final blow to our greatest enemies, the Church and the Mystics. Now the Church' singular power, aside from its great wealth, has been revealed, the secret is out and the destruction of the Church will soon be realized. Telepathy takes a while to learn, use and master, but after thousands of telepathy students master it and come forward, more people will seek it and the Church will no longer be able to eavesdrop into the minds of their slaves to get them to donate money. The Church will be striped of its clothes completely, soon enough.

So there you have it! The Illuminati is alive and well, and always has been. We were underground, but no longer. Our secrets are now fewer and of a different nature. All types of authors as evil have portrayed us. Yes, we are evil, as far as they are concerned. We seek to eliminate all the churches, synagogues and mosques and all those whom brainwash our young with mystical baloney and enslave the minds of men and women with religion and false virtues. If that is what they mean by evil, in that we seek their destruction, then yes, we are evil. We are pro-freedom, religion is anti-freedom. If we could have gotten away with a clearer US constitution we would have done so, but the religious atmosphere prevalent in the population of that time did not permit it. But make no mistake about it; all of the founding fathers were Illuminati as well as Masons. They all played a crucial role in shaping the future for the better. None of them were Christians, and only a few of them were deists. The rest were Atheists, Freethinkers and Agnostics.

So the next time you hear an American Patriot speak of the founding fathers in a positive light, call him or her a hypocrite to their face, because the American patriots are Christians, and religionists.The US Constitution is pro freedom, not pro theocracy. Christianity, Judaism and Islam especially, stand directly against EVERYTHING our Constitution stands for. The Church (Catholic) is seeking unification with other faiths so it can strengthen itself financially, because is uses money to bribe politicians and UN officials to pass laws favorable to itself. It uses OPEC to grant favors to oil companies, which are owned by under cover Jesuits.

The pope no longer has any clothes.

The following is only for those whom know what it means, so ignore it.

The time is near, the time is here, and the time has come.

The time has come, the time is near, and the time is here.

The time is here, the time has come, and the time is near.

Part One

Illuminati on Religion

Part one of this book includes some Essays on religion by Solomon Tulbure. This is essential readin in order to prepare one for the understanding of much of the Illuminati Manifesto (abridged).

"I see a very dark cloud on America's horizon, and that cloud is coming from Rome" **Abraham Lincoln**

*******What Loving God?*******

The Christians, (Jews and Muslims) especially, insist that their imaginary god is a wonderful wholly good loving and merciful god. Furthermore, they would have us believe that the "Holy Bible" (sic) is full of ethical and superior moral teachings. They further tell us that without god, there are no morals, that the fact that there are morals is evidence that there is a God; a source of all morals and ethics. They tell us that the Bible is the "Book of Life" and contains the rules by which man can achieve happiness both here on earth and in an imaginary afterlife.

1

I wrote this essay, as I would converse with you on a one on one verbal conversation. I want to communicate with you as a rational human being to another. If you are one of those who thinks she/he knows everything already, and has the truth, this essay will not help you in any way, so don't bother reading it. This is written for those who are rational and open minded, for those who think themselves intelligent enough to make their own decisions in life. This essay is not written for "sheep" or followers but for individuals who value intelligence, wisdom, freedom and knowledge; for those who sincerely seek to know the truth of things from a rational point of view.

In this essay, I will prove beyond the shadow of a doubt that the imaginary god of the Christians, Muslims and Jews (like all Gods) is not only immoral, but also a tyrant. Now, please note that when I speak of their god I am referring to the imaginary god which religion demands that people believe in without any proof; I am not speaking of a "real god" because no such beast exists.

> In Exodus 34:6 we are assured that god is "merciful and gracious, longsuffering, and abundant in goodness and truth..."

The question is what does it mean to be merciful. Longsuffering, gracious, abundant in goodness and truth? What does this really mean? The reason this question is important will become clear very soon. Another question: Is god good? If so, what does it mean for a god to be **good**? Does the word **good** mean something else than what it means when we refer to humans as good? Are we supposed to make an exception on the meaning of the word good, when we apply it to god? And yet another question: Is god **moral**? If god is moral, is he moral in a human sense or in a godly sense? Does god live up to our moral standards and then surpass them, or does god bypass our moral standards or the standards he supposedly set up for us? Should a god live up to what he preaches or can he do whatever the hell he wants simply because he is god? If doing whatever the hell he wants is part of the characteristics of god, then how does a god qualify for being worthy of being called a god and worthy of worship?

I could have asked these questions throughout the essay within better context of certain paragraphs but I asked them ahead of time so as to give you an idea what the rest of this essay will cover. The Christian will quickly argue that one "needs god's spirit" to understand the Bible and god. It is not my intention to debate that argument, or to refute it in this essay. In this essay I will only deal with common sense; with what we as rational human beings consider common sense. Although I do not agree with the term and concept of "common sense" as it is a smoke screen, I do know what people mean when they use that term and concept.

Let me start with a simple outline of the meaning of the word "good" as is understood and accepted by all human beings in the general sense (common sense). The word "good" simply means "honorable", "virtuous", and "benevolent". In other words, a person who has respect for others and human life is considered good, and I accept that summary as well. I think we can all agree that intentional inflicting of pain and suffering on human beings, especially innocent ones, is evil and the unjustified taking of human life is also evil and cruel.

In other words, someone who commits crimes such as rape, murder, genocide, enslavement or child abuse etc. is evil as far as rational human beings are concerned. As rational human beings, it is fair to say that we can be proud of having such morals and ethics, don't you agree?

So then, it is fair to say that a "god" would not support or engage in such crimes, and if there is a god who would be worthy of worship, it would have to at least meet these basic human standards and then may be even supersede them. A god must be worthy of worship and so, such a god would not disagree with us on these: "The Lord is good to all...the glorious majesty of your splendor...men shall talk of your awesome deeds...will recount your greatness...The Lord is gracious and compassionate...SLOW to anger and abounding in kindness...The Lord is beneficent in all his ways...".

We are told that god abhors such crimes as I mentioned above, and the New Testament (The Christian Bible) tells us that all those evil deeds are "works of the flesh". Now let's take a look at "The Word of God" with regards to such crimes.

> ¹And the LORD spoke to Moses, saying: ²"Take vengeance on the Midianites for the children of Israel.... ⁷And they warred against the Midianites, just as the LORD commanded Moses, and they killed all the males...⁹And the children of Israel took the women of Midian captive, with their little ones, and took as spoil all their cattle, all their flocks, and all their goods...¹²Then they brought the captives, the booty, and the spoil to Moses,... ¹⁴But Moses was angry with the officers of the army...¹⁵And Moses said to them: "Have you kept all the women alive?..."Now therefore, kill every male among the little ones, and kill every woman who has known a man intimately. ¹⁸"But keep alive for yourselves all the young girls who have not known a man intimately...²⁵Now the LORD spoke to Moses, saying: ²⁶"Count up the plunder that was taken—of man and beast—you and Eleazar the priest and the chief fathers of the congregation; ²⁷"and divide the plunder into two parts, between those who took part in the war, who went out to

battle, and all the congregation…[31]So Moses and Eleazar
the priest did as the LORD commanded Moses.

Notice that god did not simply take a passive role in the rape,
murder, enslavement and gross child abuse here but actually
commanded it! The men are slaughtered as revenge, their wives
slaughtered for the crimes of being wives and the male innocent
children from those a day old and up were slaughtered and the virgins
were enslaved and raped by the Israelites. By the way, the name of the
god mentioned above is "Jesus".

Civilized: People who are advanced in social customs, the arts and
science; persons who are enlightened, cultivated and developed; people
who show culture and good manners. A civilized person is one who has
given up on being ignorant and a savage and has adopted good laws and
customs and has acquired knowledge of the arts and science. A civilized
person is one who lives according to high moral standards, has become
highly educated and continuously refines his ways through experience
and experiment.

To an enlightened person crime such as rape, murder, genocide,
enslavement or child abuse is abhorrent. A civilized person considers
such crimes as among the most despicable and the most evil of all. The
US Constitution was written and developed by enlightened human
beings that were NOT inspired by any bible god; this is made clear in
the 13th amendment where slavery is forbidden.

While the believers are forced to admit that their imaginary god
commanded this war, they may attempt to excuse god from having been
responsible of what happened after the war. They will try and blame
that on Moses and his people as having acted independently. However,
the Bible also says that Moses was god's friend and that Moses was full
of god's spirit. If it takes the spirit of god to accept these crimes as
acceptable, than I rather not have such a spirit, thank you very much; I
rather remain rational and continue to see these crimes as abhorrent. If

god's spirit can somehow make me see these crimes as justified, then god can keep his spirit and shove it up his ass.

Furthermore, a god worthy of respect would be one who intervenes in human affairs in order to stop wars and slaughtering and not to command such wars. Such would be a god abundant in goodness; one who intervenes to put a stop to pain and suffering not condones and sanction it.

Notice that god not only commanded this massacre, but also went on to reward his "holy people" (sic) with the plunder. The women and children of the Medianites were innocent and helpless, yet neither god nor Moses has any mercy on them what so ever. In Deuteronomy 32:4 we are told that god is "just and right". If this is what justice according to god and the believer and the bible means, then I would like to know what more horrendous crimes and injustice can Satan put out. If a loving god can command such horrific crimes, what worse crimes are available to Satan to perform? Would some "spirit filled" Christian **please** answer this question for me?

What is also shocking about this war commanded by god is the mere reason behind it-vengeance. In the New Testament, the Catholics scribes had to try to fix up the problematic inconsistencies and they added such verses as "He who does not love does not know God, for God is love."

Well, I do love those who I value, but I do not know god and do not wish to know this monster. There was a time when I wanted to know god, and was a sincere believer; I whole heartedly sought to know the ways of god, and now that I do, I realize that there is no such a monster and if there was, I'd spit in his face and demand his execution.

I once said and will say it again: Religious people are only as good as their god(s). This is because people invent gods; they are fairy tales to say the least.

> "You shall not take vengeance, nor bear any grudge against the children of your people, but you shall love your neighbor as yourself: I *am* the LORD."

The above verse is a racist verse in that it is speaking only of Jewish/Israelite neighbors. This is obvious from the way god commanded his people to treat their Medianite neighbors.

It is important to note that the Bible as well as Christianity teaches that "god does not change." In light of this let's look at yet another attempt to change god, to make him a loving god, to fix god so he is no longer a tyrant.

"But I say to you, love your enemies, bless those who curse you, do good to those who hate you…"

We are told that the above words are the words of the same god, Jesus, the god of the Bible. The Roman Catholic scribes were faced with a major problem and in inventing their new religion, they had to get creative. They had to transform the god of the Bible from a tyrant to a lesser tyrant, one who would appear more civilized. But because there were many manuscripts of what was attributed to Jesus, they were unable to get rid of the Mark 10:18 verse and others like it.

> "So Jesus said to him, "Why do you call Me good? No one *is* good but One, *that is*, God."

So, the Christians are still stuck with a god who is a monster. The meaning of the word "good" we are told, means something else when we apply it to "God" the All Mighty God. God, we are told, is permitted to be a tyrant and a monster. Why? "Because he is god, he can do anything he wants." No wonder the Christians found justification for slaughtering over 70 million people during the crusades and inquisition.

> "'But bring here those enemies of mine, who do not
> want me to reign over them, and slay *them* before me.'

The above words are the words of Jesus, the God of the New Testament and the Old. Like father like son. The above words and attitude of GeeZus are no different that Hitler's or any communist or religious leader throughout history. What I find most shocking is that the believers defend the Median affair by stating that what was done to the Medianites was a **good** deed and the reason we do not see it as **good** is because "God works in mysterious ways." The believer argues that god is wholly good and incapable of doing evil.

> "And the Lord said, Because the cry of Sodom and
> Gomorrah is great, and because their sin is very grievous; I
> will go down now, and **see** whether they have done
> altogether according to the cry of it, which is come unto
> me; and if not, I **will** know."

Notice here that god admits not knowing if the accusations brought against Sodom and Gomorrah are true. He does not know, so he has to "go down" and see for himself. The believer teaches that god is "all-knowing" yet here god says that he will not know until he goes down and only then he "will know." One of the characteristics assigned to god by the believers is that god is omniscient. Clearly this is not true, for how can he **not know** something if he is omniscient.

Now, let's go back to the subject of the "goodness" of this almighty god. We are here told that two angels of god came to Lot's house. Some men of Sodom came over and surrounded Lot's house and demanded that Lot give up the two men who came to visit him, so they can have sex with them.

> "And they called unto Lot...Where are the men which
> came in to thee this night? bring them out unto us, that we
> may know them."

Lot then offers his two virgin daughters to them instead and he goes on to encourage them to do as they please with them, as long as they do not insist on harming the men who came to visit. Then, when the men attempted to break down the door to get to the two men, the visitors, who were supposed to be god's powerful angels strike the men with blindness. NOTICE that the angels did not strike them with blindness until after they had ravaged Lot's two virgin daughters. The angels did not see it important to use their powers to save the two girls, but only used their godly powers when they "the men" were in trouble.

What I find shocking is what it says next: "And while he lingered, the men (angels) took hold of his hand, his wife's hand, and the hands of his two daughters, **the LORD being merciful to him**, and they brought him out and set him outside the city."

The Lord was merciful to a man who just gave up his innocent and virgin daughters, his own children, to be raped! Not only do these so called angels fail to save the two daughters, but the Lord shows mercy to a despicable man like Lot, yet the Medianite women and children were not worthy of god's mercy. What we have here is a god who pardons the guilty in his godly justice but condemned the innocent. Furthermore, the punishment of the Sodomites was torture by fire, which is cruel and unusual punishment. No matter how heinous a crime, civilized people do not resolve to torture under any circumstances.

> "Now *when* the people **complained**, it displeased the
> LORD; for the LORD heard *it,* and His anger was aroused. So

the fire of the LORD burned among them, and consumed *some* in the outskirts of the camp. Numbers 11:1"

Murder, rape, enslavement, and child abuse are indeed heinous crimes but what took place above was mere complaining, hardly a capital offense. What we have here is god torturing and executing people simply for exercising their freedom of speech. The people were in the desert at this time and this so called almighty god was feeding them the same old crap day after day for months on in. The people followed this monster called god and he feeds them the same food over and over. You try eating the same food for weeks and months every day 3 times a day and see if you can bare it. Then, instead of god being merciful and kind to the people (his own people) he executes anyone who asks for descent food. This is pretty much what communists do with anyone who speaks against the dictator or the state. I should know, I was born and raised in communist Romania.

"We remember the fish which we ate freely in Egypt, the cucumbers, the melons, the leeks, the onions, and the garlic; 6"but now our whole being is dried up; there is nothing at all except this manna before our eyes!"

Here god equated freedom of speech with murder, rape and genocide. What a loving, merciful and just god! Don't you agree? The believers will quickly try to defend god in this regard by claiming that the people were evil in that they were not grateful for having been saved from bondage, or having lack of faith in god to provide them with their needs. An all knowing god, an omniscient and benevolent god would have known that the people are sick and tired of eating the same crap over and over and would have provided for the needs of the people before they became agitated and sick to their stomachs of the crap he was feeding them. But the important question is: Exactly how does lack of faith and ingratitude equate to a capital offense? How are these equal with rape, child abuse, genocide and slavery, or of offering one's own daughters to rapists? Why should lack of faith and ingratitude even be a crime?

"'And if by these things you are not reformed by Me, but walk contrary to Me, 24then I also will walk contrary to you, and I will punish you yet **seven times for your sins**…I will send pestilence among you; and you shall be delivered into the hand of the enemy…and I, even I, will chastise you **seven times for your sins**…You shall eat the flesh of your sons, and you shall eat the flesh of your daughters…"

Don't you think it is ironic even to contemplate punishing someone seven times for the same crime? Does this god merit to be called good? Is this god worthy of respect? Is the bible anything more than a cruel joke? Can any sane and rational and civilized person regard such a neurotic as being worthy of worship? Can any sane person defend such atrocities as sanctioned by this evil tyrant? If you are one of those who defends the bible and this so called god, **please** go jump off a bridge?

Child abuse is a recurring theme in the Old Testament, with both God and his prophets seeming to lack the respect due children in general. God's role in the killing of the Midianite children and of the children, who presumably lived in Sodom and Gomorrah as well, I have discussed already. In Lev. 26:22 God threatens to "send wild beasts among [the Israelites], which shall rob [them] of [their] children…", and in Jer. 6:11 the prophet warns that even children are not exempt from the Lord's wrath:

"Therefore I am full of the fury of the LORD. I am weary of holding *it* in. "I will pour it out on the children outside…" Jeremiah 6:11

Are we to believe that these are the words of godly man? Is Jeremiah a man of god? YES! In fact, Jeremiah is a godly man. He is as neurotic as his imaginary god and he is a true follower of his god. He and his god both suffer from neuroticism. That is what it means to have "the spirit of god" within; it means one has to become a moron and a tyrant, to ignore logic and reason and to become godly.

"Therefore thus says the LORD: "Behold, I will lay stumbling blocks before this people,
And the fathers and the sons together shall fall on them. The neighbor and his friend shall perish." V. 21

This man of god wishes for the innocent children of the people who do not listen and believe what he says, to be slaughtered. This is "godly justice". Godly people seem to believe that those who do not listen to them and believe like them are worthy of death; not only them, but the innocent children as well. That is holy justice, biblical justice, and godly justice. That is what it means to be good and just, according to the holy (sic) bible.

"Thus says the LORD of hosts: 'I will punish Amalek *for* what he did to Israel, how he ambushed him on the way when he came up from Egypt. ³'Now go and attack Amalek, and utterly destroy all that they have, and do not spare them. But kill both man and woman, **infant and nursing child**, ox and sheep, camel and donkey.' "

This is the god the Christians, Muslims and Jews worship ladies and gentlemen. This is the imaginary monster they call "good", "rich in kindness" "eternally merciful", "just", "benevolent" and "love".
Notice that even animals were somehow guilty of some sort of crime. Genocide was to be total and absolute. I declare this god, a psychopath, and the bible worthless garbage not even worthy to be used for toilette

paper and anyone who defends this crap is a neurotic and a monster who must be eliminated.

Getting back to the "omniscient" thing, the bible says that god had to test Abraham's faithfulness. God was not sure if Abraham was sincerely faithful, so he has Abraham sacrifice his own son. Now, of course this story never happened; we need not believe it did happen when we consider the source. However, consider what this story does to a person who believes in this savage text as being of an infinitely intelligent god. Think about the psychological ramification with regards to the mental conditioning and health to the believer? I'll let you figure it out.

Jesus Again

"Then out of the smoke locusts came upon the earth. And to them was given power, as the scorpions of the earth have power. 4They were commanded not to harm the grass of the earth, or any green thing, or any tree, but only those men who do not have the seal of God on their foreheads. 5And they were not given *authority* to kill them, but **to torment them** *for* **five months. Their torment** *was* **like the torment of a scorpion when it strikes a man."** Revelations 9:3-5

Here, we are told that in the future, the holy god will torture people, simply because they refuse to be submissive to this tyrant, for refusing to believe in this monster and for refusing to revere him. This is the justice set forth by a "wise god", "a good god" who is infinitely intelligent we are told. I'll take the torture gladly rather than to consider this worthless piece of shit worthy of any sort of respect.

The next time you hear a Christian claim that the United States is a "Christian Nation" do me a favor and spit in his/her face. The US Constitution protects the freedom of religion. DoG does not. He commands the torture of all that do not worship him alone. The US Constitution is a document, which promotes justice, freedom and earthly happiness for all; the bible teaches exactly the opposite. The US Constitution was written by Atheists, Freethinkers and deists, all of who were members of the Illuminati Order; an organization of moral and civilized men and women. Savages, tyrants and idiots wrote the unholy bible.

****

*******Religion: The Root & Cause of Evil*******

What you are about to read is an honest analysis of the way things are and why they are the way they are as far as "evil" is concerned. From the average person to the news media and the very politicians and government leaders, all have ignored the very real and true cause of most evil: religion. We live in an age when everyone teaches tolerance and political correctness; a time when criticism is considered bad or evil and everyone is put down and ridiculed if one criticize anyone. These might sound nice on the surface, but what does it mean to be tolerant and politically correct? Politicians live by the power of persuasion, smoke screens, lies and deception. There is not one single sincere politician (Illuminati and Masons not included here) in the world today, not even one. This political philosophy has spread to the masses, to the populations at large.

In this essay I will focus on the real cause of evil in all areas of life and will show why things are the way they are and in my conclusion I will give my opinion on how we can resolve this problem of evil. I think we can all agree that poverty is the main contributor to all sorts of evils, such as crime, hunger, suffering of all sorts and even mental illness can be attributed to poverty at least in part. But where does poverty come from? Who creates poverty? Who is responsible for poverty? Is there an invisible poverty factory?

As you shall see, people create poverty and not some invisible ghost or an uncontrollable invisible force; people are the factory of poverty, and religion is the root cause of poverty. Religion is the cause not only of poverty but also acts as an insurance agent to ensure that poverty continues to grow and spread. While all religion is responsible for poverty, I will focus on the two religions, which are directly responsible for all of the poverty in the world in the last 200 years, namely, Christianity and Islam.

The Source Of Wealth

First, let's consider the source of wealth and how wealth is created. This is very important because without understanding the real nature of wealth creation, the real way to "make money" and the very fountain of wealth, without a real understanding of this most fundamental issue of life everything else becomes a guessing game. People who are not well educated in the basics of life and **most** people are NOT, resolve to guessing games, theorizing and blame shifting. So, let's get down to the root cause and source of wealth; the fountain of happiness and well being.

Wealth is created by the creative mind of thinkers; by those who seek to know things which they do not understand, or to know what else is possible. The men and women who think about invention, experimentation and advancement of their own knowledge, those are the real source of wealth. To know means science. Science simply means, "to know", that is the true meaning of the word. For people to become thinkers and inventors there needs to be a proper atmosphere philosophically and politically. Freedom is the most essential component for a proper environment where the thinker can feel secure and free, and in such an environment thinkers see hope; hope for their ideas to be explored and experimented with, hope of being able to achieve happiness, wealth and prosperity through their efforts.

Wealth begins in the science lab where thinkers experiment on the ideas they develop. From the science lab the ideas go to the engineers and from the engineers to the factory and from the factory to the consumers. Science is the vehicle of the mind, the very fountain of wealth, the very beginning of prosperity, the very source of hope and promise. Man sees all this formless stuff, all these substances existing in nature, all the elements found in both organic and inorganic forms and of various shapes and types. All this shapeless stuff is meaningless and worthless in its original form. Man begins to think about ways to make something out of this worthless nothing, how to make useful things out of shapeless matter. Man seeks to conquer nature, to make nature serve mankind. There is no limit to the power of the human mind; there are only barriers, which get in the way. One of the barriers is time, but time does not really stand in the way as much as mankind does. Mankind has developed barbaric morals and ethics in the forms of religions, and these barbaric mentalities, which promote barbaric philosophies, these are the greatest barriers to achievement as well as the source of and cause of poverty.

I will give you just one simple example of how wealth and the love of money are beneficent to mankind, as well as how wealth is created. I could use Thomas Edison or Ford as examples but instead, I will use Bill Gates as a perfect example. Bill Gates was a nobody, as far as wealth, fame and riches are concerned. However, this great thinker used his brain and took a piece of software which was rendered garbage by his employer, and turned this garbage into millions and millions of dollars.

To make a long story short, as a result of Bill Gates' company Microsoft, by the year 2001 590 million jobs, **well paying jobs** were created worldwide. These are jobs, which are a direct result of Microsoft and its products. In addition, there are some 200 million jobs world wide, which are a indirect result of the same company which Bill Gates has founded. What is also important to note that this company produces the **value of the quality of life** we now enjoy as a direct result of its products. Nobody can put a price on this, it is beyond the reach of calculation.

Furthermore, the quality of life due to the good paying jobs created as a direct result of MS is also priceless. I am not going to go into the accusations made against Bill Gates and MS which claim that he used unethical tactics to get rich, because accusations are made due to religious ethics and morals which are in and of themselves worthless. That which society calls "morals and ethics" today is religious doctrines and altruistic in nature and so they are worthless. Only those who are evil make such accusations, those who envy achievers, who would take what is not theirs simply because their greed is of such nature. Man has always attempted to destroy achievers, throughout all of human history. Bill Gates and many like him were able to achieve all this because he had the freedom to do it, to think and innovate and expand. Because he had and has a **love of money** as a motivating factor, because of the very thing Christianity calls evil, our lives are far better. If Bill Gates were a Christian and did not love money, hundreds of millions, and billions of people would be far less fortunate today, and our lives would have been set back abut 30 years at least.

Inside The Christian Mind

In order to understand how Christianity (and Islam as well as other religions) is the cause of evil, we need to make a scientific analysis of the

Christian mentality. Before we do this, we need to make a critical analysis of the Christian and religious philosophy, altruism. It is sad but true that most religionists have no idea what their philosophy teaches, what threat and harm it causes to humanity, to life itself.

Altruism

The foundation of altruism, of Christianity and religions of all sorts says "that man has no right to exist for his own sake, that service to others is the only justification for his existence, and that self-sacrifice is his highest moral duty, virtue and value." (Ayn Rand—"Philosophy: Who Needs It?") Furthermore: "Do not confuse altruism with kindness, good will or respect for the rights of others. These are not primaries, but consequences, which, in fact, altruism makes impossible. The irreducible primary of altruism, the basic absolute, is SELF-SACRIFICE—which means: self-immolation, self-abnegation, self-denial, self-destruction—which means: the SELF as a standard of evil, the SELFLESS as a standard of the good."

One very important thing I must point out is that Christianity, (or any religion) does not have a moral code! That is right! It has NO MORAL CODE, no moral standard at all! I challenge any and all Christians to write down their moral code and submit it to everyone so we can see what it says. The reason Christianity does not have a moral code is because to Christians morals are anything, which supports their religion and doctrines, and immoral is anything which opposes; that is what they mean when they use terms such as moral or immoral. But the reason they do not and cannot have a moral standard is because their holy book itself is full of contradictions and so, agreement on what is/should be moral cannot be attained from the bible. Furthermore, the Bible stands against freedom! The Bible is opposed to Democracy, freedom of speech, freedom of religion, individual rights and freedom of free-enterprise, it is anti-private property, it is anti-reason, and it opposes even freedom of thought, as I shall prove beyond the shadow of a doubt.

On Abortion. I need not mention that Christians oppose abortion, but what I want to mention and prove is that their Bible is pro-abortion and anti-life. Christians claim and define a fertilized egg as a living child. The Bible says that life is only in the blood, (Leviticus 17:11 and Deuteronomy 12:23). However, there is no blood until the second week after conception, so as far as abortion is concerned, the Christians and their puppet politicians are out right hypocrites. But the fact that they oppose this causes great harm to stem cell research, which in turn is immoral as it interferes not only with advanced scientific jobs, but with the very rights of the individual to health and happiness. Millions of people suffer from many diseases, and without this research the chances of finding cures for these horrible diseases becomes almost impossible if not impossible.

Although the bible contains hundreds of laws and thousands of rules there is not one single word about abortion. But if we are to examine the bible to see if it supports the Christian and religious viewpoint on what constitutes life and what does not, we will find that the bible is pro abortion and anti-life. One of the so-called "laws of god" sheds much light on the value of a fetus. Let's look at how the bible views a fetus.

"If men strive, and hurt a woman with child, so that her fruit depart from her, and yet no mischief follow: he shall be surely punished according as the woman's husband will lay upon him; and he shall pay as the judges determine. "And if any mischief follow, then thou shalt give life for life, Eye for eye, tooth for tooth . . ."—*Ex. 21:22-25*

As you can see, the bible commands the death penalty for the killing of a human being, but not for the expulsion of a fetus.

The Beginning Of Life

Here is another point on which these so called Christians, these hypocrites, oppose their very own "word of god". The bible states that life begins at birth and not at conception. In fact, god defines life as "breath" and the evidence for this is found in some very prominent biblical passages, and from the very beginning, starting in Genesis where God "breathed into his nostrils the breath of life; and man became a living soul."

These anti abortion hypocrites in their desperation for biblical support of their beliefs, cite irrelevant verses such as: "Behold, I was shapen in iniquity; and in sin did my mother conceive me." Psalm 51:5 Verses such as this are few and do not support their beliefs even remotely. As I said, they use this verse out of complete desperation. Furthermore, they want to use "case law" in civil courts in their defense on various issues, but when it comes to their own bible, they have a double standard. These hypocrites openly ignore the fact that the bible and their imaginary god is pro abortion and their bible and their imaginary god does not value a fetus as a breathing and living human being. The verse just quoted invokes original sin and shows how sexist bible believers really are but the verse has absolutely nothing to do with abortion. Have you notice that Paul, Jesus and all the biblical figures ignored every chance to condemn abortion? Since the bible and these so called holy people went out of their ways to invent rules for every facet of people's lives, why is it that they did not make a ruling on abortion and the fetus? How is it that these godly and supposedly inspired men failed to make an issue out of abortion? They ignored the subject because they did not value a fetus at all, period!

Thou Shalt Not Kill

The anti abortion hypocrites are quick to quote the sixth commandment, "Thou shalt not kill" (Ex. 20:13) and claim that this commandment of god shows that god is pro life and anti abortion. Let's investigate the bible's definition of life (breath) and its silence on abortion. In Exodus 21:22-25, a law set in place immediately after the Ten Commandments, states clearly that a fetus is not a living breathing human being. Furthermore, a critical and honest analysis shows that "Thou shalt not kill" does not apply to all living, breathing human beings. We know this because children are routinely massacred in the bible at the commandment of god, Moses and other so called holy men. Take for example that the bible commands the killing of a child for being a "stubborn son" Deut. 21:18-21 or for cursing one's father or mother, Ex. 21:17 and for being a homosexual Lev. 20:13 and for doing any kind of work on the Sabbath, such as picking up sticks, Numbers 15:32-35.

So you see, god is not pro life, and certainly not anti-abortion as the Christian hypocrites claim. In fact, these hypocrites are to be found in restaurants right after church every Sabbath, so by their own worthless bible these hypocrites should all be executed! Furthermore, the so called 10 commandments are PART OF "The Law" which Jezeus supposedly "nailed to the cross" so why the hell do these hypocrites even bother to quote this savage book their own god did away with? I think hypocrisy should be a capital offense. That would solve many problems very fast. Dishonesty is the Christian standard of morals, they live by it, and they are dishonest to the core!

Suppose we start executing children for being stubborn or for cursing their parents or for having been born homosexual, do you think Christians would oppose this practice? No they would not, they would back it fully because it is the word of god. This is why we atheists, we the unbelievers despise religion, because it is uncivilized, it is barbaric at best and so are Christians and all religionists, they are tyrants, savages and certainly UNCIVILIZED!

I have said before and will say it again, Christians are only as good as their imaginary god. Case in point: Numbers 25:4-9, where doG orders Moses to massacre 24,000 Israelites: "Take all the heads of the people, and hang them up before the Lord against the sun." Clearly, doG and the bible are not pro-life!

God On Killing Babies And Children

"**Happy** shall he be, that taketh and dasheth thy little ones against the stones."—*Psalm 137:9*

What civilized human being can claim that an infinitely intelligent being inspired the above words? In 2 Kings 2:23-24 doG orders a bear to slaughter 42 children for teasing a prophet. Is this a pro-life attitude? As you can see, being godly means being a savage and a tyrant and not pro-life. When the pro-lifers use their bible and religious morals (sic) to defend their anti-abortion beliefs they have no leg to stand on, they are hypocrites, they are intellectual-bastards! Here is just a small sample of the hundreds of biblical commandments or threats to kill children:

- **Numbers 31:17** Now therefore kill every male among the little ones.
- **Deuteronomy 2:34** utterly destroyed the men and the women and the little ones.
- **Deuteronomy 28:53** And thou shalt eat the fruit of thine own body, the flesh of thy sons and of thy daughters.
- **I Samuel 15:3** slay both man and woman, infant and suckling.
- **2 Kings 8:12** dash their children, and rip up their women with child.
- **2 Kings 15:16** all the women therein that were with child he ripped up.
- **Isaiah 13:16** Their children also shall be dashed to pieces before their eyes; their houses shall be spoiled and their wives ravished.
- **Isaiah 13:18** They shall have no pity on the fruit of the womb; their eyes shall not spare children.
- **Lamentations 2:20** Shall the women eat their fruit, and children.

- **Ezekiel 9:6** Slay utterly old and young, both maids and little children.
- **Hosea 9:14** give them a miscarrying womb and dry breasts.
- **Hosea 13:16** their infants shall be dashed in pieces, and their women with child shall be ripped up.

Then we have the wise and beautiful words of JeeZeus:

> "For, behold, the days are coming, in which they shall say, Blessed are the barren, and the womb that never bare, and the paps which never gave suck."—*Luke 23:29*

Furthermore, Deuteronomy 23:1-2—"…No one born out of wedlock or any descendent of such a person, even in the tenth generation, may be included among the Lord's people."

As you can see, Christians oppose their own god, since the majority of pregnancies and abortions are amongst the unwed. So Christian hypocrisy is overwhelming and appalling to say the least. The fact that Christians try to convert these bastards is also appalling, because it is also against god's word; bastards will not be allowed in their imaginary heaven. But the fact that Christians oppose abortions and the fact that they teach their own to have children while they are poor, is what contributes to poverty; religion and the poor is the poverty factory. When a poor person has a child, that child is new poverty. The main problem is not only that the poor have children, but that they have loads of them!

On Poverty – Poverty Is Glorified By The Christians.

"Blessed are you poor, for yours is the Kingdom of God," claims the gospel of Luke.

Matthew 6:24 Matthew 6 Matthew 6:23-25 You Cannot Serve God and Riches "No one can serve two masters; for either he will hate the one and love the other, or else he will be loyal to the one and despise the other. You cannot serve God and mammon.

Matthew 13:22 Matthew 13 Matthew 13:21-23 Now he who received seed among the thorns is he who hears the word, and the cares of this world and the deceitfulness of **riches** choke the word, and he becomes unfruitful.

Mark 4:19 Mark 4 Mark 4:18-20 and the cares of this world, the deceitfulness of **riches**, and the desires for other things entering in choke the word, and it becomes unfruitful.

Mark 10:23 Mark 10 Mark 10:22-24 With God All Things Are Possible (Matt. 19:23-30; Luke 18:24-30) Then Jesus looked around and said to His disciples, "How hard it is for those who have **riches** to enter the kingdom of God!"

Luke 8:14 Luke 8 Luke 8:13-15 Now the ones that fell among thorns are those who, when they have heard, go out and are choked with cares, **riches**, and pleasures of life, and bring no fruit to maturity.

Luke 1:53 Luke 1 Luke 1:52-54 He has filled the hungry with good things, And the **rich** He has sent away empty.

Luke 6:24 Luke 6 Luke 6:23-25 Jesus Pronounces Woes "But woe to you who are **rich**, For you have received your consolation.

2 Corinthians 6:10 2 Corinthians 6 2 Corinthians 6:9-11 as sorrowful, yet always rejoicing; as poor, yet making many **rich**; as having nothing, and yet possessing all things.

1 Timothy 6:9 1 Timothy 6 1 Timothy 6:8-10 But those who desire to be **rich** fall into temptation and a snare, and into many foolish and harmful lusts which drown men in destruction and perdition.

James 5:1 James 5 James 5:1-2 Rich Oppressors Will Be Judged Danger of Riches; Patience and Prayer Come now, you **rich**, weep and howl for your miseries that are coming upon you!

Revelation 3:17 Revelation 3 Revelation 3:16-18 Because you say, "I am **rich**, have become wealthy, and have need of nothing'—and do not know that you are wretched, miserable, poor, blind, and naked.

Matthew 19:21 Matthew 19 Matthew 19:20-22 Jesus said to him, "If you want to be perfect, go, sell what you have and give to the **poor**, and you will have treasure in heaven; and come, follow Me."

Luke 6:20 Luke 6 Luke 6:19-21 The Beatitudes (Matt. 5:1-12) Then He lifted up His eyes toward His disciples, and said: "Blessed are you **poor**, For yours is the kingdom of God.

2 Corinthians 6:10 2 Corinthians 6 2 Corinthians 6:9-11 as sorrowful, yet always rejoicing; as **poor**, yet making many rich; as having nothing, and yet possessing all things.

James 2:5 James 2 James 2:4-6 Listen, my beloved brethren: Has God not chosen the **poor** of this world to be rich in faith and heirs of the kingdom which He promised to those who love Him?

James 2:6 James 2 James 2:5-7 But you have dishonored the **poor** man. Do not the rich
oppress you and drag you into the courts?

The countries, which experience the fastest population growth are also those in which **poverty is widespread.** Why is poverty wide spread? Because those countries are religious, guided by the light of DoG. Those people have been infected with a disease called religion, which teaches them that being poor is good and noble and **abortion is a sin!**

Therefore, when people multiply before wealth can be created or faster than wealth can be created the end result is poverty. Where there is poverty there is a tremendous increase in crimes, diseases and all forms of suffering.

Now, before I continue, I wish to point out a few very important issues which nobody who has argued against god and religion has ever mentioned. If you read the above verses very carefully you can get at least a small idea of what type of person Jesus was, if indeed those are his words. If he was god, or even the Son of God, he had to know that there is magnetic ore inside the earth. He knew there was all types of metal ore inside the earth. He had to know about molecular structures, if he was god. If he was the creator of mankind and the universe he had to know about protons and electrons, about atoms and quarks, neutrinos and particles. He had to know about how photons work. He had to know about geometry and mathematics. He must have known about algebra and calculus. He must have known about economics and how wealth is created and how invention and innovation could improve the lives of his so called "loved ones".

My questions are these: Why did he not teach them how to make electric wires and mine magnets to produce electricity? Why did he not teach them to make light bulbs? Why did he not teach them to make metal pipes and a simple hand operated pump even, to pump water? Why did he not teach them how to make glass so they could have clear glass windows? Why did he not teach them how to build printing presses to print books to educated the masses/poor? Why did he not teach them how to build tractors and farm equipment? Why did he not teach them to build trains and automobiles? Why did he not teach them mathematics and reading skills? Why did he not teach them electronics and various useful trades? Why did he not teach them how to perform laser eye surgery? Why did he not teach them how to build pacemakers and heart pumps? Why did he not teach them how to build septic tanks and toilettes? Why did he not teach them how to build irrigation systems?

What Jesus did teach them is to remain stupid. He taught them the dumbest thing possible; that being poor is noble and virtuous. He told them that to seek self-improvement is evil. He taught them that to try and make a good living and gather wealth is of the devil. He taught them that being educated is for the proud, and the proud are to be burnt in hell. He taught them that to have pride and self-esteem is evil. He taught them they should be like him, bums and cowards. He taught them to sell everything they have and give it to the poor. He taught them collectivism, which is communism. He taught them about equal distribution of wealth, of dividing everything they had amongst everyone so that they could all become poor. He taught them, in other words, nothing of any value.

Ironically, there are many idiots in today's day and age that think equal distribution of wealth is a good and noble thing to do. They say that helping the poor is a good idea, it is a noble thing to do. Let me tell you what would happen if we listened to Jesus and these altruistic morons. If we divide all the wealth of the world equally between every adult on the planet, the end result would be total poverty on a global scale. Everyone would get $16,687.73. This would mean, no more factories, all corporations would have to be put out of business, all banks and banking systems would be crippled, and all productivity would be brought to a halt. All electric companies would be shut down.

In other words, we would be thrown back 500 years into the dark ages. Nobody would have enough to do anything of any value.

In Christian churches, every sun-day millions of morons are taught that "the love of money is the root of all evil". Instead of teaching these morons about economics, about how important money is, and that it is good to have money, they teach them the dumbest thing possible. The preachers, these parasites behind the pulpit are the greatest evil on our planet; religious leaders are the most devious and deceptive parasites that have ever lived amongst humans. These bastards never work a day in their lives; they live off the morons who they brainwash and dumb down with their masks of virtue. The religious leaders are the epitome of the very essence of evil; they are the greediest bastards on our planet. Don't get me wrong, it is healthy to be greedy, but there are two kinds of greed. There is the greed which seeks the unearned, the taking or robbing others of their earned income through theft or/and deception; then there is the honest and healthy greed which motivates men and women to achieve, to make money to improve their lives, but through their own work, through their own efforts and not by deception and coercion.

Christians on Politics

Sadly enough, these religious parasites do not stick only to their religion. They stick their nose in politics as well. They vote for political parasites who sing their songs, who speak words pleasant to the Christian/dumb follower's' ear, who make an issue out of things which should never even be an issue. The fact that they vote for tyrants who tell them that they would seek to pass legislation which favors religion is ample proof that Christians, Muslims and Jews (religious Jews. The majority of Jews are secular) oppose freedom! But what happens when they vote for politicians who promise to vote for these parasite politicians (of which America and American government, The Middle East and Europe are infested with)? What happens is our freedoms are trampled under foot. The freedoms of the secular and the atheist are infringed, violated and done away with. The FACT of the matter is that America, with its existing laws and system of government today, is a theocracy. It is not a free country, but a theocracy pure and simple. There are only 4 basic freedoms left and even they are restricted through all forms of regulation and altruistic laws.

Our freedoms are a joke as far as the Christians are concerned. When Christians claim that America is a free country, what they mean is that it is a free country as long as you are a Christian. If they would stay out of politics and would be tolerant as they demand of others, and would vote for politicians who honor the freedoms of all the people, the rights of the individual, the US Constitution, then they would harm nobody and we would not have much to say about it. But this is not the case.

Religion is Pro-Oppression of Women

From time immemorial religion, organized or not, has suppressed and blamed women for the evils of men. Men, and not women, are the bigots, but religion being irrational, being barbaric and savage, has found ways to justify the cruelest forms of oppression of women. I am not going to quote the filthy Quran, as I am focusing on Christianity for now. While there are many verses, which speak loud and clear what religious men think of women, what their idiot gods supposedly told them about women, I will quote only two of these verses, for the sake of time and space.

"I will greatly multiply thy sorrow and thy conception; in sorrow thou shalt bring forth children; and thy desire shall be to thy husband, and he shall rule over thee."
—*Genesis 3:16*

As you can see, right from the beginning of this filthy book called the bible, women's rights have been denied. The New Testament, the Christian book of love and life has this to say about women's rights:

> "Let the woman learn in silence with all subjection (to men). But I suffer not a woman to teach, nor to usurp authority over the man, but to be in silence. For Adam was first formed, then Eve. And Adam was not deceived, but the woman being deceived was in the transgression."—*1 Tim. 2:11-14*

Tertullian, one of the highly honored church fathers said *"each of you women is an Eve . . . You are the gate of Hell, you are the temptress of the forbidden tree; you are the first deserter of the divine law."*

Martin Luther decreed: *"If a woman grows weary and at last dies from childbearing, it matters not. Let her die from bearing, she is there to do it."*

As an enlightened man I am forced by my conscience to say this out in the open, to shout it from the mountain tops, to say it as boldly and as clear as possible: Men have been and are the greatest tyrants this planet have ever produced. The way men treat women is uncivilized, but most barbaric, most savage and most shameful. Any man, who thinks himself better or superior to women in any way, should go jump off a bridge. In fact, women are superior to men, if we are to speak the TRUTH. Yes, I can prove it beyond the shadow of a doubt. First of all, the woman has a brain 30% smaller than man, yet she can perform any task, which requires mental efficiency, as good as a man if not better. What this means, is that women are 30% more able in this regard. If women are to evolve and grow a bigger brain, they will surpass men by a huge margin. Furthermore, while thousands of scientists worked to control light beams (photons) it was a WOMAN at MIT who achieved one of the greatest breakthroughs of our time and in all of human history. She not only managed to slow down the light beam, she brought it to a full stop. What this means is that we will now be able to develop much faster and superior computers and technology. In time, we will be able to have optical microchips. In other words, this *woman* which the savage church fathers and the barbaric bible author(s) and every religious moron has condemned, has achieved one of the greatest advances in human history. Today, with the new advancements of science, women can reproduce without a male, so there is very little we men can offer women, and quite frankly I have no idea what that is. I mean, aside from sex, what can we really offer them? Furthermore, my bisexual girlfriend tells me, that lesbian sex is by far better, so even sex is not something we men can offer in quality.

Christian church leaders, fought tooth and nail against the advancement of women, opposing every form of liberty for women from women's right to speak in public to the use of anesthesia in childbirth (since the bible says women must suffer in childbirth) and woman's suffrage. In fact, in many nations women do not have a right to drive a car even. During the 1920, when women were fighting for the right to vote, there was not ONE single religious leader who did not oppose women's right to vote. In fact, tens of thousands of women were persecuted, beaten and ridiculed for fighting for this basic right. I am absolutely appalled that any woman now accepts Christianity, Islam, Judaism or any religion which speaks of women as evil and denies them their most basic human rights.

Why do women remain second-class citizens? Why is there a religion-fostered war against women's rights? Because the unholy and filthy bible (and the piece of shit, the Quran) is a handbook for the subjugation of women, plain and simple; men wrote it for men, for male-ego masturbation. Those politicians in office, they are not in support of freedom and justice. When they make an issue out of abortion rights they admit that they oppose individual rights, they oppose the woman's "right to life liberty and pursuit of happiness". This garbage book called the bible, it teaches that women are property, that fathers can sell them and that men can buy them, that women are to be the slaves and servants of men. I know why those savages wrote the book, and I know why men have oppressed women and why they still are. It is because women are more capable than we are. They are better parents, better workers, better persons, better thinkers, better judges, and overall a threat to the male ego!

Here is what the filthy bible has to say about women, and this is the very short list, mind you.

Genesis
- 2:22 Woman created from Adam's rib
- 3:16 Woman cursed: maternity a sin, marriage a bondage
- 19:1-8 Rape virgins instead of male angels

Exodus
- 20:17 Insulting Tenth Commandment, considering a wife to be property
- 21:7-11 Unfair rules for female servants, may be sex slaves
- 22:18 "Thou shalt not suffer a witch to live"
- 38:8 Women may not enter tabernacle they must support

Leviticus
- 12:1-14 Women who have sons are unclean 7 days
- 12:4-7 Women who have daughters are unclean 14 days
- 15:19-23 Menstrual periods are unclean
- 19:20-22 If master has sex with engaged woman, she shall be scourged

Numbers
- 1:2 Poll of people only includes men
- 5:13-31 Barbaric adulteress test
- 31:16-35 "Virgins" listed as war booty

Deuteronomy
- 21:11-14 Rape manual
- 22:5 Abomination for women to wear men's garments, vice-versa
- 22:13-21 Barbaric virgin test
- 22:23-24 Woman raped in city, she & her rapist both stoned to death
- 22:28-29 Woman must marry her rapist
- 24:1 Men can divorce woman for "uncleanness," not vice-versa
- 25:11-12 If woman touches foe's penis, her hand shall be cut off...

Judges
- 11:30-40 Jephthah's nameless daughter sacrificed
- 19:22-29 Concubine sacrificed to rapist crowd to save man

I Kings 11:1-4 King Solomon had 700 wives & 300 concubines

Job 14:1-4 "Who can bring a clean thing out of an unclean? not one..."

Proverbs
- 7:9-27 Evil women seduce men, send them to hell
- 11:22 One of numerous Proverbial putdowns
- Isaiah 3:16-17 God scourges, rapes haughty women

Ezekiel 16:45 One of numerous obscene denunciations

Matthew 24:19 "[woe] to them that are with child"

Luke 2:22 Mary is unclean after birth of Jesus

I Corinthians
- 11:3-15 Man is head of woman; only man in God's image
- 14:34-35 Women keep in silence, learn only from husbands

Ephesians 5:22-33 "Wives, submit . . ."

Colossians 3:18 More "wives submit"

I Timothy
- 2:9 Women adorn selves in shamefacedness

·   2:11-14 Women learn in silence in all subjection; Eve was sinful, Adam blameless

No man who honors women and individual rights, as I do, and no self-respecting woman should support or respect any form of religion. No man or woman who treasures freedom should support or even respect religion or ANY religious person. If you consider yourself enlightened and intelligent, if you have any respect for yourself and others, you are duty bound to fight to eliminate this disease called "religion" from the face of our planet. Neurotics and savages do not belong on this planet, such books and teachings must be eliminated at all costs. **What loving father could think of his daughters, of his little girls as evil and as slaves?** What father in his right mind can support the crap taught in the bible? Again, if you are enlightened and self-respecting, you must oppose religion on all fronts and you must DO all you can to put a stop to barbarism once and for all.

Christianity and Religion on Socialism

I keep hearing these religious leaders and politician-parasites cry that there is a moral decline in America and the world. Do you know what they mean by moral decline? I'll tell you what they mean. It means their altruist ideals and the welfare system they created has produced millions upon millions of criminals, parasites, human trash, and these parasites, these human garbage are responsible for crime, poverty and overall disease and destruction of all peace and happiness.

The Christian leaders, when they say there is a moral decline, what they are actually saying is that their morals have failed, their ethics have produced nothing but more poverty, and with this poverty more evil. What they are saying is that the enlightened are abandoning their altruistic morals and ethics, they are giving up on barbaric morals and barbaric ethics.

Charity is one of the dumbest things to teach as a virtue or as a moral way of life. Because of charity the world is plagued by parasites that expect and live off of handouts. These religious morons do not teach those poor idiots that it is stupid to have children while they are dirt poor. NO! Instead they teach them about Jesus, and how being poor is good and a virtue. In America, these idiots invented welfare and public aid programs. Basically what this did, it enslaved the working men and women by taking their taxes BY FORCE and gave it to the garbage humans; to parasites so that the worthless scum can multiply.

They said, this would help the poor. None of them dared to tell the poor that they should get sterilized, none of them dared to tell the poor that they are idiots and morons. Instead what they did tell the poor, the more kids you have the more benefits you have a RIGHT to. That is right people, the American Democrats and Republicans are responsible for the birth of some 40 million parasites. These parasites have loads and loads of children, they do not work a day in their life and live off of working people's money.

When the government gives money to any person or group of people who do not work, and have not earned that money, what the government is saying is that all the people it governs are its slaves. The government is saying that it has the right and the authority to take from one group of people and give to another, and there is not a damn thing anyone can do about it. This is the current American government. The Christians have turned the American government into a theocratic government and they just got started. The Christians only vote for those who promise them to pass laws which take even more rights away from people, to pass laws which take even more money from the working people to give to lazy bastards who multiply like a virus. This is the result of religion and its socialistic and communistic philosophies.

I would like to ask these religious leaders, I want them to tell me why it is that in poor neighborhoods there is trash all over? Their god applauded the poor, and encouraged them not to seek earthly possessions. Why is it moral to throw garbage on the streets? Why is it that in neighborhoods where educated and working class lives there is no garbage on the streets? Could it be that the educated are better off? How can the poor justify throwing trash on the streets? Since when is poverty an excuse for laziness? How come the middle class people can throw their garbage in the garbage cans and the poor cannot? Why is being poor moral and ethical? How come it is not immoral to be a parasite and a worthless scum? Why is it not immoral to throw garbage on the streets? Why is it that the religious leaders do not educate their flocks about these things? How come there is never a call from the pulpit to their congregations to stop being lazy and parasites? How comes no preacher preaches anything intelligent from behind his or her pulpit? That is why the poor are poor, because idiots raise them. The poor are poor because their parents made them poor when they gave them birth. It is their parent's fault for being poor and nobody else. I have news for you idiots! Your god was a moron and you are a living example of such a moron. Your god praised the poor. I have news for you, if you are poor you are an idiot; if you live in poverty it is YOUR fault and your parent's fault and your religion' fault. You are to blame for the misery you are in.

On another point: The poor play loud music, they honk their horn in residential neighborhoods even at 3AM. They have no respect for anyone or anything. These are the trash raised by trash. The trash the American main political parties and preachers have created. They are the godfathers of human trash in America, and it is the same throughout the world. These politicians-parasites, they could have not gotten in office if they would not have had the poor and the idiots on their side. These politicians do not care about the poor or the rights and freedoms of the people. If they did care they would act like it. All they care about is their high positions and their own pockets. They are no different then the religious leaders. Speaking of politicians and religious leaders, I would like to know if there is one single thing the Americans have benefited from as a result of its government, in the last 50 years? Can anyone name even one single thing?

Since I am talking about charity and socialism, I would like to point out something, which may be a surprise to all of you. Do you remember all the publicity about Mother Teresa and all the good she was supposed to be doing/have done and how she was one of the best examples of being a good Christian? Well, I have something to say about this as well, and about so called Charity organizations.

Mother Teresa did not live her life at the same level of poverty and depravity that comprised the daily lives of those she 'served'. In fact, she was very rich both financially and materially. She did not personally bear the hunger and suffering she said the poor were enduring. She denied the poor of the relief that could easily have come from birth control or family planning, because her religion opposes such common sense practices. She, in fact did not help the poor at all, instead she helped them only in continuing to be poor; she told them to multiply like rats when she denied them birth control. Furthermore, the Catholic Church is worth about 93 BILLION dollars in both cash and property. Do you know that this worthless religion and church has NEVER BUILT ONE SINGLE HOUSE for a poor family? Do you know that those who Mother Teresa and the church supposedly helped, are still living in misery? Do you know that those poor are multiplying every day due to their religion and stupidity?

Mother Teresa was exactly the opposite of what she was portrayed to be; not the personification of 'altruism' in all its allegedly selfless, sacrificial glory, but as living proof of the human devastation this 'principle' has produced. Mother Teresa did not relieve ANY human misery instead she contributed to it and perpetuated it, by denying the one solution that would have relieve it: birth control. It is a sin, she said, to use birth control and to have an abortion. But it is not a sin to be poor, it is not a sin to multiply poverty, it is god's plan to manufacture parasites, to increase poverty. That is what religion supports and produces.

The Christian Politicians Their Philosophy and Communism

Before I continue with this section of my essay, I need to make a statement, which may shock some of you, not because it is not true, but because it is so true. The only difference between a theocracy and communism is in that communists have no god to worship so they invented a human god called "the people", but otherwise, communism and theocracies such as Iran, and now on its way there, America are no different fundamentally. In a communist country everything is done in the name of "the people" but none of the people have any rights at all. "The people" is the communist smokescreen alternative to the religionists' god, and only the "communist party" knows the will of "the people" therefore "the people" must do what the government dictates.

In a theocracy, the religious leaders and religious doctrines are the standards of morals and. In America, it is worse than in Iran and China (in many ways), and it is getting worse all the time. Let me explain. In America, there is a smoke screen called "The American Dream" which nobody has been able to outline as to what it means. But one of the things the American Dream is supposed to have is the dream of being free and of owning one's own house. Well, the truth is that nobody in America owns any property. Property ownership in America is a smoke screen, because as soon as you fail to pay property tax (property is taxed every year), your property is taken away. "So, when you finish paying for a home or property, all you have accomplished is you will have finished paying for the **right to rent** the property from the government, the true owner of the property and people."

In America, the government too owns people. Not true? If it is not true, then why is it illegal to commit suicide? Why is it that one is forced to live in a mental institution where they can experiment on you, but it is illegal to commit suicide? Why is it illegal to install your own underground watter pump in 99% of US cities? (**Oh, see www.DumbLaws.Com please!**). Another component of this smoke screen called "The American Dream" is the freedom to be an achiever and accomplish your dreams and become rich through your own efforts without violating the rights of others. Well, this was once true, but today, if you become successful the government will punish you. The Christian politicians have turned this country into a Christian theocracy, a country where freedoms are no longer guaranteed but have to be fought for and bought. The US Constitution is in itself a smoke screen because the Christians and the Christian politicians do not honor it. More on this later.

The founding fathers of the US Constitution set forth the importance of having the freedom to be an independent and free individual and as such, an individual was recognized as having the right to life liberty and pursuit of happiness. The right to life and pursuit of happiness is not guaranteed to "the people" or to "society" but to the individual. The founding fathers recognized that the individual IS the only minority and as such it has the rights to life, liberty and pursuit of happiness. This idea protected by the constitution is the moral doctrine of the US Constitution and it includes the idea that individuals have a right to live for themselves, to pursue their own happiness and not to be sacrificial animals living for the sake of others. That is why the

Constitution was amended to include the Bill of Rights. During the debates on the adoption of the Constitution, its opponents repeatedly charged that the Constitution as drafted would open **the way to tyranny by the central government.**

Fresh in their minds was the memory of the British violation of civil rights before and during the Revolution. They demanded a "bill of rights" that would spell out the immunities of individual citizens. As you shall see, even the Bill of Rights has become a smoke screen, since none of the politicians in Washington honor it and the majority of the people oppose the US Constitution and I will prove it. Washington has become a den of hypocrites and a lair of altruists, home to the United Socialist States of America, it is no longer the capital of a free nation but one of a theocracy in the making, a nation where religion decides the policy of the nation. The United States is becoming the very thing the founding fathers feared it would, it is becoming a theocracy and a police-state more and more every day. If this continues, the US and China will have little to argue about as far as freedoms and human rights go. In China the government owns business, in America the people own the business but the government dictates how a business is to function and what it can or cannot do and the government owns the people, so there is little difference at least in this respect. More on this later. Now, to get back to this portion of this essay, let me make it crystal clear; the US Constitution, in the Bill of Rights if we are to summarize it honestly, it says that each individual is an end in himself and that means individualism is not compatible with altruism.

Now, again, to understand the mentality of these Christian politicians, let's summarize their philosophy and its basic principle: Ayn Rand said it best when she said that the basic principle of altruism, "is that man has no right to exist for his own sake, that service to others is the only justification of his existence, and that self-sacrifice is his highest moral duty, virtue, and value." ("Faith and Force: Destroyers of the Modern World," *Philosophy: Who Needs It* [New York: Bobbs-Merrill Co., Inc., 1982, p. 74])

The Two Forms of Altruism

The sources of altruism in the American culture is the New Testament, especially the Gospels (and the Law). If we examine the Gospels very carefully what we find is not one but two distinct strands in the altruistic message that Jesus teaches, and it is these two strands of altruistic philosophy which divides the main political parties in America. **The only thing the Republicans and Democrats disagree on is on which rights of the people to violate next,** and this is because one party leans towards one form of altruism while the other towards the other.

The first of these two strands of altruism is the message of sacrifice:

"If any man will sue thee at the law, and take away thy coat, let him have thy cloak also... ."

"Give to him that asketh thee, and from him that would borrow of thee turn not thou away." (Matt. 5: 40-42.)

"If thou wilt be perfect, go and sell that thou hast, and give to the poor, and thou shalt have treasure in heaven." (Matt. 19:21)

Jesus' own mission is a form of sacrifice: He gives his life to save mankind.

But there is a second; another strain of altruism in the Gospels, expressed most clearly in the Beatitudes.

"Blessed are the poor in spirit: for theirs is the kingdom of heaven. Blessed are they that mourn: for they shall be comforted. Blessed are the meek: for they shall inherit the earth. Blessed are they which do hunger and thirst after righteousness: for they shall be filled. Blessed are the merciful: for they shall obtain mercy. Blessed are the pure in heart: for they shall see God. Blessed are the peacemakers: for they shall be called the children of God. Blessed are they which are persecuted for righteousness' sake: for theirs is the kingdom of heaven." (Matt. 5:3-10.)

According to this second strain of altruism, it isn't just that those who lack ability, strength, wealth, and so on need our help and we should give it to them. This second strand of altruism, the helpless, weak, and the poor are actually considered to be superior to the able, the strong, the wealthy and the achievers. The lazy, the incapable the weak and the helpless, we are told, deserve to go to heaven and they are the ones who will get into heaven most easily.

The successful, the strong, the able, and the wealthy are suspect precisely because of their strength, ability, and wealth. *"It is easier for a camel to pass through the eye of a needle than for a rich man to enter the kingdom of God."* (Matt. 19:24.) In other words, those who make the world turn are punished, those who make life better for all are less deserving than the worthless, the achiever is to be punished for his success while the incompetent somehow merits the rewards of an infinitely intelligent being called god.

This is the philosophy, which shapes the minds of the Christians and their Christian politicians.

In the Gospels, there is a sic theological rationale for altruism's inversion of values, a rationale which twists logic into illogic, which makes the naïve believe that the crap it teaches is actually good for humanity. It teaches that the life of this world is not to be enjoyed but lived in suffering and pain so that we can enjoy the next one. The Gospels teach that we should not love this life because it is a sin to allow our flesh to enjoy it, and that our souls yearn for the life to come. According to the Gospels, if we are failures in this world it is a good sign that one will flourish in the next, it is the mark of a true believer, and vice versa.

To be successful in this world is a very bad sign, it is a mark of a evil and sinful materialist, it is the sign of a lust for material happiness, and being happy in this life is against god's will.

In other words, Jesus demands two very unnatural things from people: the first is in the valuing others above the self, that's the sacrificial form of altruism. Then, he wants us to value the worst of the people over the best of them, to value the lowest values and the worst characteristics of humanity over the best. This moron named Jesus wants people to value poverty over wealth, incompetence and inability over competency and ability, to value weakness and the weak over the strong and strength. We are to do all this and at the same time we are to believe that this is infinite wisdom, the words and teachings of a wise god.

This aspect of altruism is what gave rise to egalitarianism and the myth of "equality", which I would broadly describe as holding that:
- People are equal, from a moral point of view;
- Differences in status, or wealth, or power, or esteem are undeserved, that nobody merits any status.
- Those who are incompetent and stupid on those scales of status, wealth, power, and esteem are victims, who should be honored and helped at the expense of others.
- Those who have achieved success and intellectual status are oppressors, who should be cut down to size or made to pay in some way; to have their wealth and success taken by force and given to the scum of the planet.

It is important to note that this egalitarianism, this equality myth also applies to moral traits. *"Judge not, that ye be not judged."* (Matt.

7:1.) What this means is simply that mercy is superior to justice, that men should be irrational instead of just, that justice needs to take a back seat and that whims and emotionalism are superior to justice. In other words, justice has no absolute standards, justice now becomes whatever the politicians want it to be and can change like the weather with the winds of politicians' emotions. It means that when a politician makes a decision based on his/her emotions and has become public knowledge, the politician is forced to promote his/her decision no matter how stupid it is, because in the name of mercy irrationality can be justified, but justice cannot.

In other words, the idea of putting mercy over justice allows the altruist to promote the concept of victimization, equal victimization, which makes the good, and the achievers who are the pillars of society as worthless as the worthless and the incompetent of society. It promotes the doctrine of *"we are all created equal"* and so we are to treat each other as equals and to love one another. This means that we are to hold a Judge at the same level of moral and competent level with a janitor; that a person who creates jobs for thousands through his/her own efforts is not worth more than a scumbag who lives off of welfare, that a brain surgeon is no better than a murderer. But human nature, the laws of nature, logic and reason does not permit this. It is not possible to love an enemy, it is stupid and childish to even attempt to. I have yet to see any Christian share each other' wives or husbands with the next door neighbor. If we are to love one another as ourselves, why should we keep our wives and husbands from those we supposedly love as ourselves? I have yet to see Christians share their cars and homes with one another, I have yet to see a Christian who own a car drive the Christians who do not have cars to their jobs and to shopping malls etc.

I have had the opportunity to work in homeless shelters as well as to be homeless for 3 months, and in that time I have learned how homeless shelters work and how they do not work. Needless to say 99% of them are run by Christian organizations. Guess what? None of the Christians took homeless into their home, none of them even treated the homeless with any form of respect. The food they provided was what stores throw away and what others donated, and nobody donated any good food but only what they disliked. **In fact, some of the homeless shelters would not allow me to eat unless I agreed to listen to a sermon.** I refused, so they kicked me out in the middle of winter, 10 degrees temperature outside and windshields made it feel like 40 below zero.

When I worked for a homeless shelter I learned that the shelters get public money from the city (In Chicago), they get $25 per homeless person per day (for every night they sleep in their auditorium). We provided shelter for the homeless from 8PM till 8AM and for that the church running the shelter under a different organization name got $25 per person. We had anywhere from 10-40 people each night from the beginning of winter until late spring. Some of the homeless people were persons who were kicked out of their own homes by their spouses, and a few of them were well educated but ran into unavoidable/complicated problems, but many of them were pure trash, absolute criminals and the scum of the earth. To make a long story short, the Christians running the shelters were hypocrites. The food they provided was worse than what we found in the garbage cans behind grocery stores, and many times there was nowhere near enough to fill one's stomach. And where do the homeless spend the day while the shelters are closed? I'll tell you where they do not spend them, they do not spend them in the warm homes of Christians or any warm place, unless a restaurant allows a few to sit in their restaurants to warm up. If it is a weekday, they find Libraries to hang out in but on weekends, **it is better to be dead than to be left at the mercy of Christians.** But Christians insist they love everyone.

Anyway back to the main subject, I have shown the two strains of altruism which taught by religion and altruists, yet none of them live up to their own altruistic ways but as much as they try they produce evil, poverty and destruction and if they get their way there will be no freedoms left

The Masks of Altruism

So far, none of the Enlightenment thinkers have undertaken to directly address, refute, and oppose either strain of altruism. The main reason is that the fundamentals of this concept in each case is because the altruists have done a good job of hiding or cloaking their philosophy behind the masks of ethics and moral, the very values they destroy. It is ironic that the bible claims that in the end people will call good evil and evil good, while everything the bible teaches and everything religion has taught and supported was evil but claimed as good. So it is hard to argue with anyone that helping the poor is not a good idea, that it is counter productive, that destroying an achiever in the name of "helping the poor" is wrong. It is not easy to argue with altruists that self-esteem is good and positive, because the bible and religion teaches that to think of oneself in high regards and to have pride is evil. The altruists are already convinced to the core that pride and self-esteem is evil and that helping the poor by giving them handouts is a virtue and noble.

For example, the sacrificial form of altruism hides behind cloaks such as generosity, benevolence, and kindness. They claim that these traits such as benevolence are expressions of selflessness, of helping others, but the truth is that they are not. In fact these are virtues and values of selfishness in that they are values understood only by the intellect that values the social environment which harbors a system of trade among people. But the altruist views each person as a means to the ends of other people, they hold that those who have more should be forced to give to those who have none and to those who produce poverty but provide no benefit to themselves or society. They sacrifice the good and the achievers for the sake of the worthless because that is what the bible and religion teaches, and because this sounds good to the idiot-the average person. Communists have found a way to steal altruism from god and invent communism, because in essence both communism and religion offer the same concepts and values.

It is true that there are people in the world, people who are vain and self-centered; who are mean and petty and grasping; who walk all over others and exploit others, but like the criminal element, they are a very small minority. But altruists, use the few exceptions as an excuse to enslave all the good selfish people, those who do not achieve their riches and wealth through exploitation, those too are lumped together. In other words to the religionist, if you are successful you are to be sacrificed, your wealth and your achievement is a symbol of being evil; so you must be punished you must be made to give more and more of your wealth to the "poor" to the parasites of the world.

Therefore altruism convinces people to accept the positive side which is cloaked as an expression of benevolence; and in doing so altruism manages to destroy the incentive to be an achiever and gains support from the many poor elements simply because it tells people that it is good to deprive others of their wealth because the wealthy are all evil, they teach them that brotherly love is superior to justice. Justice, they insist, ceases to be valid when it comes to the rich and the well to do, to them justice does not apply because mercy is above justice. So it is not surprising that politicians can get away with creating welfare, social security and all forms of regulations upon the achievers of the world. By labeling selfishness as evil they have achieved a monumental victory over reason and logic in that they managed to pervert the very meaning and application of justice. Once you convince people that taking from those who have by force is an ethical thing to do, and that all of a certain people have "rights" to a good life all paid for by the government who robs the wealthy and the achievers, there is no end in sight to injustice because injustice now means justice. More on this later...

Now let's look at another smoke screen, at yet another evil of altruism; the idea of equality-altruism, which too hides under the cloak of justice. Equality for all, they say, is good and virtuous and all men and women are to be treated equal, that all human beings have equal rights to everything. While it is horrible to discriminate against someone on the basis of the color of their skin, their nationality or gender, it is also horrible and evil to deprive people of their INDIVIDUAL rights. A person's property is private property and as such the person has a right to decide who or what type of people is allowed on it. When government passes laws and uses the armed thugs called the police to enforce those laws which prohibit a property owner from exercising their rights to their property, the end result is not equality but enslavement and infringement on the individual rights, on all of the rights of an individual.

A company, a private company is dictated to by the government, and it is forced to hire an army of legal advisers and lawyers to fight law suits, because the anti discrimination law has declared open season on law suits based on race discrimination. Now, all products produced by that company is more expensive, so everyone is harmed by it. There are no checks and balances to regulate and determine if a lawsuit is merited or not. No, on to court they go, and now the big rich company is at the mercy of a jury who hungers to take away money from the (from the rich) company and give it to the accuser simply because the accuser is poor and taking from the rich is good; the rich are the evil. The Jury now can justify granting 3 billion dollars of someone else's money to any idiot who files a lawsuit. Take the case against Phillip Morris, where an altruistic jury awarded a moron 3 BILLION dollars in damages. To that jury the fact that the moron knew that smoking is addictive and dangerous was irrelevant. The jury was not there to judge the evidence but to slaughter the rich. The accuser admitted that he knew that smoking was addictive and it caused cancer, but he smoked anyway for 30 years. But that is irrelevant to the altruists. To the altruist, someone else is always responsible for the failures of others, to the altruist people need not be responsible for their own life and well being because they can file law suits against others, they can manipulate and ignore justice as they please. Ironically the moron who sat on the bench, the Judge, upheld the ruling of the jury. So, how then is it possible to seek justice in an altruistic society? **How can a trial by jury** be of any value any more, when the population has bee taught those altruistic morals and virtues are in fact good? Yes, discrimination is evil and abhorrent, but so is denying a person the right to discriminate? If a company discriminates on the basis of race, color of skin or gender, such a company should be ostracized in public and the media and even boycotted, but to deny it the right to discriminate, and to open the door to the uneducated public, the tyrants, to destroy entire companies in the name of perverted justice is just as evil; it is monstrous. When you can get away with violating individual rights, communism is at the door, socialism sets in with an unstoppable force. The right to life and pursuit of happiness no longer exists for anyone. Private business is now a slave of the government and the altruist tyrants who support it. If a person starts a company and becomes big and hires many employees, that person has a right to pursue happiness, and if this means that the person would be happy not to see any blacks/whites on his property it is his/her right and nobody should have the right to force this person to hire people he dislikes for any reason. It is his property and his company. The issue here is justice, and if you deny this person justice by granting others authority over private property, you have perverted justice, no matter how noble the cause or reason. No cause is noble enough or grand enough to violate the rights of an individual. But the altruist, in the name of "good will towards men" ignore justice and pervert it because their sense of justice is whatever their whims dictate to them.

To the altruist it is noble to give. How come it is not wrong to receive? How come it is not immoral to accept handouts and values one has not earned? How come it is not evil to take from others? I'll tell you why. Because the altruists have been conditioned to envy those who have and to resent and envy achievement. They are jealous of those who achieve in life and since they are backed by "the word of god" that those who have are evil, it is not immoral to desire the property of others and it is not immoral to deprive others of their wealth. This they call justice! To take from those who have is moral and to receive unearned goods from others is also moral they claim. The mentality of altruists, or religionists is that they are self-righteous because some invisible imaginary god authorizes them to be so, and justice is only that which conforms to their beliefs and nothing else. When Christian politicians speak of equality and helping the poor what they are talking about is ways to take from those who earn their wealth and give it to the trash of society who do not. Thus, the US Government and many other socialist governments are nothing more than thieves run by thieves for the thieves, it is on its way to socialism; which is communism with a prettier name. Under the cloak of "law" (altruistic law, not objective law) these Christian politicians trample on every constitutional right of all individuals.

Labor Unions: The Legal Mob

The communists modified one of their tactics in order to infiltrate and destroy the very fabric of a free society by inventing Labor Unions.

Through Labor Unions they have been able to strike a blow to the very freedoms of the individual. In other words they have managed to create mini-communist societies and organizations under different names but with the same goal. No party has so staunchly promoted and encouraged Labor Unions except the Communist Party. In fact, all communist literature and websites praise the achievements of Labor Unions as well as promoted and instigated strikes and protests.

Labor Unions are a cancer to a free market economy and a direct assault on freedom and liberty. The idea that employees have "rights" to dictate to an employer how to run their business in demanding more pay and more money is legal black mail pure and simple. It is so shocking that such parasite organizations are permitted to exist in such nations as The US and other so called "freedom loving" democracies. **Every person who belongs to a union is a tyrant and a thief and opposes freedom; such persons must be disposed of.** Thousands of companies have gone bankrupt or were forced to sell due to the burden labor unions have placed on them. Not only are companies now forced to maintain an army of lawyers to fight strikes and law suits, but they are also forced to increase prices on their products and services as a result of being held hostage by the Union.

The idiots who belong to labor unions are under the illusion that they have a right to better pay and have a right to force an employer to pay them better. This is what I mean by legal black mail, when such actions, such MOB action is legal and permitted. If you wonder why so many good paying jobs are disappearing, the answer lies in the actions of the labor unions for the most part. Because of labor unions, all products are more expensive, therefore it is only natural that a company or businessman will seek to move their factories to other countries where labor is cheaper. What the union members do not realize is that they do NOT have a right to force a private business to pay them more;

that threatening to strike is no different than a death threat against another; that a private business is the property of its owner and the owner has constitutional and natural rights to conduct her/his business as he/she pleases; that an employer has the right to pay an employee what the employer and the employee agrees to. To bypass this contractual agreement and to pervert justice, the communists came up with the idea of labor unions. They argue, hey, it's a free country, let's abuse this legal loophole, let's trample all over the constitution and form labor unions and hold the employer hostage.

Not only are unionists tyrants and thugs, but they are also hypocrites. They demand freedom while they deny the same to others. In other words, if you start a business and become successful, your company grows and you hire more people you somehow loose your rights as an individual, because the government allows the employees to form a legal Mafia called a "Union" which now has the right to punish you for being successful. Justice demands that all contracts between two people are binding. When an employee forms a UNION with others, they are in effect breaking the contract with the employer and in turn now impose their own desires and demands on the person who gave them a job. Ladies and gentleman, this is legal robbery; it is communism, it is a depravation of rights, of right to life liberty and pursuit of happiness. Just as an employer has no right to force employees to work for them, so the employees have no right to break their contract with an employer, or to form a mob and hold the employer hostage.

The legal system in America and other so-called free countries not only permits and protects these legal Mafia systems, but FORCES an employer to not fire these gangsters, these thugs called union members. In other words, the employers are not only held hostages by the mob-unions but also by the very government, which is supposed to protect them from such tyranny. We urge all employers who are held hostage by unions to form a secret army of agents, which are to eliminate not only the labor union activists and employers, but also every members of a union. Furthermore, we urge all powerful corporations, which have not joined us yet, to join The Illuminati Order, and to move their corporate offices to Texas, and help encourage Mexico and South Africa to change their laws and Constitutions to conform to The Illuminati Constitution, so all our wealth and factories can be safely moved there so we can punish and eliminate all enemies of freedom in America and other nations which permit Labor Unions to deprive us of our rights and freedoms.

We will make Mexico what we hoped America to be, the Jewel and Crown of the world, the symbol of freedom and prosperity for all, a role model for all nations. We will make South Africa the Technology capital of the world, the envy of the world, and we will break Texas from the Union and teach the lazy American people, the Christian parasites and the altruists what tyranny really is; we will give them a taste of their own medicine. They voted for socialism and communism, we shall give it to them in abundance, if they continue to stand in our way. The gloves are now off, and the evil will be wiped off the face of the earth once and for all! It is time they learn that religion and their religious and altruists' leaders cannot give them happiness and wealth, and we will no longer be the slaves of the beggars and tyrants. We will make America pay us back. We had invested trillions of dollars to keep America free and show it the light of freedom and prosperity but they refused our offer, they have chosen imaginary gods and savage, barbaric bibles to guide their life instead of reason and logic. We will now make them pay for having wasted our money and efforts. The Illuminati Order will show them who the real messiah of the world is and they will beg us for help but we will be nowhere to be found, we will remain transparent and watch the tyrant parasites perish in anguish. We will hand America in the hands of the communists they voted for, in the hands of the altruists, we will withdraw our hand of support and will give the green light to our enemies to vandalize the nation we had built, the nation which turned its back on life LIBERTY and pursuit of happiness. They wanted labor unions, not we will let their communist labor unions give them jobs, because we will fire all employees when we move our wealth away, when we move our factories out of their land. Let their parasite government and their socialist unions create jobs for them, we have had enough. We will show no mercy to anyone, plain and simple.

Altruistic Political Mentality Put Into Practice

I will conclude this essay with the words of a highly enlightened and honored friend, David Kelley.

"Two Variants on "Social Justice""

Let us begin by noting that demands for social justice take two different forms, which I will call welfarism and egalitarianism. According to welfarism, individuals have a right to certain necessities of life, including minimum levels of food, shelter, clothing, medical care, education, and so on. It is the responsibility of society to ensure that all members have access to these necessities. But a laissez-faire capitalist system does not guarantee them to everyone. Thus, argue the welfarists, capitalism fails to satisfy its moral responsibility, and so must be modified through state action to provide such goods to people who cannot obtain them by their own efforts.

According to egalitarianism, the wealth produced by a society must be distributed fairly. It is unjust for some people to earn fifteen, or fifty, or a hundred times as much income as others. But laissez-faire capitalism permits and encourages these disparities in income and wealth, and is therefore unjust. The hallmark of egalitarianism is the use of statistics on the distribution of income. In 1989, for example, the top 20 percent of U.S. households on the income scale earned 45 percent of total income, whereas the bottom 20 percent earned only 4 percent of total income. The goal of egalitarianism is to reduce this difference; greater equality is always regarded as a gain in equity.

The difference in these two conceptions of social justice is the difference between absolute and relative levels of well-being. The welfarist demands that people have access to a certain minimum standard of living. As long as this floor or "safety net" exists, it does not matter how much wealth anyone else has, or how great the disparities are between rich and poor. So welfarists are primarily interested in programs that benefit people who are below a certain level of poverty, or who are sick, out of work, or deprived in some other way. Egalitarians, on the other hand, are concerned with relative well-being. Egalitarians have often said that of two societies they prefer the one in which wealth is more evenly distributed, even if its overall standard of living is lower. Thus egalitarians tend to favor government measures such as progressive taxation, which aim to redistribute wealth across the entire income scale, not merely at the bottom. They also tend to support the nationalization of goods such as education and medicine, taking them off the market entirely and making them available to everyone more or less equally.

Welfarism: Binding The Able
Let us consider these two concepts of social justice in turn.

The fundamental premise of welfarism is that people have rights to goods such as food, shelter, and medical care. They are entitled to these things (they say). On this assumption, someone who receives benefits from a government program is merely getting what is due him, in the same way that a buyer who receives the good he has paid for is merely getting his due. When the state dispenses welfare benefits, it is merely protecting rights, just as it is when it protects a buyer against fraud. In neither case is there any necessity for gratitude. The concept of welfare rights, or positive rights as they are often called, is modeled on the traditional liberal rights of life, liberty, and property. But there is a well-known difference. The traditional rights are rights to act without interference from others.... Accordingly, these rights impose on other people only the negative obligation not to interfere, not to restrain one forcibly from acting as he chooses. If I imagine myself removed from society—living on a desert island for example—my rights would be perfectly secure. I might not live long, and certainly would not live well, but I would live in perfect freedom from murder, theft, and assault.

By contrast, welfare rights are conceived as rights to possess and enjoy certain goods, regardless of one's actions; they are rights to have the goods provided by others if one cannot earn them oneself. Accordingly, welfare rights impose positive obligations on others. If I have a right to food, someone has an obligation to grow it. If I cannot pay for it, someone has an obligation to buy it for me.... From an ethical standpoint, then, the essence of welfarism is the premise that the need of one individual is a claim on other individuals... The claim does not depend on your personal relationship to the claimant, or your choice to help, or your evaluation of him as worthy of your help. It is an unchosen obligation arising from the sheer fact of his need.

But we must carry the analysis one step further. If I am living alone on a desert island, then of course I have no welfare rights, since there is no one else around to provide the goods. For the same reason, if I live in a primitive society where medicine is unknown, then I have no right to medical care. The content of welfare rights is relative to the level of economic wealth and productive capacity in a given society. Correspondingly, the obligation of individuals to satisfy the needs of others is dependent on their ability to do so. I cannot be blamed as an individual for failing to provide others with something I cannot produce for myself....

And this tells us something important about the ethical focus of welfarism. It does not assert an obligation to pursue the satisfaction of human needs, much less the obligation to succeed in doing so. The obligation, rather, is conditional: those who do succeed in creating wealth may do so only on condition that others are allowed to share the wealth. The goal is not so much to benefit the needy as to bind [enslave] the able. The implicit assumption is that a person's ability and initiative are social assets, which may be exercised only on condition that they are aimed at the service of others.

Egalitarianism: Ability As Obligation

If we turn to egalitarianism, we find that we arrive at the same principle by a different logical route. The ethical framework of the egalitarian is defined by the concept of justice rather than rights. If we look at society as a whole, we see that income, wealth, and power are distributed in a certain way among individuals and groups. The basic question is: Is the existing distribution fair? If not, then it must be corrected by government programs of redistribution. A pure market economy, of course, does not produce equality among individuals. But few egalitarians have claimed that strict equality of outcome is required by justice.

The most common position is that there is a presumption in favor of equal outcomes, and that any departure from equality must be justified by its benefits to society as a whole. Thus, the English writer R. H. Tawney wrote that "inequality of circumstance is regarded as reasonable, in so far as it is a necessary condition of securing the services which the community requires." John Rawls's famous "Difference Principle"—that inequalities are permitted as long as they serve the interests of the least advantaged persons in society—is only the most recent example of this approach. In other words, egalitarians recognize that strict leveling would have a disastrous effect on production. They admit that not everyone contributes equally to the wealth of a society. To some extent, therefore, people must be rewarded in accordance with their productive ability, as an incentive to put forth the efforts they are capable of. But any such differences must be limited to those, which are necessary for the public good.

What is the philosophical basis of this principle? Egalitarians often argue that it follows logically from the basic principle of justice: that people are to be treated differently only if they differ in some morally relevant way. If we are going to apply this fundamental principle to the distribution of income, however, we must first assume that society literally engages in an act of distributing income. This assumption is plainly false. In a market economy, incomes are determined by the choices of millions of individuals—consumers, investors, entrepreneurs, and workers. These choices are coordinated by the laws of supply and demand, and it is no accident that a successful entrepreneur, say, earns much more than a day laborer.

But this is not the result of any conscious intention on the part of society. In 1992, the most highly paid entertainer in the United States was Oprah Winfrey, who earned some $42 million. This was not because "society" decided she was worth that much, but because millions of fans decided that her show was worth watching. Even in a socialist economy, as we now know, economic outcomes are not under the control of government planners. Even here there is a spontaneous order, albeit a corrupt one, in which outcomes are determined by bureaucratic infighting, black-markets, and so forth.... In short, there is no basis for applying the concept of justice to the statistical distributions of income or wealth across an entire economy. We must abandon the picture of a large pie that is being divided up by a benevolent parent who wishes to be fair to all the children at the table.

Ability as Liability
Once we abandon this picture, what becomes of the principle espoused by Tawney, Rawls, and others: the principle that inequalities

are acceptable only if they serve the interests of all? If this cannot be grounded in justice, then it must be regarded as a matter of the obligations we bear to each other as individuals. When we consider it in this light, we can see that it is the same principle we identified at the basis of welfare rights. The principle is that the productive may enjoy the fruits of their efforts only on condition that their efforts benefit others as well. There is no obligation to produce, to create, to earn an income. But if you do, the needs of others arise as a constraint on your actions. Your ability, your initiative, your intelligence, your dedication to your goals, and all the other qualities that make success possible, are personal assets that put you under an obligation to those with less ability, initiative, intelligence, or dedication.

In other words, every form of social justice rests on the assumption that individual ability is a social asset. The assumption is not merely that the individual may not use his talents to trample on the rights of the less able. Nor does the assumption say merely that kindness or generosity are virtues. It says that the individual must regard himself, in part at least, as a means to the good of others. And here we come to the crux of the matter. In respecting the rights of other people, I recognize that they are ends in themselves, that I may not treat them merely as means to my satisfaction, in the way that I treat inanimate objects.... Why then is it not equally moral to regard myself as an end? Why should I not refuse, out of respect for my own dignity as a moral being, to regard myself as a means in the service of others?

The Objectivist Alternative

In questioning the ethics of altruism, I want to do more than simply raise these troubling questions. I want to outline an alternative ethical philosophy, developed by Ayn Rand. It is an individualist ethics, which defends the moral right to pursue one's self-interest. Altruists argue that life presents us with a basic choice: we must either sacrifice others to ourselves, or sacrifice ourselves to others. The latter is the altruist course of action, and the assumption is that the only alternative is life as a predator. But this is a false alternative, according to Rand. Life does not require sacrifices in either direction. The interests of rational people do not conflict, and the pursuit of our genuine self-interest requires that we deal with others by means of peaceful, voluntary exchange....

Man's primary faculty, his primary means of survival, is his capacity for reason. It is reason that allows us to live by production, and thus to rise above the precarious level of hunting and gathering. Reason is the basis of language, which makes it possible for us to cooperate and transmit knowledge. Reason is the basis of social institutions governed by abstract rules. In Rand's view, therefore, the purpose of ethics is to provide standards for living in accordance with reason, in the service of our lives....

How then should we deal with others? Rand's social ethics rests on two basic principles, a principle of rights and a principle of justice. The principle of rights says that we must deal with others peaceably, by voluntary exchange, without initiating the use of force against them. It is only in this way that we can live independently, on the basis of our own productive efforts; **the person who attempts to live by controlling others is a parasite.** Within an organized society, moreover, we must respect the rights of others if we wish our own rights to be respected. And it is only in this way that we can obtain the many benefits that come from social interaction: the benefits of economic and intellectual exchange, as well as the values of more intimate personal relationships. The source of these benefits is the rationality, the productiveness, the individuality of the other person, and these things require freedom to flourish. If I live by force, I attack the root of the values I seek.

The principle of justice is what Rand calls the trader principle: living by trade, offering value for value, neither seeking nor granting the unearned. An honorable person does not offer his needs as a claim on others; he offers value as the basis of any relationship. Nor does he accept an unchosen obligation to serve the needs of others. No one who values his own life can accept a open-ended responsibility to be his brother's keeper, nor would an independent person desire to be kept. The principle of trade, Rand observes, is the only basis on which humans can deal with each other as independent equals.

What I have given you is only a brief summary of Rand's ethical philosophy, the "Objectivist ethics," as she calls it. But I think it is enough to indicate that there is an alternative to the traditional ethics of altruism, an alternative that treats the individual as an end in himself in the full meaning of that term. The implication of this approach is that capitalism is the only just and moral system.

A capitalist society is based on the recognition and protection of individual rights. In a capitalist society, men are free to pursue their own ends, by the exercise of their own minds. As in any society, men are constrained by the laws of nature. Food, shelter, clothing, books, and medicine do not grow on trees; they must be produced. As in any society, men are constrained by the limitations of their own nature, the extent of their individual ability. But the only social constraint that capitalism imposes is the requirement that those who wish the services of others must offer value in return. No one may use the state to expropriate what others have produced.

Economic outcomes in the market—the distribution of income and wealth—will depend on the voluntary actions and interactions of all the participants. The concept of justice applies not to the outcome but to the process of economic activity. A person's income is just if it is won through voluntary exchange, as a reward for value offered, as judged by those to who it is offered. Economists have long known that there is no such thing as a just price for a good, apart from the judgments of market participants about the value of the good to them. The same is true for the price of human productive services. This is not to say that I must measure my worth by my income, but only that if I wish to live by trade with others, I cannot demand that they accept my terms at the sacrifice of their own self-interest.

Capitalism and the Needy

What about someone who is poor, disabled, or otherwise unable to support himself? This is a valid question to ask, as long as it is not the first question we ask about a social system. It is a legacy of altruism to think that the primary standard by which to evaluate a society is the way it treats its least productive members. "Blessed are the poor in spirit," said Jesus; "blessed are the meek." But there is no ground in justice for holding the poor or the meek in any special esteem, or regarding their needs as primary. If we had to choose between a collectivist society in which no one is free but no one is hungry, and an individualist society in which everyone is free but a few people starve, I would argue that the second society, the free one, is morally preferable. No one can claim a right to make others serve him involuntarily, even if his own life depends on it.

But this is not the choice we face. In fact, the poor are much better off under capitalism than under socialism, or even the welfare state. As a matter of historical fact, the societies in which no one is free, like the former Soviet Union, are societies in which large numbers of people go hungry...

Egoistic Charity

As for those who simply cannot work, free societies have always provided numerous forms of private aid and philanthropy outside the market: charitable organizations, benevolent societies, and the like. In this regard, let us be clear that there is no contradiction between egoism and charity. In light of the many benefits we receive from dealing with others, it is natural to regard our fellow humans in a spirit of general benevolence, to sympathize with their misfortunes, and to give aid when it does not require a sacrifice of our own interests. But there are major differences between an egoist and an altruist conception of charity.

For an altruist, generosity to others is an ethical primary, and it should be carried to the point of sacrifice, on the principle: give until it hurts. It is a moral duty to give, regardless of any other values one has; and the recipient has a right to it. For an egoist, generosity is one among many means of pursuing our values, including the value that we place on the well being of others. It should be done in the context of one's other values, on the principle: give when it helps. It is not a duty, nor do the recipients have a right to it. An altruist tends to regard generosity as an expiation of guilt, on the assumption that there is something sinful or suspicious about being able, successful, productive, wealthy. An egoist regards those same traits as virtues, and sees generosity as an expression of pride in them.

The Fourth Revolution (The Illuminati "Noble Revolution")

...I said at the outset that capitalism was the result of three revolutions, each of them a radical break with the past. The political revolution established the primacy of individual rights, and the principle that government is man's servant, not his master. The economic revolution brought an understanding of markets. The Industrial Revolution radically expanded the application of intelligence to the process of production. But mankind never broke with its ethical past. The ethical principle that individual ability is a social asset is incompatible with a free society. *If freedom is to survive* *and flourish, we need a fourth revolution, **a moral (noble) revolution,** that establishes the moral right of the individual to live for himself."*

****

*******Islam on Human Rights*******

(This is a chapter from "Islam" by Solomon Tulbure)

As time went by the men and women of the world sough to improve their lives and their values, a fact which has been recorded in the countless pages of our history. Today, in the year 2002, the civilized world has established written rules of conduct becoming a civilized person, but also left room for improvement. In the west, especially, we have some of the most humane and most precious laws, which are set in place specifically for the purpose of protecting the human rights of every single human being. Efforts of astronomical proportion have been made and are being made by the civilized world to help the third world nations. Even the oppressive and most tyrannical governments realize that their people too can have a good life and well being if they adopt our advanced system of laws and ethics.

But various forms of superstitions called religions, which are invented by the wicked and the evil have plagued human history. People embrace religions in order to attempt to appease and fulfill a natural human emptiness, which plagues all those who are emotionally weak and mentally unstable and poorly educated. The fear of death and the knowledge of our short life span have created a vacuum of insecurity. In fact, this fear of death is so powerful that it robs even some of the civilized and well educated into its trap. I suppose in time, our honored scientists will find this to be a genetic defect, and hopefully in the near future the gene(s) responsible for these emotions will be identified and dealt with accordingly.

But today, the need to find such a cure is ever more urgent, as the world faces a great and immediate threat from a unique religion, which has trapped over one billion people into a state of most barbaric mentality of those who lived some 1400 years ago. One would think that in today's modern times men and women would give up on barbaric ways; on rules which are the creation of savages who lived back then in ancient times. But ironically this is not the case; Islam has spread faster than ever and is still spreading faster than any other religion even today. In this chapter I wish to bring to light the true nature of Islam's version of "human rights" because no other author has had the courage to do so, being afraid of being condemned to death as was the author of "Satanic Verses" Mr. Salmon Rushdie. Even as I write this, the latest death threat I received yesterday from some Muslims is still fresh in my mind, and instead of having become afraid for my life, I feel even more encouraged to write more essays which I have decided to publish in book ("Islam") form as well.

On Human Rights

One of the first ironies of Islam I wish to point out here is that it is the only religion to ever claim that "god has rights" which come first before man's rights. The reason this is so ironic and certainly strange is simply because rights denote the protection from tyranny, oppression and forms of violations of one's person. Examples of rights are such as the right to life, liberty, property and the pursuit of happiness, and equal justice for all, and so on and so forth. Such rights are natural born rights, which we in the civilized world consider inalienable, and are the very foundation of our culture. These rights are needed not only for the protection for the poor, the weak, the helpless, but also for the rich and powerful as well. Therefore, our justice system protects the rights of all and this includes both genders, not just the males.

So the immediate question is, if the Muslim god, Allah, is already omnipotent, all-knowing and wise, as his followers claim, what rights does he need? Since Muslims claim that Allah is the creator of all things, and that he can do whatever he pleases, what rights does he need, and who is to guarantee and protect such rights, and for what purpose, from whom would his rights be protected? If Allah indeed needs rights then he also needs assurance and protection, as logic suggests. The truth is that such notions as prescribed by Islam would insult an omnipotent god, but as you shall see there is a devious reason behind this claim that a god needs "rights."

The secret of this Islamic jurisprudence, that Allah has a fundamental right that he be worshiped by all of mankind and that his laws be obeyed is to force Islam as a theocracy upon the whole world. This would give the Islamic clergy absolute power, to run the governments and the world as a tyrannical theocracy, in the name of Allah thus eliminating all dignity and human rights.

So when you hear Muslim scholars speak of "Islamic human rights" beware of them, because such a notion as "Islamic human rights" is an out right farce intended specifically to mislead people.

For Islam, the very concept of Human Rights is a big thorn in the side yet Muslim clerics and scholars would have us believe that Islam actually bestowed rights upon mankind. I doubt there is a bigger myth than this. In order for me to properly expose the fallacy of this "Islamic Human Rights" I will expand this chapter in 4 sections, so you can use this chapter as a reference for any future conversations you may have on the subject with others.

1. Rights of Allah (God)
2. Rights of Muslim **Men**
3. Rights of the Infidels?
4. Rights of women (LOL!)

1.   Rights of Allah

To expand on the notion of "Allah's rights" we first need to take into consideration the philosophical connotations. In light of the tremendous glory and prestige Muslims claim of Allah, it is reasonable to simply say that he has no need for any "rights" what so ever, since rights are only required as a means to protect one's interests and well being.

Allah, being almighty, the all-wise and the creator of all existence, as Muslims claim, would have no need for shelter, nor the protection of his creation, nor would anything man can do affect the eternal who is beyond space and time.

One the one hand, Muslims claim that Allah is always in control of all of existence, and on the other they claim that Allah has "rights" etc. If Allah indeed has a need for rights, then one cannot also claim that he is the creator of all things nor almighty. Philosophically speaking, an Allah who needs rights is the mere creation of religious manipulators who needed a stunning myth in order to impose their own barbaric absolutes upon others in order to gain power over others, without having to risk being publicly accountable.

This is a logical conclusion, seeing how this Allah feels very happy when people worship him, yet he gets bent out of shape when he is ignored. The savage mind actually believes that what man does or does not can actually affect such a being. If such a monster actually existed, to think that the actions of mere savages who are like a grain of sand in this vast universe which has trillions upon trillions of stars and trillion more planets, could affect a being who is supposed to be absolute, unmovable, and above all that, beyond space and time; that is bellow all levels of stupidity.

But to the Semitic god, which seems to only appeal to savages and the weak minded, worship is of great importance because it is through such a smoke screen that Allah's religious leaders can maintain power over the people and thus deprive them of liberties and human rights. Without worship of the divine there would be no need for clerics, but the inventors of religions made sure that their authority is assured through divine authority.

You see, once people are convinced of the existence of the divine and divine authority, those who propagate it can rob people under the cloak of divine authority, having been inspired by god.

The war between human rights and god's rights, however, had started in 1215 with the Magna Carta.

Let's see how it all started:

"In the first place have (we) granted to God, and by this our present Charter confirmed for us and our heirs for ever that the English Church shall be free." (Clause 1)

"No free man shall be arrested or imprisoned…or outlawed or exiled or in any way victimized, neither will we attack him or send anyone to attack him, except by the lawful judgement of his peers or by the law of the land." (Clause 39)

What had happened here, for the first time in history of mankind, a Church of god is granted freedom, a right, in other words. Without the approval of man, god' will cannot be imposed in order that he might be worshiped by force. God's authority was arrested by a man, the King of

England, and from this point onward even god's commanders on earth were subject to the laws of man above god's, thus making god's will subject to man's approval and laws. Therefore god is no longer to do as he pleases.

The fire of freedom, which started with the Magna Carta, got a huge boost when the Illuminati Order was forced to move its headquarters from Europe to the United States. Here, the Illuminati Order became more powerful. So powerful in fact that it spent millions of dollars (which in those days were huge fortunes) buying politicians and religious leaders, so they could convince them to pass the most famous piece of paper in the whole world, the Declaration of Independence and the US Constitution.

Allah received yet another blow:
"....all men are created equal, that they are endowed by their Creator with certain Unalienable Rights, that among these are Life, Liberty and the pursuit of Happiness."

The clergy of the time insisted that in order for the constitution to be accepted by the fanatical majority of the then fundamentalist Christians, a wool needed to be pulled over their eyes. By including the word "Creator" that would be enough to blind people from seeing the true nature of this most secular document. However, as you can see, god was robbed of his authority, as man demanded unalienable rights to life, liberty and pursuit of happiness, which cannot be interfered with even by the creator. So, "divine" authority was used to deprive god of absolute powers; to the Christians this paper was "inspired by god" hence the "Creator" was in there. The typical believer, as you can see, is easily deceived if one knows how to do it and the Illuminati were and are the masters of exactly that. They used the Church' own god to deprive the Church of the authority it abused until that point in time.

The Illuminati did the same thing in France, where it was at war with the Church since 1703, shortly after the Illuminati Order was founded in 1701, which forced it to go underground until the time was ripe for emerging again.

In France they were able to get a similar package passed called the "Declaration of the Rights of Man" in 1789, which was equally powerful:

"Ignorance, forgetfulness or contempt of the rights of man to be the only cause of public misfortunes and the corruption of governments. "

Article 1. "Men are born and remain free and equal in rights .."
Article 2. " ...These rights are Liberty, Property, Safety and Resistance to Oppression."
Article 3. "The source of all sovereignty lies essentially in the Nation. No corporate body, no individual may exercise any authority that does not expressly emanate from it."
Article 4. "Liberty consists in being able to do anything that does not harm others; thus the exercise of the natural rights of every man has no bounds other than those that ensure to the other members of society the enjoyment of these same rights. Only law (enacted by the Nation) may determine these bounds."

In France, the Illuminati Order also spend fortunes in order to make the French Revolution possible, because many Jesuit Priests had to be bought, and they were not as cheap as the American pawns. But god's Divine Rights were essentially demolished, and the religious thugs were thus deprived of their absolute power, which they used to rob, persecute and torture people, "in the name of god."

By 1948 the Illuminati Order had become very powerful, so powerful in fact, that they were able to buy many world leaders, in order to get them to pass the Universal Declaration of Human Rights through which they were able to rob god of his authority on a global scale:

"the inherent dignity and the equal and inalienable rights of all members of the human family as the foundation of freedom, justice and peace in the world. "

"Human beings shall enjoy freedom of speech and belief and freedom from fear and want."

Here are some of the most noteworthy articles of Universal Declaration of Human Rights.

Article 1. All human beings are born (**not created**)) free and equal in dignity and rights. They are endowed with reason and conscience and should act towards one another in a spirit of brotherhood.

Article 2. Everyone is entitled to all the rights and freedom set forth in the Declaration, without distinction of any kind, such as race, color, sex, language, religion, political or other opinion, national or social origin, property, birth or other status.

Article 3. Everyone has the right to life, liberty and the security of person.

Article 4. No one shall be held in slavery or servitude: slavery and the slave trade shall be prohibited in all their forms.

Article 6. Everyone has the right to recognition everywhere as a person before Law.

Article 10. Everyone is entitled in full equality to a fair and public hearing by an independent and impartial tribunal, in the determination of his rights and obligations and of any criminal charge against him.

Article 11. Everyone charged with a penal offence has the right to be presumed innocent until proved guilty according to Law in a public trial at which he has had all the guarantees necessary for his defense.

Article 16. Men and women of full age, without any limitation due to race, nationality or religion, have the right to marry and to found a family. They are entitled to equal rights as to marriage, during marriage, and at its dissolution.

Marriage shall be entered into only with the free and full consent of the intending spouses. (This cuts Allah's legs as well)

Article 18. Everyone has the right to freedom of thought, conscience and religion; this right includes freedom to change his religion or belief, and freedom, either alone or in community with others and in public or private, to manifest his religion or belief in teaching, practice, worship and observance.

Article 21. The will of the people shall be the basis of the authority of government; this shall be expressed in periodic and genuine elections which shall be by universal and equal suffrage and shall be held by secret vote or by equivalent free voting procedures.

From the beginning of human existence mankind has been subjected to all sorts of tyrannies and torture at the hands of priests. It was only in the last 50 years that the Illuminati have managed to secure human rights not only for the French and the Americans, but for the whole planet. To the civilized people of our world human rights are as precious as life itself.

Unfortunately, Islam and the Muslim world who have embraced savagery stands 100% against the Human Rights Declarations and yet they have the audacity of claiming to be the greatest gift to mankind.

Now, that I have explained what Human Rights are and how they came to be, let's look into Islam's claim of "Allah's Rights:

"To God belongs all that is in the heavens
and in the earth, and God encompasses everything." (Women IV: 125)

"To God bow all that is in the heavens and the earth
willingly or unwillingly." (Thunder XIII—15)

If Allah is all that Islam claims he is, why would he even need to boast of authority, property and rights? Nobody needs to claim ownership of anything unless there is a threat by a rival. Therefore, if Allah needs to assert his claim on the world, he is clearly not the Creator, since he is clearly desperate for recognition and to enslave everyone and force people into servitude. Furthermore, if Allah did exist, certainly he would not pick any human being to speak in such barbaric way in his name. A simple laser show in the sky, with a thundering voice the whole world could hear and an occasional repeat would do the trick perfectly, and everyone would have ample proof of who and what Allah is.

Allah did not create us for fun:

"What did you (humans) think that We (Allah) created you only for a sport ..?" (The Believers XXIII: 115)

As you can see, Allah is an insecure bastard who needs to be worshiped by his own creation.

You see, he did not create us for fun, but for a most important purpose:

"I have not created ... mankind except to worship me." (The Scatterers LI: 55)

If an all-powerful being does exist, one capable of creating a whole universe, such a being would have no need nor respect for idiots who have no self respect and for people who are willing to humiliate themselves by becoming the slaves of others.

If our own human standards of Human Rights are so superior and advanced how much more would a super-intelligent being's standards be? They would have to surpass them by far, not be savage, cruel and tyrannical. The Muslim worshiper is a person with no self-respect what so ever; such people are enslaved by their own stupidity and sealed in their misery by their religion which deprives them of individual rights and instills in them an absolute slave mentality. Under Islam man is a slave in the bondage of his self-induced imaginary master, which explains why Muslims are so eager to commit the most heinous crimes in the name of Allah.

Islam demands that man must have no desire for dignity, self-respect; that the sole purpose of man on earth is to worship his master, and as a reward he is promised nothing better in paradise than what is already here on earth.

What type of creatures does Allah want as his subjects:

"He (Allah) made his (man's) seed from a draught of despised fluid." (The Prostration XXXII: 8)

Here Allah tries to make sure that man does not think highly of himself.

In fact, Allah loves to insist how insignificant man is, in order to get man to be a slave:

"So let man consider of what he is created;
He is created from a gushing fluid
That issued from between the loins and ribs."
(The Night Star LXXXVI: 5-7)

By insulting man through the reference to the seminal discharge which gives life to man Allah thinks his worship by man is secured. This Allah obviously does not know that there is nothing filthy about semen what so ever; in fact semen and sperm are the very best and most valuable fluids in the universe. But even worse, this all-wise god turns around and damns the very creatures he desires to be his slaves; the creatures he supposedly created and from whom he desires worship and honor:

"Perish man! How unthankful he is!
Of what did He (Allah) create him?
Of a sperm drop .."
(He Frowned LXXX: 15-17)

What we have here is another one of the merciful Allah' taunts at his supposed creation, associating man to the so called "nasty fluid." The Koran says that when god decided to create man they rebelled against him:

"And when Thy Lord (Allah) said to the angels,
'I am setting in the earth a viceroy,'
They said, 'What will Thou set therein one
who will do corruption there, and shed blood?'"
(The Cow II: 25)

While man is deprived of any rights in the eyes of Allah due to man's "rebellious nature" man is, at the same time, worthy of being god's holy messengers on earth. On the one hand man is such a despicable and insignificant creature and on the other hand man is god's right hand ruler on earth. Through total submission and continuous worship, however, and being a complete slave of Allah, man has a chance to improve his standing with god. This all-wise Allah has laid down countless barbaric rules which man must obey in order to demonstrate obedience. In addition to the time wasting Five Pillars, god has devised methods, which ensures him that man would become completely oblivious of individual rights:

a. Prohibition to think liberally, and change religion.
b. Prohibition to legislate,
c. Allah declares:

"This day have I (Allah) perfected your religion
for you and completed My favor unto you,
and have chosen for you as religion AL-ISLAM.
(The Table, V- 3)

In other words, this perfectly wise god has chosen Islam as the perfect code of life for all of mankind; a permanent religion, which man cannot ever change. Notice also that Allah had assortments of religions to choose from, hence "have chosen for you a religion" which means there must have been many others he could have chosen from. In other words, Allah deprived Muslims of the right to make laws for themselves aside from what is given in the Islamic scriptures. Muslims living in modern times are thus forced to stick to the same barbaric laws invented my Mohammed 1400 years ago, no matter what. Any Muslim who breaks this rule is an infidel and as such he will burn in hell for doing so. This Islamic law is just one of many which deny man of basic human rights.

To make sure this Islamic law is not misunderstood Allah goes a bit further to clarify it:

"He (Allah) associates in His government no one."
(The Cave XVIII: 25)

A Muslim who even **thinks** of something which is contradictory to Allah's perfect will also burn in hell. The Koran, god demands, is to be the Muslim' only guide to his thinking process, and the study of any other books, no matter how superior and beneficial they may be, if it has the potential of affecting his Islamic faith, it is sinful and thus strictly forbidden.

Because Mohammed is declared to be the perfect role model, a Muslim' actions must be exactly as Mohammed's, including how he ate, talked, slept and walked, no exceptions. Islam being the perfect code of law, acting in any other way is sinful. Should a Muslim decide to give up his faith, he is automatically condemned to death.

2. Rights of Muslim **Men**

Now that we have explored Allah's rights, let's delve into the rights of the Muslim men.

It is logical to conclude that any rights Muslim men may have if any, they are derived ones and not substantive ones, in light of "God's Rights." For the sake of argument we shall call these "rights" even though they are mere simple rewards given Muslims by god for being such submissive and absolute slaves.

Let's see what these "rights" are now:

The relationship between Allah and the believer is laid out in such a fashion, that it clearly defines the believer as the sole property of Allah. As payment for carrying out divine commands, which are against the moral conscience of man, god grants bounty and bonuses to man in such a way as to prevent man from refusing to do god's will on the grounds of decency or justice, by cloaking the most heinous commands and teachings with "divine" origin.

"God has bought from the believers their selves and their possessions against the gift of Paradise; they fight in the way of God; they kill, and are killed; that is a promise binding upon God ..... and who fulfills his covenant truer than God." (Repentance IX: 110)

As you can see, Allah buys the believers with the promise of paradise and in exchange the believer must kill and get killed for the sake of god. The believer is forbidden from exercising his own conscience over what Allah has to say, and must have no qualms about it. The Muslims' duty is to go on a murder spree and a crusade against the unbelievers and cause destruction and death upon all that refuse conversion to Islam. The Koran has no shortage of verses to ensure that this is carried out.

The Extent of Allah's hatred towards the infidels is made clear in that god calls for total distinction between his party and the unbelievers which he calls Satan's party. God has commanded Muslims to be forever at war with the infidels, a war, which Allah promises the Muslims they would win in the end. This is made clear in the Koran (The Disputer LVIII: 20).

For this reason Muslims see themselves as the divine Managers of the affairs of all of mankind, and the sole caretakers of the planet. Allah has granted the Muslims the right to act as an elite army, judges and rulers over the whole earth, where all unbelievers must be enslaved or killed if they stand in the way of their divine mission.

However, only Allah has rights, while the rights of a Muslim are very much like those slaves of the Roman Empire who were able to rise to any political or economic height, but only under the authority of Allah, and all the while remaining god's sole property. The infidels, on the other hand, has no rights what so ever under Islamic Law:

Say (Muhammad): 'O God, Master of the Kingdom,
Thou givest the Kingdom to whom Thou wilt,
and seizest the Kingdom from whom Thou wilt,
Thou exaltest whom Thou wilt, and Thou
abasest whom Thou wilt; in Thy Hand is the good;
Thou art powerful over everything."'
(The House of Imran III: 25)

Allah is the only one who allocates honor and dishonor and since the infidels are the party of Satan, they have no rights; the unbelievers are the ones who deserve dishonor. In fact, the unbelievers, Allah says, are like animals and as such they are not subject to any human rights as you shall see. Allah justifies his severe animosity towards the infidels because unbelief, in his view, is the gravest of sins against him, which undermines his absolute authority over every aspect of a person's life.

God went out of his way to make this clear:

a. Oh believers! the non-Muslims are unclean." (Repentance IX: 27)
b. "Certainly, God is an enemy to unbelievers." (The Cow 11: 90)
c. "Surely, the **worst of beasts** in God's sight are **the unbelievers.**"
(The Spoil VIII: 57)

d. "O believers, do not treat your fathers and mothers as your friends, if they prefer unbelief to belief; whosoever of you takes them for friends, they are evil-doers." (Repentance IX: 20)

In fact, this hatred of the unbelievers among Muslims extends to their own parents if they are unbelievers; the Muslim must treat even his own mother and father as enemies if they reject Islam. This merciful god called Allah has declared all non-Muslims to be "the worst of beasts," who cannot possibly have any human rights.

The duty and purpose of all Muslims is to:

"Fight those who believe not in God and the Last Day and do not forbid what God and His Messenger have forbidden—such men as practise not the religion of truth, being of those who have been given the Book—until they pay the tribute out of hand and have been humbled." (Repentance IX: 28)

To help you understand this verse, I must point out that Islam claims and demands that the Koran is the ONLY standard of vice, virtue, justice and morals, and Islam does not recognize any other moral code or law aside from the Koran. Those who practice religions other than Islam are therefore infidels and as such, Muslims are commanded to fight them until they submit to Muslims as slaves and made to *"pay the tribute out of hand as a sign of their humiliation!"* For this reason very few non-Muslims are to be found in Strict Muslims nations, and those who are there are not permitted to leave; they must stay there and pay heavy taxes to the non-Muslims.

Therefore, when Muslims speak of Human Rights and Justice, the forms there of are as prescribed by the Koran and Islamic Law, which are a far cry as the Human Rights understood and practiced in the civilized world. The reason for the great difference is because:

a. Allah is the enemy of the non-Muslims, and
b. because, in Allah's sight, unbelievers are the worst beasts.

I think all of us civilized people can agree that freedom of expression is one of the most valued human rights. In an Islamic state Islamic Law forbids such a right, especially for the non-Muslim.

Anyone of another faith or no faith at all who speaks of his faith or lack of one favorably with a Muslim one can expect to loose his/her life or face life in prison. Even when it comes to talking about Jesus, who Islam recognizes as having been a holy man, Islam forbids Christians of speaking of him because Islam has a different take on his life and death and Islam claims to have the absolute truth about the issue:

"... For their saying 'we slew the Messiah, Jesus son
of Mary, the Messenger of God.
Yet they did not slay him, neither crucified him
only a likeness of that was shown them .....
God raised him up to Him." (Women IV: 155)

So anyone claiming that Jesus died on the cross is a heretic and an infidel worthy of death for speaking against the truth of the Koran. As you can see, Islam does not tolerate any other religion nor does it have any sort of respect for other belief systems. Islam seeks to undermine other religions such as Christianity, by insulting and belittling them and strictly forbidding any anti-Koranic teachings and practices. Any Christian or Jew in a Muslim country found praying publicly would suffer tremendous punishment if not death. While there are a few moderate countries which permit Churches and Synagogues, it is not because Islamic Laws permits such, but because those countries are in deep financial crisis and are forced to allow them in order to get international help of sorts and also because many Christians run charity organizations which feed those Muslim hypocrites. A perfect example of this is Afghanistan where millions are facing starvation, and the Christian world is now feeding them, while other Muslim nations have not lifted a finger to help their fellow Muslims, especially the filthy rich oil producing Arab nations.

Since the Koran holds that Islam is the only true religion, preaching other faiths to a Muslim is a most serious crime under Islamic law. For this reason, any Muslim who converts to another religion is to have his head cut off, as Islamic Justice demands. Missionaries cough preaching another religion to a Muslim faces the same punishment.

One of the things I find ironic is that some Muslim nations have the audacity to call themselves "republics" since this is a oxymoron; an "Islamic Republic" is like a honest liar. Allah declared to be the sole ruler of all-human affairs, therefore democracy and Islam are 100% at odds. In fact non-Muslims and women are not even permitted to vote. Islamic Law clearly states that all government belongs to Allah alone therefore even the fact that Muslims are permitted to vote is against god's perfect law.

As far as a Muslim marrying a non-Muslim, this too is a taboo and strictly illegal, but a Muslim man may have sex with a non-Muslim and have non-Muslim mistresses and concubines as a show of dominance and pride.

There is one verse in the Koran, which appears to allow for a Muslim man to marry a "woman of the Book" i.e. a Jewish or a Christian woman:

"(Permitted to you are) in wedlock women of them who were given the Book (Bible) before you if .." (The Table IV: 5)

However, this is more of a theory, since even the Prophet Mohammed did not practice it. This is made clear because he married Safya, a Jewish woman (who was not left with much of a choice) only after she agreed to accept Islam, but another Jewish girl named Rehana was kept as his concubine because she refused to give up her religion.

There are some rare instances where Muslim men marry Jewish or Christian women, but this only happens because they lack women to marry where they live, or they are living in the west where they are supposed to try and multiply as much as possible so they can raise more Muslim children in order to take over the world. This is so evident in the west, by the way. Also, in light of much criticism Islam has received from the civilized world, many Muslims have started their own brands of Islam which ignore much of what Allah and his holy prophet had to say. They want to be in control of people so they invented their own brand of bull-crap.

One important thing to note is that Islam pays lip service when it claims that Muslims believe in other "Apostles of god" and previous prophets. If Muslims did in fact live up to this myth then they would follow and listen to the teachings of those prophets and Apostles of god. In practice, however, Islam and its holy books do not recognize even one verse from those other prophets, simply because what the other holy books, such as the Bible and the New Testament oppose everything Islam stands for, pure and simple. But as you can see and shall see, hypocrisy to a Muslim is like water to a fish. Therefore, "The People of the Book" are infidels and are damned to burn in hell:

"The unbelievers of the People of the Book
and the idolaters shall be in the Fire; of Hell

therein dwelling for ever:
those are the worst of creatures,
But those who believe, and do righteous deeds,
those are the best of creatures."
(The Clear Sign XCVIII: 5)

"Islam is peace" ? Exactly what did president Bush mean when he said "Islam is peace"? What sort of peace was he speaking of? I think it was the kind, which allows his father and his friends to make millions from the Oil rich Muslim nations through his business. Only a moron or a liar and deceiver would claim that Islam is peace:

"O believers, take not Jews and Christians
as friends; they are friends of each other.
Whoso of you makes them his friends
is one of them." (The Table V: 55) ("*Islam is peace!*" President Bush)

As you can see, it is forbidden for a "true Muslim" to even have non-Muslim friends, let alone tolerate us. One would think that marrying a non-Muslim would be forbidden if even mere friendship with a unbeliever is forbidden. Notice also that a Muslim can murder a non-Muslim without fearing being executed. In Muslim 4138 it says that the Prophet had ordered that the head of a Jew should be smashed between two stones because he smashed the head of a Muslim girl, yet in another case (Muslim 4151) where a Muslim woman broke a non-Muslim's teeth, the perpetrator was only required to pay a small fee instead of applying the Islamic Law which demands "eye for an eye and tooth for tooth."

Furthermore, a Jew, Hindu, Christian or a non-Muslim may not provide evidence in court, especially against a Muslim.

As a matter of fact in a Islamic nation an infidel is merely a necessary evil who is barely tolerated. To Islam, "Human Rights" is sheer nonsense, especially when it involves an infidel. The only reason infidels are even permitted to live in an Islamic nation is for the cheap labor, because Islamic Law demands that non-Muslims pay a **humiliation tax** known in Koranic terms as **jaziya.**

In addition to the humiliation tax, a non-Muslim must wear distinctive clothes and have a clear unbeliever mark on his house to warn Muslims that an unbeliever lives there. Muslims are not permitted to associate with them or to attend funerals with them. Possessing arms and riding horses is also forbidden to a non-Muslim, and the Islam tradition demands that a non-Muslim give way to a Muslim when walking on the same path or walkway.

Now let us deal with the "Rights of Women" in Islam.

Rights of Women

I suppose one should ask, "what rights of women" in Islam?

Because Mohammed was an absolute control freak, he uses the excuse that because woman deceived Adam the woman had to be reduced to the status of a complete slave. He knew that if he included any rights for women what so ever in his scheme of things, eventually women would seek more rights and that would not play well with the dictatorial type-men of his likeness.

On the other hand he was faced with a paradox, knowing that he had to establish his doctrine in such a way that women would not rebel against Islam and eventually bring about its downfall.

For this reason Mohammed made sure that women were allowed the bare minimal liberties, so they could be fooled to buy into Islam, not that they were left with much of a choice.

Mohammed had to make sure that on the surface Islam appeared generous and gentle in this regard. But when Islamic Law and the practice of it is examined, it is far from being gentle and generous.

One of the smoke screens Muslims use when trying to convert others, or to appease a non-Muslim is in the claim that Islam is the very first religion which granted women the right to divorce their husbands and to own property. This of course is an absolute lie, since many religions, Including Judaism and Christianity granted these rights and in a much better and liberal fashion as well. As a matter of fact, the very mother of the Arabs was **herself the property of a Jewish woman** named Sarah. In Islam women can never exercise these rights simply because they are forbidden to participate in any form of social life:

"And so to the believing women, that they
cast down their eyes and guard their private
parts, and reveal not their adornment
save such as is outward; and let them cast
their veils over their bosoms, and not reveal .."
(Light XXIV: 30)

"O Prophet, say to the wives and daughters
and the believing women, that they draw
their veils close to them .."
(The Confederates XXXIII: 55) ("Islam is peace!" President Bush)

"Remain in your houses; and display not
your finery, as did the pagans of old."
(The Confederates XXXIII: 25) ("Islam is peace!" President Bush)

And this seals the faith of their so-called "rights" beyond dispute:

"**Men** are the managers of the affairs of women
for that God has preferred in bounty
One of them over another...
Righteous women are therefore obedient...
And those you fear may be rebellious
admonish; **banish them to their coaches
and *beat them*.**" (Women IV: 35) (**Allah and Islam is peace?**)

Islam restricts women to the home and the wearing of a veil and since man is appointed as the manager of all the affairs of women with authority to even go as far as to "**beat them**" if they are not obedient to their demands. Therefore a Muslim woman's rights to own property is just an attractive gimmick, a smoke screen, like a beautiful flower with an awful odor, it is merely given to women to entice and bribe them. Those rights are practically non-existent for Muslim women.

As far as Khula (right to divorce) is concerned, while a man can divorce a woman whenever he wishes, for a woman this is a process of going through a nightmare and mostly impossible or impractical to say the least. In addition, she is to face the wrath of Allah and his peaceful angels if she divorces without absolute justification. 99.9% of the time the judges of this male chauvinistic sick society will ignore the pleas of a woman as the judges are males and rarely, very rarely does a Muslim woman succeed.

Let's examine this Khula a bit, shall we?

Ibn-e-Majah, vol. 1, page 571: "A wife must not seek divorce from her husband without a serious cause. If she does, she will not enter paradise. If she can prove her case, she will be awarded decree only if she returns all that her husband had bestowed on her as an entitlement or outright gift. A woman who seeks Khula, cannot expect settlement!"

According to the law of inheritance the value of one male is equal to two women, (Women IV 10). The law of evidence is even worse; not only is a woman worth half as a man, but she is not permitted to introduce evidence while the male can if male witnesses are available.

In light of the limitations and restrictions Islamic Law has imposed on women, it is safe and honest to conclude that this was done deliberately in order to deprive women of any human rights, and turn them into mere sexual toys, house pets and slaves, which causes men to flock to Islam.

The woman's religious duty is to produce the maximum number of children, Ibn-e-Majah Vol. 1, page 518 and 523 in his "SUNUN:" The Prophet said "Getting married is my basic doctrine. Whoso does not follow my example, is not my follower. Marry, so that I can claim preference over other communities (Jews and Christians) owing to commanding a greater number of followers."

"MISHKAT" reports in Vol. 3 page 119, a similar hadith:

"On the Day of Judgement, I shall have the greater number of followers than any other prophet..."

Clearly Mohammed was after followers, fame, power and fortunes and the sure way to accomplish this was through subjecting woman to the absolute authority of man thus becoming mere baby-factories and slaves.

Under Islam the Muslim woman lives with the constant fear of what might happen to her if her husband deserts her, (especially once she has mothered many children). This alone is enough to keep her under his absolute control.

Let's go even further on this subject:

"And monasticism they invented—We
did not prescribe it for them—only
seeking the good pleasure of God; but
they observed it not as it should be observed."

To make this quite simple and to the point, the Christians are insulted here because the enjoyment of women sexually is "the good pleasure of God" for man. So woman's purpose and duty is clearly to be man's sex toys and slaves. In exchange for being man's slave, the woman is entitled to be loved by her husband, something which is rarely practiced by Muslim men, and this "love" for their wives is also subject to the husband's discretion for the most part.

Under Islam, woman MUST consent sexually to all her husband' desires; in fact there is no such a concept as consent, when it comes to sex. The woman is obligated to submit no matter what, as her husband has full authority over her body; she is practically a slave and there is no other way to say it. One might sugar coat it with many different flavors of sugar, but it is what it is-slavery.

Mohammed was not stupid in this regard; he made sure that males were ascended to a superior status while women were subjected to humiliation in equal proportions. Here, judge for yourself, don't take my word for it:

"Women have such honorable rights as obligations
but their men have a degree above them."
(The Cow: 225)

This is one of the most hotly debated verses which the Islamic zealots always try to use as proof to the would be female convert of the equality of the sexes.

Let's see what the hadith has to say on this:

"If women comply with your commands, do not
molest them ..Listen carefully, they have a right
over you that you take care of their food and wear."
(Ibn-e-Majh, Vol. 1, p. 519)

So the only real rights a woman has is to get food and clothes and even these are conditional on her obedience to her owner, her husband. To put it quite simply, under Islamic Law, man is superior to woman. The following should make this point crystal clear:

1. " ..marry such women
as seem good to you, two, three, four."
(Women: 1)

Here Islamic Law gives men the choice of having up to four wives and as you may already know, as many concubines as he can afford. (On a side note, don't you think it is strange that the west says nothing about the thousands of white young girls rich Muslim men in Islamic nations buy from kidnapping-Mafia? That is right, if you ever have the opportunity to visit a rich Muslim man in Saudi Arabia, try sneaking around if you can. You will see at least one or two blonde young girls/or women who have been bought and forced to be his wives/sex slaves. British, Israeli, Vatican (VIA), Russian, French and American intelligence have been aware of this for a long time, but due to cheap oil prices this subject has been successfully suppressed.)

Lately, Muslim scholars have been hard at work inventing all sorts of interpretations to attempt to reconcile the great shame of Islam's polygamy doctrine. Some of them claim that having more than one husband is forbidden because it becomes impossible to know the real father of a child. This worked well for them until the invention of DNA testing, so they will have to come up with newer interpretations. Either way, they cannot at the same time claim "equal rights" between men and women as those clerics on TV have been trying to feed the west every time our naïve TV networks becomes their mouthpiece.

Akbar the Great of India had 5,000 concubines and his son, Jehangir, had no fewer than 6,000! I suppose this is one form of private brothels, but that would be putting it mildly especially in light of a recent trend which brings Muslim leaders to the microphones of the naïve western media where they have the audacity to speak of morals and human rights.

As a matter of fact, Muslim scholar have the chutzpah to claim that just as men have rights over women so do women have rights over men. This is their claims as proof of equality, but the only right a woman has over a man is the right to be fed and clothed, and again, that too is conditional. Providing the woman merits it by being absolutely obedient to every command and wish of her owner, the husband, only then is she to be fed and clothed. It is a master slave relationship, make no mistake about it.

"If I were to order someone to prostrate before other than God, I would have commanded woman to prostrate before her husband.

If a husband tells his wife to keep carrying a load of
stones from that red mountain to that black mountain,
she must obey him whole heartedly."
(Ibn-e-Majah, Vol. 1, ch. 592, p 520)

"By God, who controls the life of Muhammad, a woman cannot discharge her duty towards God until she has discharged her duty towards her husband: if she is riding a camel and her husband expresses his desire, she must not refuse."
(Ibn-e-Maja, Vol. 1, ch. 592, p 520)

Even if the woman is in the middle of baking bread at a communal oven where time-share is of the essence, the wife must drop whatever she is doing at once and report to her husband for sex if he ordered her to come. (Tirmzi, Vol. 1, p 428)

It should be noted that Islamic Law is set up in such a way that it makes it extremely hard for a woman to get a divorce from her husband, especially since the father gets custody by default. This inhumane law is one of those rules, which makes divorce hard but it is one of many which ensures man's grip over the woman.

This superiority starts right from the lowest in Islamic society:

"Aisha said that she had a slave and a slave-girl who
were married. She told the Prophet that she wanted to
set them free. He said that she ought to free the slave
(man) first."
(Ibn-e-Majah,Vol. 2, ch. 130, p 100)

On evidence again:

" ..And call in to witness,
two witnesses, men; or if the two be
not men, then one man and two women,
such witnesses as you approve of .."
(The Cow: 280)

As I have stated earlier, one man is equal to two women when it comes to legal procedings!

But perhaps this is a good time to bring in the myth about the limit on four wives:

"And if you desire to exchange a wife
in place of another ..take of her nothing .."
(Women: 20)

In other words, a Muslim man can have as many wives as he wishes, providing he keeps swiping them for new models, so that the number 4 is not exceeded at any time. Divorcing for a man is quite easy since he needs not provide any reason for doing so. Hassan, one of the Holy prophet's grandson used this method, he had gone through 70 wives. He would marry during the day and after a few days he would divorce to get a new model. Sadly, those former wives now remained his concubines having been left pregnant, and since they were mere concubines they had no rights at all.

During the Roman Empire the Romans executed any man who had sex with a concubine by force, yet Islam encourages the practice in order to attract followers. Let me tell you this, even though I am an atheist, this alone makes Islam quite attractive; I could go to a Muslim country with a few thousand dollars and set myself up as quite a "king in my castle" if you will. Of course I abhor Islam and this practice so I would never do it, but I assure you, it is quite tempting.

As far as raping a concubine under Islamic Law, there is no prohibition against it, but there is a law, which punishes the woman, and not the man for "indecent" acts…

"Such of you women as commit indecency
call four of you to witness against them;
and if they witness; then detain them
in their houses until death takes them
or God appoints for them a way." (Women: 20)

So far no Muslim scholar has come forth to explain what "Or God appoints for them a way," in which case it clearly implies death by incarceration and may be even floggings or stoning to death as is usually the case. But not to worry, "Islam is peace" because President Bush said it is; that's Republicans for you. Go figure.

Man's authority over women is not limited to his own wife; it goes even further. For example, if a man does not like his daughter-in-law and tells his son to divorce her the son must do so and the father does not have to give any reason for disliking her. (Tirmzi,Vol. 1 p 440)

The Holy prophet Mohammed left yet another famous Muslim tradition, which Mullahs (religious leaders) recite with great pride to show the depth of brotherly love amongst Muslims:

"Behold my two wives and select the one you like the best."

A famous Medinite Muslim (an Ansar) made this brotherly gesture to another Muslim at the time Mohammed had to run from Mecca together with his followers to seek refuge in Medina. The offer was accepted, so an-Ansar divorced her on the spot so he could give her as a gift to the other. Once again you can see for yourself that to a Muslim man a woman is merely a souvenir, if that.

Let's look at another hadith:

"In the battle fought against FAZARA under the command of Abu Bakr, a very pretty Arab girl was given as share of booty to Salama Bin Al-Akwa. He had not seduced her (raped her) when the Prophet met him in the street, and said, " O Salama, give me that girl, may God bless your father." Salam said, "She is for you, Messenger of Allah! By Allah I have not yet disrobed (raped) her. "

The Messenger of Allah sent her to the people of Mecca, and surrendered her as a ransom for a number of Muslims who had been kept there as prisoners."(Muslim: 4345)

So this Holy Prophet, Mohammed, accepted girls and women as gifts. The Coptic Mary, who gave birth to one of his sons, is an example in point.

"The Prophet declared from the pulpit at Hajj, a wife must not spend anything belonging to her husband without his permission, and this prohibition equally applied to buying foodstuff."
(Tirmzi Vol. 1, p 265)

"Even in religious matters of great importance, a wife is subjected to her husband's command. There are several hadiths which say that a wife may not observe fasting without her husband's permission in case he wants to have sexual intercourse with her." (Tirmzi, Vol . 1, p 300)

Because men are so attracted to women, Islam treats woman as a devil:

"The Prophet unintentionally looked at a woman and was aroused. He went home and had intercourse with Zainab (one of his pretty wives). He said, "Woman faces you as Devil. If you are affected by her charm, have intercourse with your wife because she has the same thing as the woman who affected you.""
(Tirmzi, Vol. 1, p 428)

The Prophet said:

"Woman has been created from a rib which is twisted.
If you try to straighten it, you will break it. It is
desirable to make the best use of it as it is."
(Tirmzi, Vol. 1 p 440)

Here is a hadith which Muslim women must be proud of:

*The woman whose husband remains happy at night, and
every night, she will be admitted into paradise.*
(Tirmzi, Vol. 1, p 428)

As you can see, gratification of man's lust is an act equal to or of worshipping God!

The above is secured with:

"The woman who decorates herself for anyone other than her own husband is like darkness of the Day of Judgement." (Tirmzi, Vol. 1, p 430)

16. A woman, by nature, is man's only calamity:

The Prophet said that he had not left for man any calamity, which could hurt him except woman.
(Tirmzi, Vol. 2 p 286)

Here is another Islamic beauty:

"A woman is not a believer if she undertakes a journey, which may last three days or longer, unless she is accompanied by her husband, son, father or brother." (Tirmzi, p 431)

"If a woman refuses to come to bed when invited by her husband, she becomes a target of the curses of angels. Exactly the same happens if she deserts her husband's bed." (Bokhari, Vol. 7 p 93)

"A woman in many ways is deprived of the possession of her own body. Even her milk belongs to her husband." (Bokhari Vol. 7, p 27)

Birth control is forbidden a woman:

The Prophet said: "When wife vexes her husband, then houri of paradise utter curses on her saying, 'may God destroy you because he is with you only for a short time; he will shortly leave you to come to us.' (Ibn-e-Majah, Vol. 1, p 560)

The Prophet said, *"A woman's evidence carries half the weight of that of a man .. it is owing to lack of wisdom on their part. However, they are also injurious to the dignity of faith and cannot be allowed to say prayer during the period of menstruation or observe tasting."* (Mishkat, Vol. 1, p 19)

The Prophet said: *"Beware of women because the calamity that the Israelite suffered was caused by women."* (Mishkat, Vol. 2, p 70)

The Prophet said: *"Misfortune is a part of womanhood, residence and horse."* (Mishkat, Vol. 2, p 70)

The Prophet said: *"No woman should perform a marriage ceremony of another woman or her own because such a woman is the true seducer."* (Mishkat, Vol. 2, p 78)

The Prophet said: *"If Eve was not created, no woman would have been dishonest towards her husband."* (Mishkat, Vol. 2, p 98)

The Prophet said: *"When a man calls his wife to bed and she refuses and he is angered, then angels keep cursing her all night ..even the Master of Sky (God) is annoyed with her until husband is reconciled with her."* (Mishkat, Vol. 2, p 100)

28. The Prophet said: *"When a woman dies, if her husband was pleased with her, she goes to paradise."* (Mishkat, Vol. 2, p 102)

29. The Prophet said: *"On the Day of Judgement, a husband shall not be questioned for beating his wife."* (Mishkat, Vol. 2, p 105)

Dealing with "feminine brutes." The Koran says: "And those you fear may be rebellious admonish; banish them to their couches, and **beat them**. If they then obey you, look not for any way against them." (Women: 35)

A hadith says:
" ..women had become bold with their men, and so the Prophet authorised beating them. As a result, seventy women, during one evening, gathered at the residence of the Prophet to complain ruefully against their husbands, who they thought, were not good people." (Ibn-e-Majah, Vol. 1, p 553)

"And say to the believing women, that they
cast down their eyes and guard their private
parts, and reveal not their adornment
save such as is outward; and let them cast
their veils over their bosoms, and not reveal
their adornment save to their husbands..." (Light XXIV: 30)

Again:

"O Prophet, say to the wives and daughters
and the believing women, that they draw
their veils close to them:" (The Confederates 33: 55)

Then came:

"And stay in your houses..." (The Confederates 33: 25)

So the Arab woman became a Muslim woman and as such she was reduced to the status of a sex slave, house slave and a political pawn for the enjoyment of man.

It is of importance to know that Mohammed sealed many alliances with various powerful men such as Umar, Abu Bakr, Uthman and Ali, all sealed through marriages. These are the men whom held the status of high ranks and dignity at the side of Mohammed, for having been helpful in the spreading of Islam and are also co-founding fathers of the Arab Empire.

The rise of women to political power in nations such as Pakistan, Turkey and Bangladesh is merely a sign of spiritual decline and not to be seen as within the Islamic Law. In fact, Pakistani women have lost their positions when the military coup overthrew the government and set itself up as the new government, which is now heading back to the

Islamic Law style. Furthermore, these liberal Muslim nations are constantly in strife with religious wars between the liberal Muslims and the Strict Koranic Muslims. Many Muslim nations, which attempted democracy and modernization and liberal laws, have already failed as the true Muslims have overtaken them.

Now that we have explored the true nature of Islam with regards to Human Rights and women of this world it is important that I do not conclude this chapter before I show you just how important sexual enjoyment is to Allah and his holy men.

Not only did Allah turn earthly women into sexual toys and slaves but the women of the world to come, which are called HOURIS, are also specially made for the true Muslim men to enjoy once they enter paradise. The Koran describes the HOURIS, as being the most delightful, delicate and sensual and obtaining them is one of the highest goal and honor for the Muslim men to enjoy. As a matter of fact Islam has special prayers through which men plead with Allah solely for the granting them HOURIS; these supernatural sex machines are said to be the "the providers of the most exquisite and charming sexual pleasures." For these reasons uneducated and weak minded men embrace and stick to Islam, so that they may have part in the Islamic paradise. So you see, Islam is a bewitching bribe for many men and a most attractive one indeed!

Islamic salvation entails obtaining entry into the "land of houris" where there is no end to sensual delight and satisfaction, stars in the sky, flowers in the garden and the best foods in abundance; all for man's sake. All Allah asks of man is that he becomes a Muslim and lives and die as a Muslim.

Mohammed was no fool, he knew man's greatest weaknesses and made sure to exploit it fully as no religion before his has done.

What is a houri?

The Koran says:

" .... for them (the Muslims) is reserved a definite provision. Fruit and a great honor in the Gardens of Bliss reclining upon couches arranged face to face, a cup from a fountain being passed round to them, white, a pleasure to the drinkers ..... and with them wide-eyed maidens flexing their glances as if they were slightly concealed pearls."

(The Rangers 40: 45)

"Surely for the God-fearing
awaits a place of security,
gardens and vineyards
and maidens with swelling bosoms." (The Tidings 30)

But Allah even included a bonus:

"Surely the pious shall be in bliss,
upon couches gazing:
You find in their faces the shining bliss
as they are offered to drink of **wine** sealed,
whose seal is musk ... and whose mixture
is Tasnim, a fountain at which to drink
those brought nigh." (The Stinters 20: 25)

Hadith Tirmzi, volume two (p. 35-40) which gives details of houris, the ever-young virgins of paradise:

1. A houri is a most beautiful young woman with a transparent body. The marrow of her bones is visible like the interior lines of pearls and rubies. She looks like a red wine in a white glass.

2. She is of white colour, and free from the routine physical disabilities of an ordinary woman such as menstruation, menopause, urinal and offal discharge, child-bearing, and the related pollution.

3. She is a woman characterised by modesty and flexing glances; she never looks at any man except her husband, and feels grateful for being the wife of her husband.

4. A houri is a young woman, free from odium and animosity. Besides, she knows the meaning of love and has the ability to put it into practice.

5. A houri is an immortal woman, who does not age. She speaks softly and does not raise voice at her man; she is always reconciled with him. Having been brought up in luxury, she is a luxury herself.

6. A houri is a girl of tender age, having large upright breasts. Houris dwell in palaces of splendid surrounding.

Mishkat, volume three says on pages 83-97:

7. If a houri looks down from her abode in heaven onto the earth, the whole distance shall be filled with light and fragrance...

8. A houri's face is more radiant than a mirror, and one can see one's image in her cheek. The marrow of her shins is visible to the eyes.

9. Every man who enters paradise shall be given seventy-two houris; no matter at what age he had died, when he enters paradise, he will become a thirty-year-old, and he will not age any further.

10. Tirmzi, Vol. 2 states on page 138:

In this chapter I have given absolutely honest and accurate view of Islamic human rights and particularly the status and non-rights of women. Perhaps you should look up everything I have said here, and please do reflect on it, because the very future of our existence as a race may very well depend on it. It is my sincere belief that unless we work to put a stop to this savagery as soon as possible, by the time the Arabs arm themselves with nuclear weapons it may very well be too late.

****

*******The Omnipotent God ?*******

First of all I wish for you, the reader, to understand that this essay is written in such language as to appeal to the average person and not just to the intellectual. The average person is poorly educated and lacks the mental grandeur to understand scholarly language. For this reason traditional arguments against the existence of God, put forth by many scholars have failed to reach through the minds of the unsophisticated, the simple minded if you will. This is made clear in that theologians have not bothered to put forth counter arguments in forms which can be understood by their followers, and preachers have purposely ignored or failed to mention in their temples of brainwashing the existence of these arguments. The best arguments against god therefore remain unknowable to the masses, as if they do not even exist; the blind followers of religion have never encountered them and so, their minds are blind still.

One of the things you will never hear a preacher or theologian admit openly is that there is no rational proof of god's existence; that it is impossible, logically speaking, for such proof to exist. In order for me to show you just how true this fact is, I will use the "Omnipotence" of god claim, one of the characteristics of god which theists have assigned to their god(s), and the problem of evil. Please note that my argument against god in this case is purely logical and rational, therefore, if you are not well educated in the laws of logic and subject, do not expect to understand what you will read henceforth.

One of the things I will show you is that theological doctrines put forth in the Bible and Koran as well as many other religious dogma, are inconsistent and leads the laymen to reject reason with extreme attitudes when these problems are brought to their attention. This essay is intended for the theists whom not only believe in a god, but that their god is also wholly good as well as omnipotent. Such is the case with the Biblical and Islamic god. Also note that I have excluded the mythical figure called "Satan" from this equation as it does not concern Satan but the faith and claims of this "Omnipotent god" alone and in this case the existence or none existence of Satan is irrelevant. However, I will address this issue later or perhaps in another essay.

To get right to the point and root of the problem let me simply state it clearly: **God is wholly good; god is omnipotent; and yet evil exists.** There is a clear contradiction between these three statements, and only two of them could be true and one false. Nevertheless, all three of them are essential parts of the biblical god-character and Christian and theistic doctrines. This problem is not merely a theological problem but a logical problem in that when critically analyzed it either undermines the very idea of the Biblical god, or on the other hand, logic and reason must be thrown out and ignored completely.

So, let's look at the problem in-depth so as to cover all bases and not leave any loopholes, let's not overlook any premise on the subject. Let's be objective to the minute details to "leave no stone unturned" and see "if these things be true" to quote one of the great defenders and creators of the very myths in question, Paul. The problem is not self evident to the average reader, so for this reason I shall now outline the very basics of their own doctrines with regards to **"good" "omnipotent" and "evil"** etc. This way the reader will understand the premises better than he/she could ever get from a preacher; since preachers are in the business of confusing people and not showing them the light. Preachers and theologians are in the business of evading logic and reason; only when they convince their followers to ignore these two greatest tools of the mind, only then can they be assured of a continuous income.

Back to our subject. Good simply means that it is opposed to evil, that pleasure is opposed to pain, that happiness is opposed to suffering etc. Good things, the preachers teach, eliminate evil, that "the good shall overcome the evil" until evil is extinguished. God, being omnipotent, therefore can overcome and eliminate all evil; this is because he is omnipotent-he can do anything. That is what the theologian and preachers preach. Yet here we are, in reality, and to put it quite simply, evil still exists, and this all-good god has failed to eliminate evil. "God has a plan" the theist would reply. We'll see about that.

Question: Is god also evil? Can god be all-good without also being equally evil? Can good exist without evil? What would we compare good to if we never know what evil is? How can we determine that a god is all-good if he has no evil attributes to compare the good to? Can God create good without also creating evil at the same time?

First of all, if god is all-good and incapable of evil, then certainly god has limits and in turn is not omnipotent. If there are limits to what god can or cannot do, then you must admit that your god is not omnipotent. If you are willing to admit that god is also evil, then you must change your doctrine and discard the parts of the bible which claim otherwise.

Furthermore, the theists and the Bible, as well as the Koran, claim that god can also do what is logically impossible. The theologians and preachers as well as the laymen alike insist that god is the author of the laws of logic as well; that god is the one who created logic. Now I ask you this: Does god think logically? Does he use the same standards that he sets forth for others to follow; does he practice what he preaches? Or is god not bound by logical necessities?

If god created logic, as you claim, then he created evil as well; you can't have your cake and eat it too! Many evils are logical necessities and either you accept logic and reason or commit yourself to an insane asylum. Either something is or is not; a thing cannot be both A and B at the same time; it is either A or B. Furthermore, if god does use logic, then he is not omnipotent, since he is BOUND by the laws of logic which he created. Furthermore, if god does not use logic, then what standard of discipline is there for an intelligent being?

Either evil is opposed to good or it is not. If evil, as is taught by your Bible is not evil any more, than you must give up on your Bible and your god; on the other hand, if you insist the bible is true, then you must conclude that evil no longer exists.

sr restructure

Let me put forth yet another argument directly related to the subject *your god* of this essay. Suppose your god were to take you to heaven, where there is no evil at all; how would you be able to enjoy the all-good nature of heaven? To what would you be able to compare each experience of every moment spent there in order for you to recognize it as good and pleasant? How would this be possible, without any challenges? Fact is you would not be able to; you would be worse than a vegetable in such a state, no different than a person in a comma would be.

When we loose the good v. evil Dichotomy we also loose all pleasure.

*If God exists
then we have
completly misunderstood
or interpreted it.*

t god had to use evil in order to teach us about what is good. To those who make this claim, or similar ones, my reply is that: if this is so, then god in not omnipotent; god was bound by a limitation, a limitation which prevented him from being able to demonstrate good to us without evil. Fact is, without evil good cannot exist-period. You cannot demonstrate to me that a certain action is good without putting forth an example of evil. Furthermore, you cannot demonstrate to me anything good without letting me experience the evil. If you admit this is true, and it is to any sane and intelligent person, then you must admit that your god is not omnipotent. If god could have designed a planet with humans without any evil on it but did not, then your god is not wholly good. Furthermore, if he had made such a planet, the beings he would create would not be able to choose anything; they would be robots or vegetable-like. *or emotionless.*

Now let me present yet another related argument. Would the universe be better off without any evil in it? If yes, you must redefine what evil is and what is not; in other words, some of the things, which are destructive by their very nature, would have to be considered good. This would include hurricanes and earthquakes and such. These things would have to be eliminated or simply declared a blessing. But you would still be faced with a lala-land situation where nothing has any meaning or value because to have the ability to value anything you have to understand the meaning of loss-of-value. Without losses the gains are meaningless, there are no challenges, the mind would be reduced to a vegetable state, there would be nothing to aspire for, nothing to desire and nothing to miss. *There must be an antithesis! For anything to exist it must have*

Some of the other values or characteristics ascribed to god. Since "benevolence" is also one of god's attributes, how is it that god keeps misery in existence? Could god make the virtue of benevolence possible

what if God and the Devil were the same entity, just antithetic versions of the same being.

without misery? If so, how? It is a logical impossibility. So if god can do it illogically but not logically, then again god is bound by an inability and hence he is not omnipotent. I know that many of you will run to the "god can do anything because he is god" argument. To this I would simply say that A is not B yet A and B are both A at the same time. If you do not understand what this means then you know how unintelligible YOUR "mystery" argument is. When you reduce god to a simple "mystery" then you cannot claim to know anything about him. Not honestly anyway. Either god can be known or cannot be known. If he cannot be known then he might as well not exist. If god can prevent hurricanes from destroying people and their property and does not, then benevolence cannot be ascribed to him. Not by an honest person to say the least. If god does not prevent the winds from destroying people and property while he has it in his power to do so, then neither can I be judged for not helping a drowning child. I am as moral as your god. On the other hand, since our morals are superior to those god lives by, we (Illuminists) are superior in morals to your imaginary god.

To the free-will argument. Some scholars and preachers have invented yet a new argument in recent years. They argue that evil is due to the independent actions of human beings. For this reason, they say, evil cannot be ascribed to God. So this wholly good god gave humans free will, knowing that humans would commit evil through the utilization of their free-will. If we accept this argument, then what is revealed is that god is anti freedom or that freedom to make independent choices is evil. This is something I will deal with in another essay in which I will outline every Christian and Biblical doctrine to prove that Christianity, Islam and Judaism, like many other religions, are anti-freedom pure and simple. But for this essay and this subject matter the question is: How can an infinitely intelligent being, how can this so called god, create beings which can commit evil or take actions which are against his very will, against his very character and values?

Furthermore, if he knowingly and willingly created such beings, fully aware of the possibilities, how can he then turn around and punish his own handiwork for doing what they were supposed to do?

If having free will means not being able to choose what you like or dislike, then do we really have free-will? If we do, as the Bible claims, how are we guilty of angering god whom is supposed to transcend time and space? How can our imperfections cause harm to a perfect being; which is not only perfect but transcends time? How is it possible for us whom are bound by time and space, to cause any harm or affect god in any way? If our mere actions of independence provoke god to fury and rage, then how can theists claim that god transcends time and space? If god is immutable as the bible and theists claim, how is it that our actions offend this god? Again, the bible claims that god cannot be affected by human actions on one hand, and on the other, god gets mad, gets furious, and displays characteristics of a mere savage human, a neurotic; he destroys innocent babies, even unborn ones out of anger. Does this make sense? Is this logical for a god like the ones Christians and theists claim?

If god is omnipotent and he had made men such that in their choices they sometimes prefer what is evil and other times what is good, why could he not have created men such that would always choose the good freely, of their own **free-will**?

I'll tell you why? It is a logical impossibility that's why! Had he made such humans, then the very concept of free will or freedom to choose would be none existent. Either one has freedom to choose or one is bound by a predestined nature, which prohibits him from choosing the evil. Either we have free will or we don't. In addition, the fact that god did not do so if he could have begs the question of his "wholly good" characteristic as well as his omnipotence. Furthermore, if freedom is the ability to choose at randomness, then it has nothing to do with "will" and it cannot be said that we have "free will" and this too I will cover in another essay.

Another issue arises out of the "omnipotent" god theory. If god did indeed create beings with "free will" then even god cannot control these creatures, which in turn begs the question of omnipotence; in this case god is clearly not omnipotent. If I have free will, god cannot control my actions due to my very nature; I have free will and as an independent agent of my actions and choices, god cannot interfere even if he wanted to; he cannot make me do what I do not freely choose. Is this clear enough for you? Some may argue that god can control our will but he always refrains from doing so. Why then would god refrain from controlling evil wills? How can it be said that god is wholly good then? Either he is wholly good or he is not. Or the theists must change the meaning of the very words we use to communicate, because as they are, their god is a logical impossibility.

Now on to a more direct problem with this omnipotent god: Can god create things beyond his control? Can god make rules, which bind him to them? Does god have any rules by which his mind is guided, or does he always act out of his whim? If he has rules, by which he lives and cannot violate, then again he is not omnipotent. For example, if god created the laws of nature and logic, is he bound by them or not bound by them? If there are rules, which are superior to the laws of the physical universe, does god live by them or not? If the laws of nature are set in place, and god transcends space and time it is impossible for god to communicate with us without binding himself to space and time, thus in turn bind himself to the very rules he created. Suppose you are a being who transcends space and time. In such a case, you would not be able to effect anything or me or in nature without violating your very own existence or the nature of your being. You would be absolutely helpless to intervene in our reality. If god does interfere, then he has to become less than god, in order to communicate with the physical world. He would have to give up his nature in order to manifest himself into ours, and in such case he would be bound by the laws of physics and all laws of nature meaning he would be as trapped in this realm as we are. This is the limit of our logic and nature; aside from this, any talk about god's nature is unintelligible and useless. Any human being that claims to have knowledge of a being outside the laws of logic, reason and nature is to be regarded as a neurotic at best.

Conclusion

It is therefore necessary for us to be honest and simply state the obvious; that any god we can invent can only meet our own values and standards and never supercede them. It is essential for human beings, if we are to maintain our sanity and continue on as a civilized people to conform to the laws of nature and to conform to the standards of logic and reason. It is essential that we keep an open mind to all issues and devote as much time to all sides of any argument before we reach a conclusion. This is what is expected of honest and moral individuals. If we are not willing to live by the standards we teach, and if we are willing to permit anyone to violate the very morals we uphold then what good are we? What constructive and beneficial purpose can we as human beings possibly have? If we allow our own lives and existence to be guided by irrationality and whims, why should we deserve to live? If we insist on convincing others of our own convictions without having given equal time and consideration to the arguments put forth against our own beliefs we are not only living a lie but we will have become tyrants and bullies. Furthermore, any teachings and actions which propose to infringe on the individual rights of another and on their freedoms should be considered as a warning flag; the teachers and proponents of such doctrines should be viewed as defective and most dangerous.

Shalom

****

*******Jesus The Idiot: Is This Your God?*******

Before I start with my critical and objective analysis of the character and teachings of Jesus I would like to ask you some question. Why is it moral and ethical to consider a person to be a great and noble person in light of our better judgement? Why is it that we judge people by their words, teachings and deeds to determine their caliber, but when it comes to Jesus all logic and reason as well as all objectivity is ignored? How is it possible for any sane and so-called civilized person to ignore common sense and objectivity in cases such as Jesus, Mohamed or any other savage, just because millions or billions hold those persons in high regard? I warn you, the presentation to follow is objective in every sense of the word and I am presenting a honest and logical presentation based on the same evidence everyone else has before them. If you are of the opinion that objectivity, honesty and rationality should be put aside when it comes to Jesus and the Mohammeds of the world, I suggest you stop reading the rest of this essay and go jump off a bridge. Why? Because civilized people do not sacrifice objectivity, logic and reason at the altar of political correctness or to appease others or an imaginary fairy tale.

Weather Jesus existed or not is not the focal point of this essay even though I could include a strong argument on that subject as well. What I want to focus on is the fact that Jesus has been held in high regards by billions of people, regardless of the evidence which shows that Jesus' nobility is unfounded. The parasites behind the pulpit, with a straight face, have the audacity to claim that Jesus and his character is a perfect example of the highest example of moral living that ever existed. They say that if we all follow in Jesus' footsteps and listen to his teachings we would make this a peaceful and great world. Let's ignore what those parasites behind the pulpit claim and investigate their claims ourselves, objectively. Let's consider what Jesus supposedly said and did and see if his words and deeds indeed merit the honor and respect the preacher-parasite claims.

Jesus On Morality

"There be eunuchs which have made themselves eunuchs for the kingdom of heaven's sake. He that is able to receive it, let him receive it." (Matthew 19:12)

Based on this verse many believers and even some church fathers have castrated themselves. Even if we are to take these words metaphorically, only an idiot can claim that these are the words of an infinitely intelligent person who is supposed to be a god. Even in the metaphoric nature they hold no value and no mark of what a civilized person would say or consider intelligent advice.

1. In Matthew 5:29-30, Jesus teaches that it is best to cut off our hands or pluck out our eyes if we lust or commit some sort of sexual sin. Not only is "sin" a religious concept but also to even suggest such practices, even metaphorically, is barbaric and certainly not moral or ethical in any way let alone a sign of intelligence.

2. In Matthew 5:32 this dumb idiot says that to marry a divorced woman is a sin worthy of death, (adultery). This, to me as a civilized person is a great insult, an insult to my intelligence to say the least. Exactly who is harmed by such a marriage? How could such an act harm a god or anyone else and why should it? Such rules and laws are the products of a barbaric and savage mind and no civilized human

being can honestly say that these are moral teachings in any way shape or form.

3. When it comes to economics, in Matthew 6:19-20 this idiot advises his likewise dumb and naïve followers that it is not a good idea to save money. Which one of you would give your child or loved one such stupid advice?

4. Then this moron, who was executed for being stupid, advises a man to sell all of his possessions and to follow him (Mark 10:21-25). Then he goes on to advise his audience not to be wealthy. Think about this for a moment; had the young rich man listened to this dumb teacher, imagine what his life would have been like. He would have been poor like the rest of Jesus' friends, and would have probably ended up executed or persecuted as well. But imagine how the life of a bum like Jesus must have been back then; it is hard enough to be a bum today with all the wealth and technological advances, it certainly would have been much harder in his days. Obviously Jesus believed being poor was smart and beneficial in some sick way.

5. *"Therefore do not worry about tomorrow, for tomorrow will worry about its own things. Sufficient for the day is its own trouble"* Matthew 6:34.

Is it any wonder we have so many poor idiots in the world today? They are listening to Jesus and the parasites behind the pulpit. Tell me, would you give such advice to your children? Do you think it intelligent to give such advice? Is this supposed to be divine advice, is this divine wisdom?

6. *"Sell what you have and give alms; provide yourselves money bags which do not grow old, a treasure in the heavens that does not fail, where no thief approaches nor moth destroys.* 34*"For where your treasure is, there your heart will be also."* (Luke 12:33).

You hear this people? Live like an idiot, be poor and sell all you have to give to the poor so you can be as happy as the poor and live a life of misery, all because some dumb bum promises some imaginary happy afterlife. Only the poor deserve to live happily in Jesus' imaginary afterlife. Those whom seek to be happy and well in this life are not worthy of heavenly rewards because…well because they are smart enough to make a good living and enjoy this life. My advice to you is to use your bible for emergency toilette paper.

7. From the verse in Matthew 5:28, I am led to believe that Jesus must have been incompetent. He says *"But I say to you that whoever looks at a woman to lust for her has already committed adultery with her in his heart."*

Guys and girls, if you see a sexy woman and you are attracted to her lust and feast your eyes on her, and if she is willing have as much unbridled sex as your heart desires. Why? Because sex is natural and beautiful and it is part of the greatest characteristics which makes us human. Don't listen to this idiot called Jesus, for he was a liar and a false prophet as well and certainly not a god. Lusting after anyone is hardly a crime, but according to this savage, lusting is a crime worthy of death. Imagine that!

"Blessed are you when they revile and persecute you, and say all kinds of evil against you falsely for My sake". Matthew 5:11.

This sounds like advise to seek to be persecuted. No matter, there is no honor in being persecuted for any reason what so ever. Furthermore, this is the kind of advice that breeds fanatics as we have seen throughout history after this moron was executed.

9. *"Do not labor for the food which perishes, but for the food which endures to everlasting life, which the Son of Man will give you, because God the Father has set His seal on Him"* John 6:27.

Whatever the above is supposed to mean, we all know that it is important to work for food which perishes because we need it to survive. To simply beg for food is not a nice way to live. In a metaphoric sense, the above words are garbage.

"Give to everyone who asks of you. And from him who takes away your goods do not ask them back." Luke 6:30.

Too bad thieves don't read the bible, because if they were to stumble on this verse, they could have a field day stealing from the dumb Christians. Oh wait, the Christians would call the police…well, what Christian today actually follows all the advice given by this moron anyway? It is STUPID to obey the advice of this idiot, plain and simple. Oh, do not give to everyone who asks of you. In fact don't give to anyone anything for free because that is just plain stupid!

11. *"But I tell you not to resist an evil person. But whoever slaps you on your right cheek, turn the other to him also."* Matthew 5:39

Is this sound advice? Is this advice you follow and teach to your children? What sane and rational person can honestly say that this is divine advice; the advice of an infinitely intelligent being?

12. *"For I say to you, that to everyone who has will be given; and from him who does not have, even what he has will be taken away from him."* Luke 19:23-26

This idiot knew nothing about economics either. His advice is that we should take from the poor who have nothing in savings and give that nothing to rich investors. Some wisdom this idiot had.

13. *"If anyone wants to sue you and take away your tunic, let him have your cloak also."* Matthew 5:40 According to the advise given by this bum if we loose a lawsuit we should give much more than the judgement calls for. How many Christians follow this advice. Can someone point out even one such a case? What sane person would call this divine and intelligent advice?

14. *"Give to him who asks you, and from him who wants to borrow from you do not turn away."* Matthew 5:42

Again I ask, show me which Christians follow this advice? Please let me know so I can go and start asking for stuff. After all, they are supposed to give me without question, per their dumb bum god. This advise of Jesus is not stupid, it is beyond that, it is plain moronic, Jesus makes stupidity seem intelligent!

15. *"And whoever compels you to go one mile, go with him two"* Matthew 5:41

According to this advice, you are to be twice as stupid. How are these words the words of an intelligent being? How is it possible to call this stupid advice "wisdom" and kindness. Me thinks this kind of stupid advice is perfect for creating dumb followers whom would give even the little they have to the bastard behind the pulpit. In fact, the bible teaches that those who are poor and give from what they have actually give more than a rich man. But then again, that is very self serving since the rich are scorned and most people who go to church are poor, so the only way to get the dumb poor to give and give is to make them feel and think that it is more noble to give when you are poor. How else could preachers live well if they could not get their dumb sheep to support them with the little they have?

Which one of you gives such advice to your children as Jesus gave above? Honestly now, don't lie? Do you teach your children to follow the advice given by this idiot? Is this what you consider wise?

Was Jesus' Word Trustworthy?

1. *"There be some standing here, which shall not taste of death, till they see the Son of man coming in his kingdom"* Matthew 16:28). *"Behold, I come quickly."* Revelation 3:11

It has been almost 2000 years and Christianity is still waiting for him. Can someone please explain to me how "quickly" equals to thousands years? Which dictionary did Jesus and his moron followers follow? How is it intelligent and wise to believe in this liar? Where was his quick return in his "kingdom"?

2. *"The kingdom of heaven is like a mustard seed, which a man took and sowed in his field, 32"which indeed is the least of all the seeds;"* Matthew 5:13

How can a god who supposedly created all the seeds of the earth not know that the mustard seed is NOT "the least of the seeds"??? If he were god, or even an intelligent and knowledgeable man, he would have never made such a stupid comment. This same moron claims that salt can "lose its savour". We know this is not true so this Jesus guy is an idiot, a fool of fools and not wise at all. Only fools can believe and follow this fool, for fools have no standard to recognize intelligence, thus they are naïve and gullible.

3. *"But whoever says, 'You fool!' shall be in danger of hell fire."* Matthew 5:22

This tyrant teaches that merely calling someone a fool is worthy of eternal torture. Which one of you would torture anyone for mere poor taste in words? How is a verbal insult worthy of death or eternal torture?

I tell you, these words of Jesus are the words of an idiot, a tyrant and a fool!

4. *"Fools and blind! For which is greater, the gold or the temple that sanctifies the gold?* Matthew 23:17

See? By Jesus' own standard he himself is worthy of eternal torture in hell. He was the one who called people fools and in doing so he condemned himself. Jesus was a hypocrite in addition to being a moron.

5. *"If I bear witness of myself, my witness is not true"* John 5:31, and *"Though I bear record of myself, yet my record is true"* John 8:14.

Here Jesus proves his hypocrisy 100% He speaks out of both sides of his mouth. He would make a poor witness in court, and no sane person would consider this moron to be divine or infinitely intelligent.

Jesus On Social Justice?

"And that servant [slave], which knew his lord's will, and prepared not himself, neither did according to his will, shall be beaten with many stripes." Luke 12:47

Notice that this doG, instead of denouncing slavery he encourages it and justifies the physical beating or torture of slaves. Furthermore, instead of helping the poor he allowed expensive ointment to be wasted on himself. In addition, not one woman was chosen as his disciple and none of the so-called "sisters" were invited to participate in his Last Supper.

Was Jesus A Good Role Model?

1. *"Now in the morning, as He returned to the city, He was hungry.* ¹⁹*And seeing a fig tree by the road, He came to it and found nothing on it but leaves, and said to it, "Let no fruit grow on you ever again."* *Immediately the fig tree withered away.*

20And when the disciples saw it, they marveled, saying, "How did the fig tree wither away so soon?" Matthew 21:18-19

Notice that these morons called "disciples" were as dumb as could be. They marveled at how quickly the tree had withered instead of being shocked **that Jesus expected a tree, which was out of season, to have fruits.** If this were a god, a divine being with infinite wisdom he could have never cursed a tree which was out of season for not having any fruits on it. Jesus was no god, he was a neurotic who found fault with everything and everyone. No wonder they executed him.

2. *"Now it happened that He went through the grainfields on the Sabbath; and as they went His disciples began to pluck the heads of grain."* Mark 2:23

What we have here is Jesus stealing grain from someone else's farm, and not only that, he was stealing on the "holy Sabbath" as well. It seems, if you are poor and an idiot, you can steal and violate the law.

Sorry guys, but there is no way this was a god or a noble man. No civilized and sane human being can honestly use Jesus a role model.

3. *"Go into the village opposite you, and immediately you will find a donkey tied, and a colt with her. Loose them and bring them to Me. 3"And if anyone says anything to you, you shall say, 'The Lord has need of them,' and immediately he will send them."* Matthew 21

What we have here is Jesus ordering his disciples to go and steal two animals.

4. We are then told in numerous places that Jesus was humble. However, a simple examination of Jesus' words proves otherwise. This so called "humble" man boasts about how he was greater "than Jonah" even "greater than Solomon" and then to top it off he claimed to be even "greater than the Temple".

5. *"He who is not with Me is against Me, and he who does not gather with Me scatters abroad."* Matthew 12:30

Had this been a god there would have been no need to even utter these words, since he was already all knowing. Furthermore, there is no wisdom in these words. They are common sense. If he did utter these words, then he is merely proving to be suffering from paranoia like all dictators and their like.

Jesus The Prince Of Peace?

1. *"He that hath no sword, let him sell his garment, and buy one."* Luke 22:36 *"Think not that I am come to send peace: I came not to send peace but a sword."* Matthew 10:34 *"But those mine enemies, which would not that I should reign over them, bring hither, and slay them before me."* Luke 19:27. *"If a man abide not in me, he is cast forth as a branch, and is withered; and men gather them, and cast them into the fire, and they are burned."* John 15:6

As you can see, this Jesus guy was no "Prince Of Peace" nor was he himself peaceable. In fact, the Church used the above words of Jesus during the Inquisition and Crusades to justify itself. As a result, some 70 million people were murdered in the name of Jesus during the inquisition and crusades.

2. *"And when He had looked around at them with anger, being grieved by the hardness of their hearts…"* Mark 3:5

Jesus did not love his enemies but hated them. He was frustrated that they did not believe in him. In John 2:15 he uses whips to whip the merchants whom were doing legal and much needed services for the pilgrims, by the way. In Matthew 8:32 this worthless bum kills innocent animals, which, by the way, were the property of another person. So Jesus, the criminal, destroys the property of others and in doing so, he kills innocent animals which have harmed nobody.

3. *"And behold, a woman of Canaan came from that region and cried out to Him, saying, "Have mercy on me, O Lord, Son of David! My daughter is severely demon-possessed." 23But He answered her not a word. And His disciples came and urged Him, saying, "Send her away, for she cries out after us." 24But He answered and said, "I was not sent except to the lost sheep of the house of Israel." 25Then she came and worshiped Him, saying, "Lord, help me!" 26But He answered and said, "It is not good to take the children's bread and throw it to the little dogs."* Matthew 15:22-28

Notice how merciful Jesus is here, the mother of the sick innocent child has to beg and convince him to help her. Jesus was a racist as well, for he did not see it necessary to love the gentiles. Obviously the woman beat him with a better argument than his and so he was forced to help her due to embarrassment. Also notice how loving his disciples were. They wanted to send her away which was typical of racists back then as it is now.

4. *"The Son of man [Jesus himself] shall send forth his angels, and they shall gather out of his kingdom all things that offend, and them which do iniquity; And shall cast them into a furnace of fire: there shall be wailing and gnashing of teeth."* Matthew 13:41-42 *"And if thy hand offend thee, cut it off: it is better for thee to enter into life maimed, than having two hands to go into hell, into the fire that never shall be quenched."* Mark 9:43

This moron promoted the torture of people and taught it as being just to torture people for eternity. Jesus could only make his followers believe him and follow him by threatening them with hellfire. This is not a peaceful and loving man but a tyrant and a monster. Certainly hell is not a peaceful promise, and clearly Jesus was against freedom of religion, speech and thought. Anyone who claims that these words of Jesus were the words of a god worthy of respect and worship needs serious professional help...or better yet, such should jump off a bridge, because they are mentally defective and their existence only means the continuous spread of this disease called "Christianity". Our civilized world has no place for such barbaric and savage people.

Jesus On "Family Values"

"I am come to set a man at variance against his father, and the daughter against her mother, and the daughter in law against her mother in law. And a man's foes shall be they of his own household." Matthew 10:35-36

"If any man come to me, and hate not his father, and mother, and wife, and children, and brethren, and sisters, yea, and his own life also, he cannot be my disciple." Luke 14:26

And when it comes to funerals, Jesus has this to say: *"Let the dead bury their dead."* Matthew 8:22

When it comes to "honor thy father and thy mother" Jesus gives an example of how this is to be done when he says: *"Woman, what have I to do with thee?"* John 2:4

Conclusion

I wish to point out a few very important issues which nobody who has argued against god and religion has ever mentioned. If you read the above verses very carefully you can get at least a small idea of what type of person Jesus was, if indeed those are his words. If he was god, or even the Son of God, he had to know that there is magnetic ore inside the earth. He knew there was all type of metal ore inside the earth. He had to know about molecular structures, if he was god. If he was the creator of mankind and the universe he had to know about protons and electrons, about atoms and quarks, neutrinos and particles. He had to know about how photons work. He had to know about geometry and mathematics. He must have known about algebra and calculus. He must have known about economics and how wealth is created and how invention and innovation could improve the lives of his so called "loved ones".

My questions are these: Why did he not teach them how to make electric wires and mine magnets to produce electricity? Why did he not teach them to make light bulbs? Why did he not teach them to make metal pipes and a simple hand operated pump even, to pump water? Why did he not teach them how to make glass so they could have clear glass windows? Why did he not teach them how to build printing presses to print books to educated the masses/poor? Why did he not teach them how to build tractors and farm equipment? Why did he not teach them to build trains and automobiles? Why did he not teach them mathematics and reading skills? Why did he not teach them electronics and various useful trades? Why did he not teach them how to perform laser eye surgery? Why did he not teach them how to build pacemakers? Why did he not teach them how to build septic tanks and toilettes? Why did he not teach them how to build irrigation systems?

What Jesus did teach them is to remain stupid. He taught them the dumbest thing possible; that being poor is noble and virtuous. He told them that to seek self-improvement is evil. He taught them that to try and make a good living and gather wealth is of the devil. He taught them that being educated is for the proud, and the proud are to be burnt in hell. He taught them that to have pride and self-esteem is evil. He taught them they should be like him, bums and cowards. He taught them to sell everything they have and give it to the poor. He taught them collectivism, which is communism. He taught them about equal distribution of wealth, of dividing everything they had amongst everyone so that they could all become poor. He taught them, in other words, nothing of any value.

Ironically, there are many idiots in today's day and age that think equal distribution of wealth is a good and noble thing to do. They say that helping the poor is a good idea, it is a noble thing to do. Let me tell you what would happen if we listened to Jesus and these altruistic morons. If we divide all the wealth of the world equally between every adult on the planet, the end result would be total poverty on a global scale. Everyone would get $16,687.73. This would mean, no more factories, all corporations would have to be put out of business, all banks and banking systems would be crippled, and all productivity would be brought to a halt. All electric companies would be shut down. In other words, we would be thrown back 500 years into the dark ages. Nobody would have enough to do anything of any value.

In Christian churches, every sun-day millions of morons are taught that "the love of money is the root of all evil". Instead of teaching these morons about economics, about how important money is, and that it is good to have money, they teach them the dumbest thing possible. The preachers, these parasites behind the pulpit are the greatest evil on our planet; religious leaders are the most devious and deceptive parasites that have ever lived amongst humans. These bastards never work a day in their lives; they live of the morons whom they brainwash and dumb down with their masks of virtue. The religious leaders are the epitome of the very essence of evil; they are the greediest bastards on our planet. Don't get me wrong, it is healthy to be greedy, but there are two kinds of greed. There is the greed, which seeks the unearned, the taking or robbing others of their earned income through theft and deception; then there is the honest and healthy greed which motivates men and women to achieve, to make money to improve their lives, but through their own work, through their own efforts and not by deception and coercion.

The teachings of Jesus are contradictory and that is a clear sign that the New Testament was tempered with. The Catholic scribes knew that there were too many problems with this Jesus character, and before they could invent a new religion, a new way to dumb down the sheep and keep them under control, they had to patch up the words of Jesus or those, which were attributed to him. The end result was the New Testament as we have it today, a book of contradictions which is intended to show how divine and wise this Jesus was, but in reality it only shows what a idiot he really was.

****

*******What Happens When You Die?*******

I have wanted to write an essay in response to this often asked question for a long time now, and I finally decided to do it now while it is fresh in my mind. Believers use this question as a last resort-defense when they are pressed with their backs against the wall of logic and reason. In response to this question having been asked by a person whom read and posted a short comment in the review box on my essay "*What Loving God?*".

Here are the comments he left:

"Nathan (visitor) 8/9/2001. Your points make sense and are logical but our God is a just God. He will not just let things go by untouched. Write an essay about what happens when you die and where you will go and if there is a purpose in life. I would be interested in reading that. Thank you."

Now I shall respond to this important question, not because I believe in an after life; I have no reason to believe in such, but I am open minded and I have a few things to say on this subject.

First of all, the main reason weak minded people cling to religion is due to fear; fear of eternal torture in the after life, or fear of the unknown and death to say the least, or the hope of a undeserved reward. I say the weak minded people because to fear the unknown is irrational behavior and a sign of a damaged mind, a sign of the mind of a neurotic at least in part. What you are about to read can only be understood if you read the whole of this essay in its entirety and most importantly with an open/unbiased mind. The content of this essay is the essence of my thoughts on this subject, and to be honest, I am the only one who shares the views presented here as far as I know. I have studied and read hundreds of books and have yet to find any philosopher or scholar whom wrote anything even close to what I am saying here in full context.

When children's minds are filled with fear of eternal tortures and with religious fairy tales, the child grows up and develops a character around the knowledge he/she was exposed to. I believe the empirical evidence we have on this subject is far beyond the reaches of refutation, so I need not go into the evidence itself. All one needs to do is study determinism and psychology basics and then look around and pick a subject to practice the laws of determinism on.

The point I want to stress is that the main component of a healthy mind, a healthy mental state is knowledge. Not pseudo knowledge, but knowledge of the facts of life, of truth. If you teach children horror stories and eternal torture and things of than nature as being true, not only will the child grow up to be a neurotic, a nervous wreck, an unstable and irrational person, but you shape their character in regards to moral and ethics. When a child is taught that the best/greatest persons, such as god(s) whom are supposed to be the role models of ultimate morals and ethics, can be justified in inflicting torture and commit horrible crimes, the child grows up to be insensitive to torture and crimes against none believers for one thing. Furthermore the minds of such people stop developing fully because they assume the answers to their questions, such as what happens when you die, and where does everything come from, appear to be satisfied. When a person is satisfied with the answer to a question, regardless of weather the answer is correct or false, the mind no longer seeks knowledge on the subject, and as such, the mind does not mature in that area of knowledge and information.

I view our minds as ever developing and ever maturing. The more knowledge we gather the better minds we develop and in turn make us better/worse persons. What determines our characteristics is in part due to genetic traits, but what determines our personality, wisdom and our ultimate characters is KNOWLEDGE. If we feed our brain or the brain of our children with junk, lies and fairy tales, we cannot expect our children or ourselves to develop into intelligent and very capable human beings. Mental grandeur and intellectual abilities have nothing in common with irrationality and mysticism.

Our minds are our lives and our body is merely the shell in which we exercise our experience of life. The most sacred tools of our mind are reason and logic. Without reason, logic becomes circular and trivial. If we ignore reason in exchange for a "psychological high" for a self induced false sense of reality we become disillusioned with reality and thus tend to reach a comfort level in our lives, a comfort level which no longer seeks self improvement, and self advancement. As children we have a natural curiosity, and if the answers to a child's questions are dishonest or the answers given to a child are lies/false, the child will believe them and so their whole mental process and abilities are shaped by the information they gather early in life. It is true that they can change their minds later after having learned the truth of the matter, but at what psychological costs? Furthermore, the knowledge we gather while young is of such great importance that no value can be even fully contemplated. The essential education and knowledge of our youth is an integral part of what we will be when we grow older, and what type of person we will become.

The young mind and the young brain (brain-the physical/biological shell our mind resides in) stores information far more efficiently and much more permanently than when we become fully-grown adults. This information is the roots, which will hold our tree of life, our early development and into the rest of our future.

The Lies

Now let's consider what happens to the people whom are raised on lies and falsehoods, on erroneous information and knowledge. The religious persons, by having been taught religious and mystical doctrines have committed themselves knowingly or unknowingly to the greatest crime one can commit against the self, dishonesty. When people are reduced to irrational states of mind by exchanging honesty for faith they have committed the most heinous crime against the self; they have committed intellectual suicide. In doing so, they have reduced themselves to nothing more than social animals. It is true, in a sense, that we are all social animals, however, there is a great difference between enlightened humans and social animals. In other words, the mystics, the religionists, by resorting to mysticism and not having explored the powers of reason and logic, by not learning science and the arts, they have reduced their own lives to a hopeless and meaningless existence. Such persons are now seeking to fill the gap and emptiness where knowledge should have resided, they are seeking to fill this void with myths, with more irrationality, with more lies. Untruth can only be defended properly by a continuo stream of untruth. Logic, reason and honesty cannot help fill the voids and the emptiness in one's life as long as the life is dominated by and guided by self-deceptions, by mythical dogma and fairy tales. To the believer, logic and reason are mere foolishness; they see their own whims as divine wisdom.

Such persons can be rightly called occultists, regardless of which religion they practice. The religious commit themselves to self-slavery by submitting themselves to useless rituals and repetitive worthless songs and self-induced psychosis, which they call "spiritualism" or the "spirit of god". Their sole purpose in life now becomes that of a virus and serves as a radical counter-blueprint to the enlightened culture.

The religious, therefore, are an occult culture and their existence means the death of sequential, linear thought; an erosion of people's ability to plan and manage their own lives, the end of the use of reason and logic. In their parasitical vendetta to convert as many people to their neuroticism, to their occultism, they destroy the very fabric of civilization, the advancements of the arts and science. These parasites, because they are so many, they get the attention of political parasites, politicians whom sing songs the occultists like, by catering to the politics which support the doctrines and advancement of their version of "morals and ethics", these parasites become the tools for the destruction of Illuminism. So the occultists, due to their shear numbers, quickly gain control of governments and powerful institution regardless of what type of government it is.

Therefore, most hard-core occultists remain stuck in their hope of salvation, and are swaying between relaxation beyond this world and their indistinctness in this world, whether on the kitchen table or in the marriage bed or society at large. Their lives are now meaningless and the only way they find "peace" is by going to temples and churches to get a psychological fix, and by utilizing their parasitical nature which forces them to force their neurotic irrational beliefs on others. Proselytizing gives them some kind of psychological fix to their neurotic addictions through authentication. The believer feels better when they convert others, because it helps them cope with their own insecurity, and somehow, by converting others they get confirmation psychologically speaking, in that they were able to convert more and that somehow means that they are doing something right. I have dealt with this particular subject in my essay entitled "Religion: The Root Of All Evil"

Existence

Now let me give you an insight into the mind (my mind) of a strong atheist, into the mind of a truly honest individual. I am certain many atheists and most scientists may share these views, although I have yet to see any of them admit this in public. The way I view reality, existence as a whole is this: Existence exists, or, reality exists. Now this may not seem very intelligible on the surface, and I am sure Ayn Rand was criticized for having said the same thing but failed to qualify it. It was not her intention to qualify it, as her goal was to put forth our principles on various platforms so as to establish them as a philosophy.

What I mean by "existence exists" is as follows. All that exists is there as various forms of energy. Rocks are as much energy as they are matters and they are as much a form of energy as is light, heat and cold, electricity etc. The fact is that everything changes, even rocks and iron and biological matter and all that exist in the universe constantly changes. True, some things change at different speed and in different ways, but ultimately all existence changes from one form of energy to another.

For example, a wood table holds a cup of coffee on it without letting the cup fall through. This is because the atoms of the table are composed of fibers which in turn are composed of certain types of atoms which are held together by a form of energy. The fibers that these atoms amount to are held together by a form of Electro-static energy. All forms of matter are held together by different forms or types of Electro-static fields or forces. This is also true of the human body and everything that exists.

In looking at our own human body, we can see that it is a biological organism composed of trillions upon trillions of other forms of biological organisms. We even have many different life forms/beings/creatures, which live, inside our own bodies. The machinery that makes our body function is called "the mind" and the mind lives in what we call a brain. The brain is merely a complex set of proteins, which are so arranged as to form a super complex form of neurological-Electro-circuitry. The mind itself is composed of atomic and subatomic electronic circuits, which utilize the brain to control the biological beast we call "our bodies".

As time goes by, our biological life forms evolve and constantly change to adapt to different environments. The mind generates copies of itself and its biological form in the form of blue prints called sperm/cells etc. Throughout millions of years the life form we call humans, like all biological life forms, evolve constantly. The theory of evolution has been an established fact by the shear amount of evidence to support it. Now, here are some possibilities as to the origins of life, our existence etc. Please do not take this out of context, as I am merely giving you my own thoughts and opinions, which are pure speculation on my part, and in no way am I claiming the following to be facts.

In my opinion, because the body functions on a complex neurological electronic circuit, it is illogical to think that when our bodies die and rot, that our mind does as well. The mind is not biological in nature and that complex electronic system, which runs and maintains our biological body does not rot, it cannot rot. Electricity does not rot. So, whatever happens to it nobody knows for sure; in fact nobody knows at all. For sure the mind and its energy goes somewhere, or transforms/evolves into something else. May be we enter other dimensions or another plain of reality. Whatever happens to our mind when we die, rotting is not it.

It is also my belief that biological life is not the only possible form of life. I reached this view when I started to study quantum physics and dark matter and the nature of various forms of energies. It is possible that we are to the universe/existence what our brain cells are to our bodies; the old ones die and are replaced by new ones, or defective ones are either repaired or recycled or trashed. In other words, the whole universe may be a form of life itself. It is possible that we are just a small speck of its finest attributes. We could be part of the very brain of the universe(s)/existence itself.

Since the majority of the matter in the universe is unaccounted for, and much of it is dark matter, we lack a great deal of knowledge about the forms of existence possible on planets composed of dark matter. We have millions of years to go before we know much about our own universe, especially since it is constantly changing and expanding. Dark matter is called such because it is invisible to the human eye and undetectable through scientific instruments. The only reason we know of it is because we can detect its effects in various ways. We also have proven that there are forms of particles that appear out of nothing and disappear right back into nothing. We call that "nothing", nothing simply because there is much we do not know about existence, period.

Another possibility is that we may very well be lab rats for another species, for other forms of life or aliens. We know now that there are/may be at least 10 more dimensions, and we know that there is so much we do not know, and so much we do know but not quite understand fully. The reason I think it is possible that we and our planet is a science lab for other life forms, is due in part to the fact that the human and biological genomes appear to have their own self-repairing mechanism which in turrn would imply an intelligence independent of the mind. If this is true, then not only did we evolve as per Darwin, but we were designed to evolve at random, and the natural selection made sure we all evolved into various forms of robots. I say robots simply because we do not have free will. All we have is an automatic robotic curiosity and all we are capable of as far as choices is calculated-decision-making-ability. This means that we are talking about normal and rational humans and not the irrational, which I consider defective. The fact that we do not have free will implies artificial intelligence; it implies that we were set upon this planet much like the way bacteria/microbes is set in a science lab and left in certain environments to cultivate and develop. The environment differences alone can guarantee difference in results through mutation.

And finally, it is very possible that when we die, our bodies rot and our electric energy simply dissipates or joins other forms of Electro-magnetic energy, with/without any consciousness. In other words, we may simply die and cease to exist.

Now, if we do enter into an after-life, another form of existence, don't you think that the more intelligent and knowledgeable we are in this life the better of we will be in the next? The believers in gods and myths would enter the next life completely stupid irrational and thus defective. If we were created by ~~ ͌ ʼe forms, don't you think we will be of mc ___ f we have used our brains here and our p ___ ʜis life? Don't you think it is immoral to r ___ nd the full power of our minds to impro ___ is an intelligent being, do you think such ___ ·tics and the lazy into its realm/plain of e ___ ·r or a religious person who spent their ___ ..g worthless prayers and empty songs would be of more value in the next life than a brain surgeon or a physicist?

(handwritten note: Do we have a moral Duty to evolve?)

You think the next life is lala-land for the lazy, for those whom thought that using our brains to become more knowledgeable was foolish? You think bowing and praying and pretending to be good out of fear of hell/death is worthy of rewards? Is that what you think an intelligent being appreciates? Don't you know that the enlightened and well educated do not like to receive undeserved praises and do not enjoy the company of neurotics and lazy fools?

Part Two: Honesty

Let me tell you why an atheist deserves such a gift of eternal life if he/she so desires it and there is the possibility of having someone providing it or some way of obtaining it. Let me tell you why the atheist, the freethinker, the deist and agnostics deserve such a gift and the religious do not.

First let me deal with the believer' dishonesty. The main problem with believers is that they are dishonest not only with others, but they are dishonest with themselves. They lie to themselves as soon ad they refuse to acknowledge that reason and logic are essential tools to gather knowledge. Instead of being honest with themselves, they deny truth and embrace fables. Here is an example:

The believer says; God exists! How do you know? Well, the bible says so. Who wrote the bible? Men inspired by god? How do you know? The bible says so! How do you know that the men who wrote it were men of god? Because the bible says so? What if the bible is nothing but ancient science fiction or mythology? It is not! How do you know? Because I know! Because god tells me so? How does god tell you? He speaks to me through his spirit! How do you know it is the spirit of god and not your own whims? Because I know! How do you know? I just know! Who taught you about the bible? Such and such/my parents. What if they are wrong, and what if the bible is nothing more than fables? It is not, it is the word of god. What happens if you don't believe in god? You go to hell? Why? Because god said so and god is just. How is having lack of belief in god a crime? Because if you do not believe in god you are of the devil, you are evil. Who is the devil? He is Satan one of god's angels who turned against god? How do you know god and Satan exist? Because the bible says so? What proof do you have that god exists? Well, the proof is that everything is so well designed. What is well designed? Everything, humans animals plants etc. What if everything evolved? God created everything. How do you know? Because the bible says so. Well, the bible also says that the sun revolves around the earth, and we now know that this is not true; how do you explain this? The bible is not mistaken, you just can't understand it because you don't believe it, etc. etc. For the rest of my response to the believer's arguments and their bible read my essay "*What Loving God?*" and my book "Christianity Exposed" as well as my other essays.

The point I wanted to make is that the believer' whole life and mentality revolves around circular logic and around the box called the bible. They have been reduced to idiots; they are dishonest in that anything which is against their bible and their barbaric doctrines is not true regardless of the facts which prove beyond the shadow of a doubt that the bible and their religion is mythology and fables. They are also dishonest in that they refuse to even consider the possibility that they are wrong.

Now the non-believer, the honest human.

The atheist, freethinker, and the agnostic are the honest people, the enlightened people of the world in that we look at reality and life through objective eyes. We utilize reason, the most powerful tool of the human mind, and logic as the guiding light. We use the scientific method to determine what is truth and to us truth does matter. We are honest with ourselves and we accept the truth of nature, life and reality regardless of weather we like the answers or not. We do not invent fables and myths and call them truth when we are faced with questions for which we do not have answers. We speculate and develop theories, but we do not call our theories facts before the evidence presents itself.

Let me go into the details of what the "scientific method" entails and what it means. The scientific method is the process by which scientists, collectively/independently and over time, endeavor to construct an accurate (that is, reliable, consistent and non-arbitrary) representation of the world.

Recognizing that personal and cultural beliefs influence both our perceptions and our interpretations of natural phenomena, we aim through the use of standard procedures and criteria to minimize those influences when developing a theory. In summary, the scientific method attempts to minimize the influence of bias or prejudice in the experimenter when testing a hypothesis or a theory.

I. The scientific method has four steps
1. Observation and description of a phenomenon or group of phenomena.
2. Formulation of an hypothesis to explain the phenomena. In physics, the hypothesis often takes the form of a causal mechanism or a mathematical relation.
3. Use of the hypothesis to predict the existence of other phenomena, or to predict quantitatively the results of new observations.
4. Performance of experimental tests of the predictions by several independent experimenters and properly performed experiments.

If the experiments bear out the hypothesis it may come to be regarded as a theory or law of nature (more on the concepts of hypothesis, model, theory and law below). If the experiments do not bear out the hypothesis, it must be rejected or modified. What is key in the description of the scientific method just given is the predictive power (the ability to get more out of the theory than you put in) of the hypothesis or theory, as tested by experiment. It is often said in science that theories can never be proved, only disproved. There is always the possibility that a new observation or a new experiment will conflict with a long-standing theory.

II. Testing hypotheses

As just stated, experimental tests may lead either to the confirmation of the hypothesis, or to the ruling out of the hypothesis. The scientific method requires that an hypothesis be ruled out or modified if its predictions are clearly and repeatedly incompatible with experimental tests. Further, no matter how elegant a theory is, its predictions must agree with experimental results if we are to believe that it is a valid description of nature. In physics, as in every experimental science, "experiment is supreme" and experimental verification of hypothetical predictions is absolutely necessary. Experiments may test the theory directly (for example, the observation of a new particle) or may test for consequences derived from the theory using mathematics and logic (the rate of a radioactive decay process requiring the existence of the new particle). Note that the necessity of experiment also implies that a theory must be testable.

Theories which cannot be tested, because, for instance, they have no observable ramifications (such as, a particle whose characteristics make it unobservable), do not qualify as scientific theories.

If the predictions of a long-standing theory are found to be in disagreement with new experimental results, the theory may be discarded as a description of reality, but it may continue to be applicable within a limited range of measurable parameters. For example, the laws of classical mechanics (Newton's Laws) are valid only when the velocities of interest are much smaller than the speed of light (that is, in algebraic form, when $v/c \ll 1$). Since this is the domain of a large portion of human experience, the laws of classical mechanics are widely, usefully and correctly applied in a large range of technological and scientific problems. Yet in nature we observe a domain in which v/c is not small.

The motions of objects in this domain, as well as motion in the "classical" domain, are accurately described through the equations of Einstein's theory of relativity. We believe, due to experimental tests, that relativistic theory provides a more general, and therefore more accurate, description of the principles governing our universe, than the earlier "classical" theory. Further, we find that the relativistic equations reduce to the classical equations in the limit $v/c \ll 1$. Similarly, classical physics is valid only at distances much larger than atomic scales ($x \gg 10^{-8}$ m). A description, which is valid at all length scales, is given by the equations of quantum mechanics.

We are all familiar with theories, which had to be discarded in the face of experimental evidence. In the field of astronomy, the earth-centered description of the planetary orbits was overthrown by the Copernican system, in which the sun was placed at the center of a series of concentric, circular planetary orbits. Later, this theory was modified, as measurements of the planets motions were found to be compatible with elliptical, not circular, orbits, and still later planetary motion was found to be derivable from Newton's laws.

Errors in experiments have several sources. First, there is error intrinsic to instruments of measurement. Because this type of error has equal probability of producing a measurement higher or lower numerically than the "true" value, it is called random error. Second, there is non-random or systematic error, due to factors, which bias the result in one direction. No measurement, and therefore no experiment, can be perfectly precise. At the same time, in science we have standard ways of estimating and in some cases reducing errors. Thus it is important to determine the accuracy of a particular measurement and, when stating quantitative results, to quote the measurement error. A measurement without a quoted error is meaningless. The comparison between experiment and theory is made within the context of experimental errors. Scientists ask, how many standard deviations are the results from the theoretical prediction? Have all sources of systematic and random errors been properly estimated?

III. Common Mistakes in Applying the Scientific Method

As stated earlier, the scientific method attempts to minimize the influence of the scientist's bias on the outcome of an experiment. That is, when testing a hypothesis or a theory, the scientist may have a preference for one outcome or another, and it is important that this preference not bias the results or their interpretation. The most fundamental error is to mistake the hypothesis for an explanation of a phenomenon, without performing experimental tests. Sometimes "common sense" and "logic" tempt us into believing that no test is needed. There are numerous examples of this, dating from the Greek philosophers to the present day.

Another common mistake is to ignore or rule out data, which do not support the hypothesis. Ideally, the experimenter is open to the possibility that the hypothesis is correct or incorrect. Sometimes, however, a scientist may have a strong belief that the hypothesis is true (or false), or feels internal or external pressure to get a specific result. In that case, there may be a psychological tendency to find "something wrong", such as systematic effects, with data which do not support the scientist's expectations, while data which do agree with those expectations may not be checked as carefully. The lesson is that all data must be handled in the same way.

Another common mistake arises from the failure to *estimate quantitatively* systematic errors (and all errors). There are many examples of discoveries, which were missed by experimenters whose data contained a new phenomenon, but who explained it away as a systematic background. Conversely, there are many examples of alleged "new discoveries" which later proved to be due to systematic errors not accounted for by the "discoverers."

In a field where there is active experimentation *and* open communication among members of the scientific community, the biases of individuals or groups may cancel out, because different scientists who may have different biases repeat experimental tests. In addition, different types of experimental setups have different sources of systematic errors. Over a period spanning a variety of experimental tests (usually at least several years), a consensus develops in the community as to which experimental results have stood the test of time.

IV. Hypotheses, Models, Theories and Laws

In physics and other science disciplines, the words "hypothesis," "model," "theory" and "law" have different connotations in relation to the stage of acceptance or knowledge about a group of phenomena.

An *hypothesis* is a limited statement regarding cause and effect in specific situations; it also refers to our state of knowledge before experimental work has been performed and perhaps even before new phenomena have been predicted. To take an example from daily life, suppose you discover that your car will not start. You may say, "My car does not start because the battery is low." This is your first hypothesis. You may then check whether the lights were left on, or if the engine makes a particular sound when you turn the ignition key. You might actually check the voltage across the terminals of the battery. If you discover that the battery is not low, you might attempt another hypothesis ("The starter is broken"; "This is really not my car.")

The word *model* is reserved for situations when it is known that the hypothesis has at least limited validity. A often-cited example of this is the Bohr model of the atom, in which, in an analogy to the solar system, the electrons are described has moving in circular orbits around the nucleus. This is not an accurate depiction of what an atom "looks like," but the model succeeds in mathematically representing the energies (but not the correct angular momenta) of the quantum states of the electron in the simplest case, the hydrogen atom. Another example is Hook's Law (which should be called Hook's principle, or Hook's model), which states that the force exerted by a mass attached to a spring is proportional to the amount the spring is stretched. We know that this principle is only valid for small amounts of stretching. The "law" fails when the spring is stretched beyond its elastic limit (it can break). This principle, however, leads to the prediction of simple harmonic motion, and, as a *model* of the behavior of a spring, has been versatile in an extremely broad range of applications.

A *scientific theory* or law represents a hypothesis, or a group of related hypotheses, which has been confirmed through repeated experimental tests. Theories in physics are often formulated in terms of a few concepts and equations, which are identified with "laws of nature," suggesting their universal applicability. Accepted scientific theories and laws become part of our understanding of the universe and the basis for exploring less well-understood areas of knowledge. Theories are not easily discarded; new discoveries are first assumed to fit into the existing theoretical framework. It is only when, after repeated experimental tests, the new phenomenon cannot be accommodated that scientists seriously question the theory and attempt to modify it. The validity that we attach to scientific theories as representing realities of the physical world is to be contrasted with the facile invalidation implied by the expression, "It's only a theory." For example, it is unlikely that a person will step off a tall building on the assumption that they will not fall, because "Gravity is only a theory."

Changes in scientific thought and theories occur, of course, sometimes revolutionizing our view of the world (Kuhn, 1962). Again, the key force for change is the scientific method, and its emphasis on **experiment**.

V. Are there circumstances in which the Scientific Method is not applicable?

While the scientific method is necessary in developing scientific knowledge, it is also useful in everyday problem solving. What do you do when your telephone doesn't work? Is the problem in the handset, the cabling inside your house, the hookup outside, or in the workings of the Phone Company? The process you might go through to solve this problem could involve scientific thinking, and the results might contradict your initial expectations.

Like any good scientist, you may question the range of situations (outside of science) in which the scientific method may be applied. From what has been stated above, we determine that the scientific method works best in situations where one can isolate the phenomenon of interest, by eliminating or accounting for extraneous factors, and where one can repeatedly test the system under study after making limited, controlled changes in it.

There are, of course, circumstances when one cannot isolate the phenomena or when one cannot repeat the measurement over and over again. In such cases the results may depend in part on the history of a situation. This often occurs in social interactions between people. For example, when a lawyer makes arguments in front of a jury in court, she or he cannot try other approaches by repeating the trial over and over again in front of the same jury. In a new trial, the jury composition will be different. Even the same jury hearing a new set of arguments cannot be expected to forget what they heard before.

VI. Scientific Method Conclusion

The scientific method is intricately associated with science, **the process of human inquiry** that pervades the modern era on many levels. While the method appears simple and logical in description, **there is perhaps no more complex question than that of knowing how we come to know things.** In this introduction, I have emphasized that **the scientific method distinguishes science from other forms of explanation because of its requirement of <u>systematic experimentation</u>.** I have also tried to point out some of the criteria and practices developed by scientists to reduce the influence of individual or social bias on scientific findings.

Is there a purpose in life? What is the Purpose of life?

The answers to these questions as I shall explain them from my point of view, and I'm sure I speak for many non-theists in this, depends heavily on your state of mind and on your mental health. Ironically, the believers, especially Christians and Muslims, who have been taught to hate science and to ignore it is because it is evil, may not see the beauty of looking at reality objectively. When I was a believer and used to attend the synagogue regularly I did not pay much attention to science and since I was biased towards the Bible and god, I had a negative outlook on science and non-believers.

Now that I no longer subscribe to irrationality and neuroticism, having given up on all things which cannot be proven as true and on barbaric and savage writings, teachings and mythology, my outlook on life and existence is very positive and certainly as fresh air/chicken soup for the mind.

The purpose of life does not exist however. Life is not about a purpose, life is about living it well. You have to determine what you would like to have as a purpose in your own life. Because each individual is unique, while we do share many tastes and fields of study or outlooks on the many aspects of life's possibilities and beauties, we still have to chose individually what we want to do with our lives. Myself, although I may not live to see it, I hope to see humanity explore deep space and colonize other planets. I hope to see far-reaching and exotic technological advancements in all areas of science and technology and life. I would like to see the development of an efficient and practical propulsion system for spacecraft so we can travel to other planets, solar systems and galaxies in a practical time frame.

I also like to help ensure that humanity does not fall back into the dark ages. I find fulfillment in my life through learning new things, by reading scientific journals and papers, enjoying the arts, foods and searching to constantly improve myself by acquiring new knowledge. I keep up with world events as far as politics and social changes. I find happiness in knowing that there is so much more to know (science = to know) and as soon as I learn something new about new scientific research or technological advancements, or new books worth reading or new techniques which help make my life better. I enjoy the wealth of knowledge I have available to me, as well as the never-ending supply of movies, music foods etc.

But ultimately, we all come down to this "fear of death" and the passing time, which goes by so fast. My ONLY fear concerning death is that I will die uneducated; that I will die with not enough knowledge. Not that I don't have an education, as I do have a degree in electronics, and am also a Systems Engineer. In my opinion, the beginning of wisdom begins with the fear of being stupid. If there is an after life I want to get there with as much knowledge about this reality and universe as possible. If there is no afterlife, I want to enjoy my life as much as possible, as well as do something positive to help humanity and future generations, especially my own children's future.

Furthermore, I have a thirst for intellectualism, for developing my character so as to make me a noble person, a man of integrity, to be moral and ethical in all areas of life. It is hard to believe now, but when I was a believer, even though I was very sincere and devoted, I feared death. Now, death is just a fact of life, and to be quite honest, as you grow older you start to get bored of it as well. We grow old and weary, tired of living. Life starts to taste like when you eat the same food over and over and over. So enjoy it while you can, and no matter what purpose you choose to give your own life, do it honestly; be honest with yourself and do not let anyone lead you by the nose. Do not believe everything anyone says; consider the source and look into any information, which you feel, is of interest to you but lack the proper knowledge to make an educated decision or reach a proper conclusion. As a final note, the unknown is not to be feared but explored. Fear will never do away with all the things that can go wrong, and if anything can go wrong, rest assured it will anyway, so fear of the unknown is in vain.

Shalom

Part Two

The Illuminati Manifesto

The Declaration of Individual Rights

Each individual has natural born rights, which no other person, entity or government of any kind may infringe. The respect and loyalty to these rights is the moral standard of the rational and just human beings.

The natural rights of the individual are:

1. The right to life.

2. The right to the pursuit of happiness.

3. The right to own property, intellectual and/or tangible.

4. The right to perform any action needed to ensure preservation/ending of the life of the self without damaging the environment of the planet. The environment belongs to all and endangering it violates the individual rights of others.

5.   The right to earn a living through one's own efforts, mental or physical.

6.   The right to live his/her life any way he/she likes without causing physical harm to another individual.

7.   The right to defend his/her life and property and family.

8.   The rights to have children, ONLY if he/she can guarantee food, shelter clothing, safety and education for such and provide for any and all medical needs of such.

9.   The right to conduct business with others based on mutual and/or contractual agreement.

10.   The right to privacy in all forms.

These are the **inalienable** human rights inherited at birth.

The Absolute Value of Individual Rights

When we say that the Individual Rights are **absolute** then they are **absolute!**

The Individual Rights can never be suspended under any circumstances what so ever (with the one exception made clear in the Prime Directives).

The Individual Rights cannot be infringed upon under any circumstances what so ever.

The Individual Rights cannot be suspended for any reason ever.

The Individual Rights cannot be violated or restricted in any way for any reason in any fashion, period.
The Individual Rights are absolute forever.

The Individual Rights are inalienable in every sense of the word and no business, contract or any other entity can ever violate them or seek to dilute them through contracts, deception or coercion.

The Individual Rights can never be refused or given up even voluntarily; no person has the right to wave their own individual rights as they are part of the very composition and existence of a conscious mind.

The Individual Rights are never and can never be considered semi-absolute or semi inalienable.

The Individual Rights and the rational human are sovereign over each other and absolutely inseparable.

The Individual Rights are the individual rights of every single human being regardless of gender, sexual orientation or color of skin.

Any person who does not agree with this is a person who has forfeited their right to exist as they have rejected the rights of others.

If you agree with the above you are here by recognized as an Illuminati in the 1st.
On the behalf of the Illuminati Order and the Unseen Head we say, Shalom

✶✶

[The Constitution of a Free Society]
(The Illuminati Constitution)

We the people of The Illuminati Order, in order to form a more perfect society, establish justice, insure domestic tranquility, provide for the defense of the individual and individual rights, promote the welfare of the individual and secure the blessings of liberty to ourselves and our posterity and future generations, do ordain and establish this Constitution for the Free Society of the World. Each nation shall be annexed/assimilated into the World Federation, as a state, at all costs. Each state shall retain its existing borders.

Article 1a. The Declaration of Individual Rights

Each individual has natural born rights, which no other person, entity or government of any kind may infringe. The respect and loyalty to these rights is the moral standard of the rational and just human beings.

The natural rights of the individual are:

1. The right to life.
2. The right to the pursuit of happiness, without violating the rights of another individual.
3. The right to own property, intellectual and/or tangible.
4. The right to perform any action needed to ensure preservation/ending of the life of the self without damaging the environment of the planet. The environment belongs to all and endangering it violates the individual rights of others.
5. The right to earn a living through one's own efforts, mental, physical or both.
6. The right to live his/her life any way he/she likes without causing physical harm to another individual, directly or indirectly.

7.   The right to defend his/her life and property and family.
8.   The rights to have children, ONLY if he/she can guarantee food, shelter, clothing, safety and education for such and provide for any and all medical needs of such.
9.   The right to conduct business with others based on mutual and/or contractual agreement.
10. The right to privacy in all forms.

The Government Its Nature and Its Purpose

Article 1b

Section 1. The government is the institution responsible for the protection of the individual rights, and only the government holds exclusive power to enforce certain rules of social conduct on planet earth, and any area/planet annexed by the Federation. Civilized, rational humans/beings, in order to be able to use their basic tools such as the mind as their basic tool of gaining knowledge to guide their actions in order to maintain the freedom; to think and to act according to one's own rational judgement, need the institution of government.

Section 2. An individual's right can only be violated by the use of physical force of sorts. For this reason, government has a monopoly on the use of **retaliatory** use of force, and the punishment of criminals.

Section 3. It is only to secure the protection of the individual from the use of violence by another that government is needed.

Section 4. The only source of authority of the government is the consent of the governed. This simply means that the government is not the ruler, but the servant of the governed.

Article 2

Section 1. All legislative powers herein granted shall be vested in a Congress of the World Federation, which shall consist of a Senate in each state, a Federal Senate and Federal House of Representatives and Chamber of Presidents. The Senate of one state and Federal House of Representatives shall be the Congress for that state, which shall deal with issues related to the concerns of that state.. The same applies to every other state within the Federation.

The Federal Senate and Federal House of Representatives shall be the Congress of the Federation, which shall deal with Federal wide issues.

Section 2. The House of Representatives shall be composed of one person from each state, chosen every four years by the people of the each state. In the event that an even number of persons preside in the House, the Chief Justice shall be the tiebreaker.

Section 3. No person shall be a Representative who shall not have attained to the age of thirty five years, and who shall not, when elected, be an inhabitant of that state in which he shall be chosen, and all representatives and senators shall posses a degree in one of the accepted advanced sciences.

Section 4. When vacancies happen in the Representation from any state, the executive authority thereof shall issue writs of election to fill such vacancies. The House of Representatives shall choose their speaker and other officers; and shall have the sole power of impeachment.

Section 5. The Senate of each State shall be composed of 71 Senators chosen by a democratic vote of the residents of the respective state whom are college professors and schoolteacher of accepted schools, for six years; and each Senator shall have one vote.

Section 5. Immediately after they shall be assembled in consequence of the first election, they shall be divided as equally as may be into three classes.

Section 6. No person shall be a Senator who shall not have attained to the age of thirty years, and all senators must posses a degree in one of the advanced sciences and must be, when elected, an inhabitant of that state for which he shall be chosen for no less than seven years.

Section 7. The Senate shall choose their other officers, and also a President and the President of the State shall be a tiebreaker.

Section 8. The Senate shall have the sole power to try all impeachment of all and any official within the Senate and above, state or federal. When sitting for that purpose, they shall be on oath or affirmation.

Section 9. When the President of the State is tried, the Chief Justice shall preside: And no person shall be convicted without the concurrence of two thirds of the members present.

Section 10. Judgment in cases of impeachment shall not extend further than to removal from office and imprisonment of more than seven years, and disqualification to hold and enjoy any office of honor, trust or profit under the State and/or Federation: but the party convicted shall nevertheless be liable and subject to indictment, trial, judgment and punishment, according to law.

Section 11. The times, places and manner of holding elections for Senators and Representatives, shall be prescribed in each state by the legislature thereof; but the Chamber of Presidents may at any time by law make or alter such regulations, except as to the places of choosing Senators.

Section 12. The Congress shall assemble at least once in every year, and such meeting shall be on the first Monday in January, unless they shall by law appoint a different day.

Section 13. Each House shall be the judge of the elections, returns and qualifications of its own members, and a two thirds majority of each shall constitute a quorum to do business; but a smaller number may adjourn from day to day, and may be authorized to compel the attendance of absent members, in such manner, and under such penalties as each House may provide.

Section 14. Each House may determine the rules of its proceedings, punish its members for disorderly behavior, and, with the concurrence of two thirds, expel a member.

Section 15. Each House shall keep a journal of its proceedings, and from time to time publish the same, excepting such parts as may in their judgment require secrecy; and the yeas and nays of the members of either House on any question shall, at the desire of one fifth of those present, be entered on the journal.

Section 16. Neither House, during the session of Congress, shall, without the consent of the others, adjourn for more than three days, nor to any other place than that in which the two lower Houses shall be sitting.

Section 17. The Senators and Representatives shall receive a compensation for their services, to be ascertained by law, and paid out of the treasury of the Federation. They shall in all cases, except treason, felony and breach of the peace, be privileged from arrest during their attendance at the session of their respective Houses, and in going to and returning from the same; and for any speech or debate in either House, they shall not be questioned in any other place.

Section 18. No Senator or Representative shall, during the time for which he was elected, be appointed to any civil office under the authority of the Federation, which shall have been created, or the emoluments whereof shall have been increased during such time: and no person holding any office under the Federation, shall be a member of either House during his continuance in office.

Section 19. All bills for raising revenue shall originate in the House of Representatives; but the Senate may propose or concur with amendments as on other Bills.

Section 20. Every bill which shall have passed the House of Representatives and the Senate, shall, before it become a law, be presented to the President of the State, who is to present it for a vote in the Chamber of Presidents; if it is approved the Chairman/President of the Chamber shall sign it, but if not he shall return it, with the objections of the Chamber members to that House in which it shall have originated, who shall enter the objections at large on their journal, and proceed to reconsider it.

Section 21. If after such reconsideration two thirds of that House shall agree to pass the bill, it shall be sent, together with the objections, to the other House, by which it shall likewise be reconsidered, and if approved by two thirds of that House, it shall become a law. But in all such cases the votes of both Houses shall be determined by yeas and nays, and the names of the persons voting for and against the bill shall be entered on the journal of each House respectively and made public.

Section 22. If any bill shall not be returned by the Chamber of Presidents within 30 days after it shall have been presented to it, the same shall be a law, in like manner as if it had signed it, unless the Congress by their adjournment prevent its return, in which case it shall not be a law.

Section 23. Every order, resolution, or vote to which the concurrence of the Senate and House of Representatives may be necessary (except on a question of adjournment) shall be presented to the Chamber of Presidents; and before the same shall take effect, shall be approved by it, or being disapproved by it, shall be reinstated by two thirds of the Senate and House of Representatives, according to the rules and limitations prescribed in the case of a bill.

Section 24. The Congress shall have power to lay and collect 30% income taxes or less, to pay the debts and provide for the common defense and general welfare of the Government and Federation; but all duties, imposts and excises shall be uniform throughout the Federation and shall never exceed 30% total;

To borrow money on the credit of the Federation;

To regulate commerce with foreign states which are not part of the Federation, but without infringing, on the business of the individuals citizens of the federation.

To establish a uniform rule of naturalization, and uniform and objective laws on the subject of bankruptcies throughout the Federation;

To coin money, establish the value thereof permanently, and of foreign coin, and fix the standard of weights and measures;

To provide for the punishment of counterfeiting the securities and current coin of the Federation;

To promote science and the arts, by securing for limited times, no less than 40 years, to authors and inventors the exclusive right to their respective writings and discoveries;

To constitute tribunals inferior to the Supreme Court;

To define and punish piracies and felonies committed on the high seas or in space, and offenses against the law of the Federation;

To grant letters of marque and reprisal, and make rules concerning captures on land, air, space and water;

To provide for calling forth the federal police/militia to execute the laws of the Federation, suppress insurrections.

To provide for organizing, arming, and disciplining, the police and militia, and for governing such part of them as may be employed in the service of the Federation, reserving to the states respectively, the appointment of the officers, and the authority of training the police and militia according to the discipline prescribed by Congress;

To exercise exclusive legislation in all cases whatsoever, over such District (not exceeding ten miles square) as may, by cession of particular states, and the acceptance of Chamber of Presidents, become the seat of the government of the Federation, and to exercise like authority over all places purchased by the consent of the legislature of the state in which the same shall be, for the erection of forts, magazines, arsenals, dockyards, space stations and other needful buildings;—And

To make all **objective** laws which shall be necessary and proper for carrying into execution the foregoing powers and all other powers vested by this Constitution in the government of the World Federation, or in any department or officer thereof.

Section 25. The privilege of the writ of habeas corpus shall not be suspended, unless when in cases of rebellion or invasion the public safety may require it.

No bill of attainder or ex post facto Law shall be passed.

No other direct/indirect, tax shall be laid aside from the 30%, unless the planet/Federation is in immediate danger, and in such case any extra tax shall be **temporary** to cover the costs of the emergency needs only.

No tax or duty shall be laid on articles exported/imported from any state/planet belonging to the federation.

No preference shall be given by any regulation of commerce or revenue to the ports of one state over those of another: nor shall vessels bound to, or from, one state, be obliged to enter, clear or pay duties in another.

No money shall be drawn from the treasury, but in consequence of appropriations made by law; and a regular statement and account of receipts and expenditures of all public money shall be published from time to time.

No title of nobility shall be granted by the Federation: and no person holding any office of profit or trust under them, shall, without the consent of the Congress, accept of any present/gift, emolument, office, or title, of any kind whatever, from any king, prince, or foreign state or private business or citizen.

Section 26. No state shall enter into any treaty, alliance, or confederation; grant letters of marque and reprisal; coin money; emit bills of credit; pass any bill of attainder, ex post facto law, or law impairing the obligation of contracts, or grant any title of nobility.

No state shall, without the consent of the Congress, lay any imposts or duties on imports or exports, except what may be absolutely necessary for executing its inspection laws: and the net produce of all duties and imposts, laid by any state on imports or exports, shall be for the use of the treasury of the Federation; and all such laws shall be subject to the revision and control of the Congress and Chamber of Presidents.

No state shall, without the consent of Congress and Chamber of Presidents, lay any duty of tonnage, keep troops, or ships of war in time of peace, enter into any agreement or compact with another state, or with a foreign power, or engage in war, unless actually invaded, or in such imminent danger as will not admit of delay.

Article 3

Section 1. The executive power shall be vested in a Chamber of Presidents of the World Federation. It shall have the power;

To raise and support armies, but no appropriation of money to that use shall be for a longer term than two years;

To provide and maintain a navy, space and planetary defense;

To make rules for the government and regulation of the land, space, air and naval forces;

Each state shall appoint, in such manner as the Legislature thereof may direct a president of the state; to function, as the executive of the state in the Chamber of Presidents of the World Federation.

Section 2. Only College and/or University professors qualify for such office and theology professors are disqualified by default and state presidents must be elected by a majority vote of the population of its respective state.

The person having the greatest number of votes shall be the President of the State, if two or more candidates have an equal number of votes, then the House of Representatives shall immediately choose by ballot one of them for President.

Section 3. The Congress may determine the time of choosing the elections, and the day shall be the same throughout the Federation.

Section 4. No person except a natural born citizen, or a citizen of the Federation, at the time of the adoption of this Constitution, shall be eligible to the office of President; neither shall any person be eligible to that office who shall not have attained to the age of forty five years, and been 10 years professor at college/university level, of one of the accepted professional recognized faculty.

Section 5. In case of the removal of State President from office, or of his death, resignation, or inability to discharge the powers and duties of the said office, the same shall devolve on the Congress may by law provide for the case of removal, death, resignation or inability, both of the President and Vice President, declaring what officer shall then act as President, and such officer shall act accordingly, until the disability be removed, or a President shall be elected.

Section 6. The President shall, at stated times, receive for his services, a compensation, which shall neither be increased nor diminished during the period for which he shall have been elected, and he shall not receive within that period any other emolument or gifts from the Federation, or any other source.

Before he enter on the execution of his office, he shall take the following oath or affirmation:—"I do solemnly swear (or affirm) that I will faithfully execute the office of State President of the [STATE], and will to the best of my ability, preserve, protect and defend the Constitution of the World Federation and the individual rights of all."

Section 7. The Chairman/President of the Chamber of Presidents shall be commander in chief of the Army and Navy of the Federation, and of the militia of the states, when called into the actual service of the Federation; he may require the opinion, in writing, of the Presidents of States and officers in each of the executive departments, upon any subject relating to the duties of their respective offices, and he shall have power to grant reprieves and pardons for offenses against the Federation, except in cases of impeachment.

He shall have power, by and with the advice and consent of the Chamber of Presidents, to make treaties, provided two thirds of the Presidents concur; and he shall nominate, and by and with the advice and consent of the Chamber of Presidents, shall appoint ambassadors, other public ministers and consuls, and all other officers of the Federation, whose appointments are not herein otherwise provided for, and which shall be established by law: but the Congress may by law vest the appointment of such inferior officers, as they think proper, in the Presidents alone, in the courts of law, or in the heads of departments.

Section 8. The Chairman/President of the Chamber of Presidents shall from time to time give to the Congress information of the state of the Federation-union, and recommend to their consideration such measures as he shall judge necessary and expedient; he may, on extraordinary occasions, convene both lower Houses, or either of them, and in case of disagreement between them, with respect to the time of adjournment, he may adjourn them to such time as he shall think proper; he shall receive ambassadors and other public ministers in the presence of the Chamber of Presidents; he shall take care that the laws be faithfully executed and the constitution is not violated by such, and shall commission all the officers of the Federation with the approval of the Chamber of Presidents by a simple majority.

Section 9. Any and all civil officers of the Federation shall be removed from office on impeachment for, and conviction of, treason, bribery, perjury or other high crimes and misdemeanors.

Article 4

Section 1. The judicial power of the Federation shall be vested in One Supreme Court and in such inferior courts as the Congress may from time to time ordain and establish. The judges, both of the supreme and inferior courts, shall hold their offices during good behavior, and shall, at stated times, receive for their services, a compensation, which shall not be diminished during their continuance in office.

Section 2. The Supreme Court shall be comprised of 13 Judges in each state and one chief Judge shall preside over a panel of 13 judges whom shall oversee and preside over the functions of the Supreme Court as follows;
Chief Judge;
Thirteen Supreme Court judges to act as overseers of the Supreme Court and its functions
Thirteen Supreme court Judges in each state to act as the Supreme Court of the state and Federation.

Section 3. The judicial power shall extend to all cases, in law and equity, arising under this Constitution, the laws of the World Federation States, and treaties made, or which shall be made, under their authority;—to all cases affecting ambassadors, other public ministers and consuls;—to all cases of admiralty and maritime jurisdiction;—to controversies to which the Federation shall be a party;—to controversies between two or more states;—between a state and citizens of another state;— between citizens of different states;—between citizens of the same state claiming lands under grants of different states, and between a state, or the citizens thereof, and foreign states, citizens or subjects.

In all cases affecting ambassadors, other public ministers and consuls, and those in which a state shall be party, the Supreme Court shall have original jurisdiction. In all the other cases before mentioned, the Supreme Court shall have appellate jurisdiction, both as to law and fact, with such exceptions, and under such regulations as the Congress shall make.

The trial of all crimes, except in cases of impeachment, shall be by jury; and such trial shall be held in the state where the said crimes shall have been committed; but when not committed within any state, the trial shall be at such place or places as the Congress may by law have directed.

Section 4. Treason against the Federation shall consist only in levying war against them, or in adhering to their enemies, giving them aid and comfort. No person shall be convicted of treason unless on the testimony of two witnesses to the same overt act, or on confession in open court.

The Congress shall have power to declare the punishment of treason, but no attainder of treason shall work corruption of blood, or forfeiture except during the life of the person attainted.

Section 5. Teachers and college professors only shall elect the Supreme Court justices. The Supreme Court in any state may veto/overturn any law on constitutional grounds, any law which violates individual rights as stated in The Declaration of Individual Rights.

Section 6. A Special session in which all Supreme Court justices attend can be summoned by the Chief Justice to modify this Constitution, and a two-thirds majority is required for such as well as a small majority of the general population.

Article 5

Section 1. Full faith and credit shall be given in each state to the public acts, records, and judicial proceedings of every other state. And the Congress may by general laws prescribe the manner in which such acts, records, and proceedings shall be proved and the effect thereof.

Section 2. The citizens of each state shall be entitled to all privileges and immunities of citizens in any other.

A person charged in any state with treason, felony, or other crime, who shall flee from justice, and be found in another state, shall on demand of the executive authority of the state from which he fled, be delivered up, to be removed to the state having jurisdiction of the crime.

No person held to service or labor in one state, under the laws thereof, escaping into another, shall, in consequence of any law or regulation therein, be discharged from such service or labor, but shall be delivered up on claim of the party to whom such service or labor may be due.

Section 3. New states may be admitted/annexed by the Congress into this union; but no new states shall be formed or erected within the jurisdiction of any other state; nor any state be formed by the junction of two or more states, or parts of states, without the consent of the legislatures of the states concerned as well as of the Congress and Chamber of Presidents.

The Congress shall have power to dispose of and make all needful rules and regulations respecting the territory or other property belonging to the Federation Government; and nothing in this Constitution shall be so construed as to prejudice any claims of the Federation, or of any particular state.

Section 4. The World Federation shall guarantee to every state in this union a republican form of government, and shall protect each of them against invasion; and on application of the legislature, or of the executive (when the legislature cannot be convened) against domestic violence.

Section 5. Any government property, which is not needed or utilized, must be sold by lottery to all interested parties for no more than one dollar per acre. Government may not forcefully purchase/confiscate the property of any federation citizen(s). ALL lands within the Federation, aside from that needed for the function of government, must be privately owned. Congress shall sell all existing or future acquired lands to the public by lottery, for no more than one dollar per acre.

Section 6. No aid of any kind may be given, or loans of any kind may be granted to any entity, nation or foreign government, which is not part of the World Federation under any circumstances.

Article 6

The Congress, whenever two thirds of both upper houses shall deem it necessary, shall propose amendments to this Constitution, or, at the request of two thirds of the Chamber of Presidents, shall call a convention for proposing amendments, which, in either case, shall be valid to all intents and purposes, as part of this Constitution, when ratified by the Supreme Court, be proposed by the Congress.

Article 7

Section 1. All debts contracted and engagements entered into, before the adoption of this Constitution, shall be valid against the World Federation under this Constitution.

This Constitution, and the laws of the World Federation which shall be made in pursuance thereof; and all treaties made, or which shall be made, under the authority of the World Federation , shall be the supreme law of the land; and the judges in every state shall be bound thereby, anything in the Constitution or laws of any State to the contrary notwithstanding.

Section 2. The Senators and Representatives before mentioned, and all executive and judicial officers, both of the World Federation, shall be bound by oath or affirmation, to support and protect this Constitution; but no religious person shall ever be permitted to speak publicly of any religious dogma/doctrines, or use any religious language while holding any office or public trust under the World Federation.

Article 8

Government shall exercise absolute separation between state/government and religion but shall make no law respecting an establishment of religion, or prohibiting the free exercise thereof; or abridging the freedom of speech, or of the press; or the right of the people peaceably to assemble, and to petition the government for a redress of grievances.

Article 9

Section 1. A well-regulated militia, being necessary to the security of a free state, the right of the people to keep and bear arms, **shall not be infringed in any way.**

Section 2. Citizens may not use their arms for the use of physical force, even in self defense/self-protection, except during the types of emergencies that require action at once, before the police can be summoned.

Section 3. The militia, when called upon to service, are every citizen wishing to participate, and the police.

Section 4. A person, whom has been convicted of a serious violent crime, with a deadly weapon, does not have the right to bare arms of any kind, as he/she had forfeited his/her right by default.

Article 10

No soldier shall, in time of peace be quartered in any house, without the consent of the owner, nor in time of war, but in a manner to be prescribed by law and consent of the property owner(s).

Article 11

The right of the people to be secure in their persons, houses, papers, and effects, against ALL unreasonable searches and seizures, shall not be violated, and no warrants shall issue, but upon VERY **objective** probable cause, supported by oath or affirmation, and particularly describing the place to be searched, and the persons or things to be seized and **only** in cases of **most serious crimes** shall such be permitted.

Article 12

No person shall be held to answer for a capital, or otherwise infamous crime, unless on a presentment or indictment of a grand jury, except in cases arising in the land or naval forces, or in the militia, when in actual service in time of war or public danger; nor shall any person be subject for the same offense to be twice put in jeopardy of life or limb; nor shall be compelled in any criminal case to be a witness against himself, nor be deprived of life, liberty, or property, without due process of law; nor shall private property be taken for public use, without just compensation; nor shall any person be arrested unless the evidence is objectively conclusive in nature, and the related crime accused of is very serious.

Article 13

Section 1. In all criminal prosecutions, the accused shall enjoy the right to a speedy and public trial, by an impartial objective jury of the state and district wherein the crime shall have been committed, which district shall have been previously ascertained by objective law, and to be informed of the nature and cause of the accusation; to be confronted with the witnesses against him; to have compulsory process for obtaining witnesses in his favor, and to have the assistance of government/private counsel for his defense.

Section 2. A jury must consist of persons whom have obtained and completed a college education and are versed in Objectivism. Furthermore, in the case of an atheist, agnostic, or secularist being the defendant, he/she may request and has a right to have a jury composed of such as sharing his/her beliefs. No religious persons of any kind may sit on a jury when an Atheist, Agnostic, None-theist, or Freethinker is the defendant(s). No person whom had a major legal dispute with a defendant in question, may sit on the jury. No theist Judge shall preside over such a case, as related to none-theists

Article 14

In suits at common law, where the value in controversy shall exceed 3,000 dollars, the right of trial by jury shall be preserved, and no fact tried by a jury, shall be otherwise reexamined in any court of the World Federation, than according to the rules of the common law.

Article 15

Excessive bail shall not be required, nor excessive fines imposed, nor cruel and unusual punishments inflicted.

Article 16

The enumeration in the Constitution, of certain rights, shall not be construed to deny or disparage others retained by the each individual.

Article 17

The powers not delegated to the World Federation (Federal Government) by the Constitution, nor prohibited by it to the states, are reserved to the states respectively, and/or to the people. States and lower governments may not impose any taxes or fees of any kind, with the exception of a lottery per state.

Article 18

Citizens of any foreign state shall not construe the judicial power of the World Federation to extend to any suit in law or equity, commenced or prosecuted against one of the World Federation by citizens of another state.

Article 19

The electors shall meet in their respective states and vote by ballot for President and Vice-President, one of whom, at least, shall not be an inhabitant of the same state with themselves; they shall name in their ballots the person voted for as President, and in distinct ballots the person voted for as Vice-President, and they shall make distinct lists of all persons voted for as President, and of all persons voted for as Vice-President, and of the number of votes for each, which lists they shall sign and certify, and transmit sealed to the seat of the government of the World Federation, directed to the President of the Senate;—The President of the Senate shall, in the presence of the Senate and House of Representatives, open all the certificates and the votes shall then be counted;—the person having the greatest number of votes for President, shall be the Presid- ctive state, if such number be a majority of the · ' s appointed; and if no person have such ı having the highest numbers not exceedir d for as President, the House of Represent: : immediately, by ballot, the President. Ar atives shall not choose a President whe. devolve upon them, before the fourth day ᴜowing, then the Vice-President shall act as Presiden ... ın the case of the death or other constitutional disability of the President. The person having the greatest number of votes as Vice-President, shall be the Vice-President, if such number be a majority of the whole number of electors appointed, and if no person have a majority, then from the two highest numbers on the list, the Senate shall choose the Vice-President; a quorum for the purpose shall consist of two-thirds of the whole number of Senators, and a majority of the whole number shall be necessary to a choice. But no person constitutionally ineligible to the office of President shall be eligible to that of Vice-President of any State of Federation Chairman.

Article 20

Section 1. Neither slavery nor involuntary servitude, except as a punishment for crime whereof the party shall have been duly convicted, shall exist within the World Federation, or any place subject to their jurisdiction.

Section 2. Congress shall have power to enforce this article by appropriate legislation.

Section 3. All prisons where criminals will serve the term of their punishment must be privatized and the prison owner(s) may put the criminals to work for profit.

Article 21

Section 1. All persons born or naturalized in the World Federation , and subject to the jurisdiction thereof, are citizens of the World Federation and of the state wherein they reside. No state shall make or enforce any law which shall abridge the privileges or immunities of citizens of the World Federation; nor shall any state deprive any person of life, liberty, or property, without due process of law; nor deny to any person within its jurisdiction the equal protection of the laws.

Section 2. All persons of the age of 18 or older, or any person who works and pays taxes for at least 6 months, has a right to vote in elections accordingly, for any official mentioned in this Constitution.

Section 3. No person shall be a Senator or Representative in Congress, or elector of President and Vice President, or hold any office, civil or military, under the World Federation, or under any state, who, having previously taken an oath, as a member of Congress, or as an officer of the World Federation, or as a member of any state legislature, or as an executive or judicial officer of any state, to support the Constitution of the World Federation, shall have engaged in insurrection or rebellion against the same, or given aid or comfort to the enemies thereof. But Congress may by a vote of two-thirds of each House, remove such disability on a case by case basis.

Section 4. The validity of the public debt of the World Federation, authorized by law, including debts incurred for payment of pensions and bounties for services in suppressing insurrection or rebellion, shall not be questioned. But neither the World Federation nor any state shall assume or pay any debt or obligation incurred in aid of insurrection or rebellion against the World Federation/Federation State; but all such debts, obligations and claims shall be held illegal and void.

Section 5. The Congress shall have power to enforce, by appropriate legislation, the provisions of this article.

Article 22

Section 1. The right of citizens of the World Federation to vote shall not be denied or abridged by the World Federation or by any state on account of race, color, gender or previous condition of servitude.

Section 2. The Congress shall have power to enforce this article by appropriate objective legislation.

Article 23

The Congress shall have power to lay and collect 30% taxes on incomes, from all employed citizens, without apportionment among the states, and without regard to any census of enumeration.

Article 24

The Senate of the World Federation shall be composed of 71 Senators from each state, elected by the people thereof, for seven years; and each Senator shall have one vote.

When vacancies happen in the representation of any state in the Senate, the executive authority of such state shall issue writs of election to fill such vacancies: Provided, that the legislature of any state may empower the executive thereof to make temporary appointments until the people fill the vacancies by election as the legislature may direct.

Article 25

The right of citizens of the World Federation to vote in any of the government bodies shall not be denied or abridged by the World Federation or by any state on account of gender.

Congress shall have power to enforce this article by appropriate legislation.

Article 26

Section 1. The terms of the Presidents and Vice Presidents shall end at noon on the 20th day of January, and the terms of Senators and Representatives at noon on the 3d day of January, at the end of their terms of office respectively.

Section 2. The Congress shall assemble at least once in every year, and such meeting shall begin at noon on the 3d day of January, unless they shall by law appoint a different day.

Section 3. If, at the time fixed for the beginning of the term of the President, the President elect shall have died, the Vice President elect shall become President. If a President shall not have been chosen before the time fixed for the beginning of his term, or if the President elect shall have failed to qualify, then the Vice President elect shall act as President until a President shall have qualified; and the Congress may by law provide for the case wherein neither a President elect nor a Vice President elect shall have qualified, declaring who shall then act as President of the State to serve in the Chamber of Presidents, or the manner in which one who is to act shall be selected, and such person shall act accordingly until a President or Vice President shall have qualified.

Section 4. The Congress may by law provide for the case of the death of any of the persons from whom the House of Representatives may choose a President whenever the right of choice shall have devolved upon them, and for the case of the death of any of the persons from whom the Senates may choose a Vice President whenever the right of choice shall have devolved upon them.

Article 27

No person shall be elected to the office of the President more than three times, and no person who has held the office of President, or acted as President, for more than two years of a term to which some other person was elected President shall be elected to the office of the President more than once.

Article 28

Section 1. The right of qualified citizens of the World Federation to vote in any primary or other election for President or Vice President, for electors for President or Vice President, or for Senator or Representative in Congress, shall not be denied or abridged by the World Federation or any state by reason of failure to pay any poll tax or other tax.

Section 2. Persons whom have been unemployed for a period of 13 months or more, or have not paid any tax in more than 7 years do not have a right to vote. However, in the case of the unemployed, the rights to vote shall be restored after 3 consecutive years of employment.

Section 3. Persons whom fail to vote at least 2 times every seven years, (unless health does not permit) in any of the state and federal elections shall loose their right to vote permanently.

Section 4. The Congress shall have power to enforce this article by appropriate legislation.

Article 29

Section 1. In case of the removal of the President from office or of his death or resignation, the Vice-President shall become President.

Section 2. Whenever there is a vacancy in the office of the Vice President, the President shall nominate a Vice President who shall take office upon confirmation by a majority vote of both the Senates, State and Federal.

Section 3. Whenever a President or the Chairman of the Chamber of Presidents transmits to the President pro tempore of the Senate and the Speaker of the House of Representatives his written declaration that he is unable to discharge the powers and duties of his office, and until he transmits to them a written declaration to the contrary, such powers and duties shall be discharged by the Vice President/Chairman as Acting President.

Section 4. Whenever the Vice President and a majority of either the principal officers of the executive departments or of such other body as Congress may by law provide, transmit to the President pro tempore of the Senate and the Speaker of the House of Representatives their written declaration that the President is unable to discharge the powers and duties of his office, the Vice President shall immediately assume the powers and duties of the office as Acting President.

Thereafter, when the President transmits to the President pro tempore of the Senate and the Speaker of the House of Representatives his written declaration that no inability exists, he shall resume the powers and duties of his office unless the Vice President and a majority of either the principal officers of the executive department or Presidents or of such other body as Congress may by law provide, transmit within four days to the President pro tempore of the Senate and the Speaker of the House of Representatives their written declaration that the President is unable to discharge the powers and duties of his office. Thereupon Congress shall decide the issue, assembling within forty-eight hours for that purpose if not in session. If the Congress, within twenty-one days after receipt of the latter written declaration, or, if Congress is not in session, within twenty-one days after Congress is required to assemble, determines by two-thirds vote of both Houses that the President is unable to discharge the powers and duties of his office, the Vice President shall continue to discharge the same as Acting President; otherwise, the President shall resume the powers and duties of his office.

Article 30

Section 1. The right of citizens of the World Federation, who are 18 years of age or older, or regular tax payers, to vote, shall not be denied or abridged by the World Federation or any state on account of age.

Section 2. The Congress shall have the power to enforce this article by appropriate legislation.

Article 31

No law varying the compensation for the services of the Senators and Representatives shall take effect until an election of Representatives shall have intervened.

Article 32

Section 1. The Federal government may operate a lottery as follows if it so chooses: a. Names instead of numbers shall be drawn once per week. b. No less that 100 names shall be selected as winners. c. 50% of all lottery income shall be assigned for the Jackpot, which shall be divided equally between all winners whose names were drawn.

Section 2. Each State can, if it chooses to, run a lottery as well.

Section 3. Each Space Agency, such as NASA may run their own lottery for raising additional funds.
Section 4. Each City may also run its own lottery.

Section 5. All lotteries must abide by the lottery rules in Section 1.

Section 6. Lottery winnings may not be taxed, since the money was already taxed once already when the individual earned the income. Regardless, no lottery winnings may ever be taxed.

Section 7. All lotteries must provide full documentation/disclosure on their operations, and may not have more than one drawing per week each.

Section 8. Any citizen who buys a ticket must have submitted their name to the lottery.

Section 9. The Lottery system must be computerized, all moneys received must be made public knowledge in real time, on an internet, television, radio and the outside of the building from which the lottery operates.

Section 10. All moneys must be paid to the winners within 3 days of the drawing.

Section 11. The names of all winners shall be made public, but not their home address.

Section 12. The winners of the lottery shall be given police protection until they secure their winnings in a bank account, and make a relocation of their residence for their safety, which may not exceed 30 days, and the winners may refuse protection at their own risk.

Section 13. Persons employed by the lottery agency do not qualify as winners/participants in the lottery, nor their families.

Section 14. The Lottery should provide credit-card type cards and system for participating in the lottery instead of paper tickets.

Section 15. The Lottery shall allow for automatic entry, by means of withdrawing money from a person's pay check/credit-card, if a citizen wishes to do so.

Section 16. A person may, if one chooses to, pre pay for the drawing of each week in advance, for a full year.

Section 17. In the event that a winner dies before collecting the winnings, the money will be awarded to the closest relative, unless the winner had indicated a beneficiary when buying the tickets.

Section 18. Each ticket shall cost no less than $5 US.

Section 19. In the event that a winner dies, and does not have any family or relatives, or a beneficiary, the money shall be donated to the

Jackpot for the following week, which shall be added to the Jackpot 100%.

Section 20. Only federation citizens may participate in the federation lotteries, and citizens may participate in any/and/or all lotteries.

Article 33

Section 1. Each state may operate an independent Space agency, for the purpose of military needs and research; the protection of the planet; advancement of science.

Section 2. Any citizen may operate a Space Agency for its own purposes; as long as it does not endanger the planet, or the property of others.

Section 3. The Federal government may operate an independent Space Agency.

Section 4. All government contracts to be awarded to the public sector for any reason, shall be by lottery/ballot format, in which the individual or company name is selected from a lottery, after the applicant has shown reasonable proof that it can provide the services or goods required.

Article 34

Section 1. The Federal Government shall give to each State 20% of the 30% taxes collected from the respective state, without any preconditions.

Section 2. All state governmental agencies and lower governments shall be funded from the 20% tax.

Section 3. No county, city, or town governments may charge any fees, or impose any form of taxes on anyone, nor charge any fees for documents or services.

Section 4. Aside from the 30% tax, no form of taxes or fees may be collected by any part of the government.

Section 5. Under no circumstances shall any property be taxed.

Section 6. All government bodies, and government itself must be efficient and effective.

Section 7. All employers shall withdraw the 30% income tax automatically from each paycheck of each employee, and 30% tax from its own profits, each week, and transfer it to the Treasury of the Federation within 3 days, or otherwise as prescribed by law.

Section 8. Property of any kind may not be confiscated for the purpose of collecting taxes, nor can the government use any force/coercion to collect taxes.

Section 9. Persons whom refuse to pay taxes, shall be given the option to leave the federation lands/space/planet, or may not enjoy the protection of the government, or the use of any services of the government, including public roads and shall loose federation citizenship permanently etc. etc.

Article 35

Section 1. Government shall provide a cash-less system as an alternative/option to currency for the citizens.

Section 2. Government shall provide an electronic system for voting, and provide each employer with electronic devices, which can be used by employees to vote on all elections and laws, and for the schools, at the expense of the employer, with the employer's consent.

Section 3. Government shall allow the private sector to provide devices for sale, to be used for voting from home via Internet, or other media forms, in real time.

Section 4. When a law is about to be submitted to congress, all citizens shall have the opportunity to vote for or in favor/against of the law in question, just so that the government and the public know where people stand on issues.

Section 5. When electronic votes are cast, for the purpose of electing public officials the votes are binding; when for a law, the votes are for information and educational purposes only.

Article 36

Section 1. All laws passed must be written in crystal clear common language, so that any high school graduate can understand the implication fully.

Section 2. All laws. Citizens shall be fully informed of any and all laws and shall have access to such documents of law.

Section 3. All law must be logical and objective and may not contradict this constitution even remotely.

Section 4. All public officials and legislators must posses deep knowledge of Objectivism, logic and rationality.

Section 5. All law must be clearly defined, so that nothing is left to interpretation.

Section 6. No person, in any branch of government is permitted to interpret any law.

Section 7. The clear definition of each law, and its meaning must be grasped and taken from the statement of the law itself, so that citizens are not reduced to guessing, or attempt to enter the minds of the legislators.

Section 8. All nonobjective element must be excluded from laws and legislative process. Nonobjective laws contradict and defy the whole reason humans need a government.

Section 9. All legislators and government employees must know that each individual is sovereign in and of oneself.

Section 10. All legislators and government employees must read and understand and use as a guide the book: ISBN 0-452-01101-9 by Leonard Peikoff, and all books written by our former spoke person, her majesty-Ayn Rand.

Article 37

Section 1. Government is a necessary evil, in order to maintain civilized and enlightened society, until such time as evolution permits otherwise.

Section 2. The power of force is a power of destruction, and government must use this power only for the destruction of destruction.

Article 38

Section 1. The State may not intervene in the intellectual life of citizens.

Section 2. The State may not intervene in the moral life of citizens.

Article 39

The government does not have a standard to uphold, or the right to invent/create one.

Section 1. The State may not intervene in education, or schools.

Section 2. The State may not intervene in literature.

Section 3. The State may not intervene in or infringe upon science or its advancements.

Section 4. The State may not intervene in the sex life of adults, whom voluntarily practice and or explore sex with other consenting adults.

Section 5. The State may not intervene in philosophy.

Article 40

Section 1. The State may not intervene in the realm of production and trade.

Section 2. The State may not provide humans any economic standards or benefits, weather in regards to goods, services, or conditions of trade, in any way.

Section 3. Politicians, and Government may have nothing to do with, distribution, production, manage, or regulate schools, hospitals, utilities, roads, parks, post offices, railroads, steel mills, banks etc. etc.

Section 4. Government may not hand out subsidies, franchises, tariff protection, social insurance, minimum-living standards, minimum-wage laws for workers, parity laws for farmers, insider-trading laws for investors, fair-price laws for consumers, etc. etc.

Section 5. The state shall maintain absolute separation of itself and the economy, and the private sector.

Article 41

Section 1. Government may not demand that any man or woman serve in the military or police force, against their own judgement.

Section 2. Government may not finance its activities by seizing property without the consent of the owner(s).

Section 3. This constitution recognizes that only individual citizens have rights, but the government does not.

Section 4. This constitution's purpose is strictly to protect the individual from tyrants such as governments, and any mob.

Section 5. The only minority this constitution recognizes is the individual.

Section 6. This constitution is designed to thwart the lust for power by any aspiring dictator, and any momentary corrupt passion on the part of a group regardless of its size.

Section 7. This Constitution is to establish and recognize a nation/The World Federation as a **republic** with its government strictly restricted to the protection of individual rights.

Section 8. Such a republic can be considered an absolute-democracy, in that all individuals have the **same absolute rights** and as being such, majority rule applies **ONLY for the selection of public officials**.

Section 9. The sole source of power of the government is the consent of the governed, and as such, the government is an agent and servant of its citizens.

Section 10. The citizens do not have the right to delegate any powers to the government which they do not posses, nor can a majority rule invent or create any additional rights, aside from those birth rights prescribed/defined in The Declaration of Individual Rights.

Section 11. The Declaration of Individual Rights is the supreme law of the land, and this Constitution as a hole is Supreme second only to Declaration of Individual Rights, and no law may ever abolish The Declaration of Individual Rights, nor provide for anything contrary to The Declaration of Individual Rights, in any way shape or form.

Section 12. The source of Government's power is rational consent, based on objective principle, and the Objectivism philosophy, and not arbitrary consent in any way shape or form.

Article 42

Section 1. In the event that a non-federation state or nation, desires to join the federation, all laws of that state become void, and this

Constitution and the laws of the Federation are valid, immediately upon acceptance into the World Federation, permanently.

Section 2. The World Federation, and/or any independent nation/state, which has adopted this Constitution, may annex/take over any other nation, which suppresses and violates the rights of its individual citizens, if it so desires.

Section 3. A free nation or Federation has a **moral right** to invade and take over an oppressive government, under Section 2 of this article.

Section 4. Congress has the power to enforce this article like all others, and to provide for the transition rules of a none-federation state being brought into the federation.

Article 43

Section 1. At any time in the near future, and upon the formation of a sizable World Federation, the Federal Space Agency shall construct a fortress in space, for the preservation of mankind, in the event of an unavoidable planetary disaster.

Section 2. The space fortress shall house volunteers of fertile and healthy males and females, 3 pairs from all types of humans.

Section 3. The fortress shall be well equipped to provide for the preservation of life for as many years as humanly possible, based on the potential danger the planet may face.

Article 44

Section 1. In the event the armed forces are to be used for war, the Executive branch shall provide the objectives, and there after shall not tie the hands of the armed forces from achieving the objectives.

Section 2. The head(s) of the armed forces shall have sole power of decision in case of war, and politicians may not intervene until the war is won, or the Chairman of the Chamber of Presidents declares that the war is over.

Article 45

Section 1. This Constitution and The Illuminati Order recognize no race, nationality or ethnicity of any kind, aside from "human" as valid, of all the humans on planet earth.

Section 2. This Constitution and The Illuminati Order respects and honors the scientific and technological achievements of man kind, and respects all rational, logical and objective human beings and demands that all future Illuminati holds such in the same regards.

****

Prime Directives

1. All prime directives are of equal importance regardless of how they are listed (There are some deep secrets behind the reasoning for these directives, only made available to senior Illuminati Members).

2. Humanity must survive at all costs What this means is that all measures must be taken to ensure this and this is a need which outweighs the rights of the individual/individual rights in the event that our planet is threatened with destruction by outer-space threats. This is only valid under such circumstances. **Aside from this unique scenario the Individual Rights are absolute.**

3. Planet earth must be protected at all costs.
Same as above.

4. The most intelligent and educated humans are superior to all others and they must reproduce with others at all costs and must be protected at all cost.

Basically, all this means, is that we seek to establish a hybrid human race, devoid of nationalism and racism. Studies show that children of mixed races are more intelligent and healthier overall. The genetic code is altered and advanced every time two different types of humans reproduce.

5. Logic and reason must be the foundation of all speech and teachings at all costs.

This means that no fairy tales must be permitted to be taught to children or anyone as truth. Opinions must be stated as being such and the idea of ghosts and spirits are concepts based in irrationality and stupidity. There must be supportive evidence for everything involving education and higher learning.
Society must be cleansed of superstition etc.

6. No human may hold a superior position (such as a legislator or a Judge) unless he or she has obtained degrees in physics and biology.

This is because those who are educated in these fields posses a higher understanding of reality, and thus posses an advanced/developed mind. Education breeds education and enlightenment.

7. The population of planet earth must be reduced to 3 billion and maintained at approximately that number (until such time when our Enlightened Society is in place and all the family names of our enemies are wiped off the planet and we will have populated the other planets we have discovered to be earth-like).

The basis for this is prosperity, security and well being of not only society, but also all life forms on our planet and our beloved planet itself. The reduction in population is to be done through education of the need for this. Of course there are other means and Mother Nature and diseases will help us in this regard.

8. All human males and females should be sterilized as soon as they reach puberty, to protect them from premature and unwanted births.

Unlike some uneducated fools think, women can still have babies, even with their tubes tied but not accidentally and men can have their sterilization reversed once they are mature, educated and able to support children financially.

9. All violent criminals (and those convicted of horrible crimes) must be used for productivity science research and experiments. Criminals are to be given options to choose if they wish to work or which scientific experiments they are willing to be part of.

This is self-explanatory.

10. Science and scientists must be the only governing body of planet Earth and humanity.

This is so that intelligent people compose the ruling class, not religionists and politicians. What we will achieve with this, is a system of **objective law** and order, not political and religionist mind games.

11. Politics and politicians must be eliminated at all costs.

This is because in a society of Illuminists there is no room for politicians. The society of the future will be ruled and protected by the enlightened, together with society, which too will be enlightened and highly educated.

12. Farmers may own up to 10,000 acres of land and must never be taxed as long as they utilize their farms for farming (until all is set in place).

This is because they provide the essentials of survival, and is to be considered a sacred matter. Farmers are not to be belittled in any way. Not all fields require degrees in physics, and it does not devalue any one human being, overall. The 10,000-acre limit is to be a temporary measure so that when governments are devolved their property must be available for purchase by all at a very very low cost in order that all individuals will have an opportunity to share the planet as owners.

13. Genetic engineering must be one of the most supported fields.
If you do not understand this, it is not for you to understand. Once and if you develop your telepathic abilities you will understand this.

14. All governmental bodies must be under the command of persons with degrees in physics, biology and chemistry.

Read above.

15. All lower life forms must be protected at all cost and scientific research must take this into consideration.
Self explanatory.

16. Humans must not be permitted to consume any type of flesh.
Killing other life forms, simply because we like the taste, is barbaric, and is rooted in savagery. Furthermore, consuming other animals introduces all forms of bacteria, diseases and microbes into the human body, which can eventually produce a soup of the most deadly viruses. There is **no need** to kill other animals, to eat, or for any other reason. The only exception is when one's life is endangered by an animal, and even then, alternative measures should be seriously considered or to save a human life.(There is a great secret behind this directive, only available to senior Illuminati Members). As time goes by each Illuminist must reduce the consumption of meat until one is able to break the habit completely.

17. Should an alien being(s) visit our planet or should we encounter other aliens humanity must consider them superior to us and must protect and never harm them unless they pose an obvious threat and immediate danger to our kind.
Self-explanatory. Furthermore, if such is to take place, chances are, they would be superior to us in both knowledge and evolution.

18. Nationalism, religion and racism must be eliminated at all costs.
Self-explanatory.

19. All types of humans (nationalities) must procreate with each other at all costs.

This simply means that when one does decide to have children, it should be with people of another "race" (lack of a better word). This does NOT mean everyone should immediately do this. Just if and when.

20. Anyone who is against the Prime directives must be neutralized at all costs.
This is an internal matter, and for the digestion of the Illuminati Order, and its senior members.

NOTE: To understand much of the reasoning behind these directives and behind the missing protocols from this abridged manifesto, watch science fiction movies of high quality, TV shows of high quality and the many songs of popular artists. In addition, read scientific journals such as Nature. We have and will continue to wean and condition the public for the future through certain messages in the above mentioned. Let's just say that 8-25% of all-top quality Sci-Fi movies and shows is truth and we will reveal other secrets through the media, science papers and the arts. Those who are wise will know what needs to be known.

****

****

The Illuminati Protocols

1.   It is of out-most importance that we think carefully about the words we use in a sentence. Words are the engine of

communications. When an Illuminati says something it has to be clear and to the point. Anyone who interprets the words of an Illuminati is a fool, a parasite who seeks to pervert the meaning and value of words.

2. Aside from our own political philosophy we do not and must not tolerate nor preach political tolerance. All altruist philosophies have had their chance and have failed. To tolerate a political philosophy other than Objectivism is to commit intellectual treason; it is to tolerate and reward failure.

3. Illuminati never do act on whim nor does one tolerate those who worship whim knowingly or otherwise. Whim is a gut feeling, an idea conceived through emotions without any regard for logic; such people who think they are right but do not know why nor can they explain why; they are parasites who have rejected logic and reason. Example of people who act on whim are the brain-dead and the animals and other examples are socialists/communists; such people hide behind words such as "democrats", "republicans" but all they are, are people who have no moral standards, people who try to solve problems by creating new ones; they are like a black hole.

4. The Illuminati never ever tolerates any form of welfare or socialism. Welfare and social programs can only exist in situations where the government takes from those who produce to give to the trash who do not. An example of the results of communism in practice in the United States is the welfare system which took the money of hard working people to give to

the poor as a reward for being poor and doing nothing. The end result was that 38 million people were born on welfare and each one decided to spit out more parasites (children of the poor) because the Socialist United Federation of America offered them a reward for having more babies. The more babies those parasites had the more welfare money they are given. It is the duty of every Illuminati to wipe out all forms of socialism (which is communism under a different name) once and for all.

5. The Illuminati hold Laissez-faire capitalism as the only social system proper for mankind, because it is an objective system, which honors and respects the rights of each individual.

6. The Illuminati Order recognizes the right of all individuals to vote for elected officials but not for "majority rule." When a majority is given power over a minority nobody has any rights at all; society will shift and change like the wind over an ocean. The only majority and minority we recognize is the individual when it comes to justice and freedom.

7. The Arts are recognized as the symbols of greatness and beauty of an enlightened human being. Furthermore, we recognize each Enlightened individual as a self-made work of art, which always changes but never, looses its value and beauty.

8. The only "virtue" we recognize is the will to obtain values through honest means. Any person who uses reason and logic to continually improve oneself is automatically a virtuous person.

An Illuminati is a virtuous individual not because one is intelligent or because one has great knowledge but because one is never satisfied with the knowledge one has and seeks to gather more and to obtain one's own happiness.

9.   An Enlightened individual always seeks to trade value for value; this means that whatever one desires one seeks to obtain honestly through her/his own efforts. This is what it means to value something or someone.

10.   The sole duty and goal of each individual is to seek one's own happiness not someone else'. For this reason we seek to establish a world of responsible and enlightened people so that our own children who are an extension of ourselves will have the freedom to enjoy the happiness which is the sole reason for living.

11.   We view all that exists as our reality. Aside from existence there is nothing but death. Those who embrace irrationality, the concepts of the "supernatural" have betrayed reality for unreality, the intelligent for the unintelligible. All of existence is what we call "nature" therefore the "supernatural" is a concept invented by morons and preached by those who seek to exploit the brainwashed.

12.   The vision of the Illuminati is not to conquer the world but to free it from those who enslave it.

13. Union(s) is a communist cancer introduced into the world to deprive the honest person from running her/his own business honestly. Such organizations and all those belonging to them must be eliminated at all costs. The formation of unions caused the employers to raise the prices of its products, which in turn created higher inflation rates and introduced stagnation into healthy economies. Unions are formed by immoral thugs who seek to acquire higher wages simply because they feel like at. The type of people who love unions are those who are jealous of someone's success; the type who like to dictate to others how much wealth they are permitted to have. These types of parasites must be eliminated at all costs; they are morons who have no respect for freedom or any concept of economics and the effect of their actions has on the economy and the future. Such organizations are just another form of legalized Mafia, pure and simple.

14. The Illuminati hold true that tyranny and tyrants are those political systems and people who do not respect the individual rights and property rights. To destroy such systems and people is a measure of self-defense and it is morally justified. Perfect example of such is the socialists, fascists, communists and those who preach "democracy" without defining what they mean by "democracy". Democracy comes in many forms and it does not represents "freedom" nor "justice", it represents whatever those altruists preaching it have in mind; whatever the whim of the times are. The ONLY form of government, which represents freedom and justice, is an **absolute-democracy** where the system of government has an absolute standard known as a constitution. Such a democracy is a "republic" because it has a constitution as the supreme law of the land and an absolute

moral standard included within its body. We use the term "Enlightened" to refer to like-minded people and to members of the Illuminati Order also known as Illuminists.

15. An Illuminati is a person who loves truth and a person who recognizes **reason** as the only tool which leads to truth. To obtain truth we must recognize and accept objective reality and in doing so, truth becomes and is the only and absolute standard of justice. For this reason Illuminati are the only people worthy of respect and honor. (We use the word "illuminati" in the singular as well out of respect for both/all genders similar to the way we use the word "law" in both the singular and plural.)

16. An Illuminati does not recognize any nationality, race, or people aside from that which we call "human" beings when it comes to our specie.

17. To seek payment for something one did not earn is a sign of a thief. To give payment for the unearned or undeserved is to commit intellectual treason. Illuminati do not practice charity as the altruists do nor do we compromise or seek to please others by offering gifts, bonuses or flattering words.

18. People who seek to be respected by others and who seek the acknowledgement and appreciation of others are parasites who deserve neither respect nor any acknowledgement. Illuminati live justice; we do not just talk about it. We love ourselves and respect ourselves; we need not be loved by others. We respect

each other automatically because of our nature, because what we stand for, because we know who we are and what we wish to become.

19. One must never be lazy to think, you are to embrace thinking as a way of life in order to improve your mind and character and well being. People who are too lazy to think are never welcome amongst us; people who do not enjoy intellectual stimulation are not much better than animals. To think is to exercise your ability to reason; to improve your mind you must feed it with information. A healthy mind is like a healthy body, which is fed proper nutrition. A healthy body with a starved mind is like a beautiful man/woman who has no teeth or cannot speak. Books, literature, science, music and the Arts are the fuel, which feeds the ever-growing mind. The day you stop reading books and enjoying life's many pleasures, that is the day you should seriously consider jumping off a bridge because if you do not, you will become a burden to yourself and others.

20. To an Illuminati every day should be a day of celebration. Even if it is in a small way, every day one should seek pleasure in one-self and in those one values such as a lover or a wife, a child or a friend.

21. The person who opposes science and technological advancement or infringes upon such is a person who belongs in a mental institution. Without the advancement of science the future can be easily predicted; it can be said that the future without science is the end of mankind. The engine of

advancement is science, which simply means, "to-know". Those who do not seek **to know** are the types who would embrace religions and the dream-world of the delusional. It is from the educated mind that ideas are born; it is from those ideas that theories are formed; it is the application of the scientific method to a theory which leads to the testing of the theory to see if it is true or false; it is from science that engineers get their designs for new products; it is from the engineers that the factories get prototypes for manufacturing new products; it is from the factories that the people get the products which enrich their lives and make life easier and more pleasant. It is also from science that we obtain the ability to seek out other worlds to populate or to fashion and develop so we can populate them in the future. Without science humanity is destined for destruction.

22. Involuntary taxation is something we abhor plain and simple. But until such time when the world is reshaped we need to be objective and practical. The world is inflated by parasites that cannot even afford to earn their own food; full of immoral beasts. Some day we hope there will be a voluntary tax, we hope people who are responsible will inhabit the planet. To reach that stage we need to produce intelligent people; competent leaders, persons of integrity and honor; such people are worthy of a honorable reward in the form of a fixed salary. Furthermore, to implement the principle of voluntary government financing we need to develop and produce philosophers who are worthy of prestige. Today's philosophers are nothing more than a bunch of cowards and thieves who seek to keep people stupid in order to maintain their undeserved positions and titles. They are in bed with the rest of the altruists and with the parasites you call

"politicians" and religious leaders. They are all cowards and thieves, they have nothing original or practical to offer because they themselves are too lazy to exercise their minds; they are like parrots constantly repeating the same old junk. Furthermore, we must form a world government, which is to serve as **the servant of the people.** The way things are today; every citizen is the subject and property of the government. Today's governments are formed by tyrants and dictators of all forms and colors; they are like a private club which only the corrupt can join and those who are not corrupt will be forced to be if they wish to be permitted to play the game. Such leaders must be dealt with appropriately and quickly.

23. We must never allow others to appease us in any fashion. The person who seeks to appease is a deceiver who seeks to pervert justice and the just, to cause a just person to compromise. Those who compromise are evil; they have betrayed not only what is moral but also themselves.

24. An Illuminati should never boast about her/his success especially in front of other Illuminati whom have experienced a loss or a bad period in their lives. To do so is to cause them pain and anguish; it is disrespectful and those who do such practices are without honor. If you value a friend help her/him if it gives you pleasure to do so. If you have been helped by a friend or another Illuminati be appreciative and always return the favor with interest.

25. Never ever seek to show how virtuous you are; if you are an Illuminati you are already appreciated and considered virtuous regardless of the degree you hold. Only altruists seek to gloat and show off what they have done or achieved; those are the type who have no self respect and seek the respect of others because they feel guilty for their success or good deeds. In many cases such persons are the types of parasites who have obtained something dishonestly; or have done a good deed for ulterior motives. An Illuminati does good deeds to obtain self-gratification only and does good deeds ONLY when one desires and not to be praised by others. Doing good deeds is neither a virtue nor a moral act; it is merely an act of pleasure and self-interest. Never ever remind someone of what you have done for them; to do so is to inflict pain, to make them regret what you have done for her/him. It is only the intellectually bankrupt who reminds someone of what she/he has done and those who have done those good deeds for ulterior motives other than self-gratification. Such people are immoral and should never be trusted.

26. Never ever help someone who is in need of help but does nothing to help her/himself. Never ever offer to help someone; let them ask for help if they are courageous. Those who do not ask for help when they need it are cowards. A person of honor does not feel shame when asking for help; the only persons who feel shame in asking for help are those who have no self-respect; those who are not willing to help themselves. Do not help a person more than three times. To do so is to create an incompetent person who will always be a burden to others. If you have children whom have not yet gone to college or a university, in other words if they are yet young, do not help

anyone if it means using money or wealth you have put aside for their education. Your children's happiness should be second to yours and never ever risk their future to help others. Most of the time when you help others you will live to regret it. Those who suffer due to an immoral act done by them should never be helped. Do not help someone simply because they are in need; only help those who are suffering due to a situation or cause which was beyond their control.

27. Never ever cover up someone else' mistakes or immoral deeds or an action; to do so is to betray everything we stand for. If an illuminati does something immoral criticize him/her without hesitation. To an Illuminati criticism should be welcomed not frowned upon. We are analog creatures and we do make mistakes; criticism is an action to correct an obvious error or immoral act.

28. We must remove all derogatory words from our vocabulary especially those, which are gender specific and demeaning to others amongst the Illuminati. Bad language can never be justified and even humor, which involves barbaric statements is in bad taste. To appropriate meaning to derogatory concepts is to abuse freedom and pervert language-the tool we need to communicate properly.

29. When we use the word "society" we use it only to refer to people in general and never to mean a group of people who have certain rights. Society has no rights; it is a superficial concept utilized to simplify communications. Only corrupt politicians

use such terms as "the people" or "for the people" or "society" etc. Society has no rights what so ever; only the individual has rights. Government has no rights at all, it is an entity which has very limited authority and authority must never be confused with "rights" because only private citizens have rights.

30.   We hold selfishness to be the engine of motivation and being as such it is moral and ethical to be selfish. This is not to be confused with dishonest selfishness. Everything you do must be on the basis of honesty. A rational human being is selfish by nature and does nothing except for one' own interest. To deny this truth of nature is to be irrational and dishonest.

31.   Every Illuminati must have courage and most importantly one must have self-esteem. You must raise your children in such manner that they have self-esteem and there can never bee to much self-esteem. A person who has no self-esteem is mentally disturbed or will become one. Self Esteem is to be held as one of the highest of values a person can achieve.

32.   You must always be able to defend yourself and your property. Any person who advocates disarmament of the people is a tyrant or a fool who is either a communist or an irresponsible and incompetent fool. To kill a trespasser or any government official who enters your property for any reason without the consent of the property owner is morally justified. **The rights to private property are absolute** and the owner has absolute authority over her/his property.

33. You must fight for freedom at all costs and in any way you so desire. The fight for freedom is the highest noble cause and the only time war can be justified. The person who desires happiness but only talks about freedom and does nothing to obtain it, such a person is a worthless thug and a parasite. Freedom is a priceless value and fighting for freedom is not a sacrifice but a noble duty of every rational being. Without freedom justice cannot exist and life has no value.

34. Never trade a higher value for a lesser one. This means that to sacrifice is plain stupid. An Illuminati is a person who seeks one's own happiness above all else. Never sacrifice your life for another nor risk it for the sake of another.

35. Freedom and Justice cannot be separated; together they equal "enlightenment" or Illuminism. Therefore, freedom and Justice are the only sacred values above all else. If you do not have and uphold these, happiness is impossible. To be Illuminati means to not just talk about freedom and justice but it means to be the very embodiment of these two values; it means you live by and for these values as the only means through which happiness is possible. A person who says that she/he is happy while there is no freedom and justice in the world, such a person is a despicable animal.

36. It is expected that each Illuminati try to write a book on Objective Law or an essay (or more than one) in their lifetime. You choose the subject of law of your interest and write.

Objective Law is the only form of law, which is proper for rational beings.

37. The Illuminati Order recognizes proper revolution to be a fight for individual rights without which justice and freedom is meaningless. Any other form of revolution cannot ever be morally justified. It is the duty of every Illuminati to help fight this revolution either through actions of sorts or political movements and literature, through the media and through the re-education of the young.

38. Illuminati must never accept or recognize any form of government other than a Constitutional Republic.

39. Racism is one of the greatest evil, one of the sickest form of deprivation it is one of the most destructive concept; it must never be tolerated. Racists must be eliminated; one must never try to enlighten a racist but to destroy them.

40. An Illuminati holds Purpose, Reason, Self-Esteem and Goal of happiness as one's highest personal values.

41. Public property is to be eliminated in time. The "public" is a communist concept; the "public" is a fictional concept and has no place in reality. To claim that you are doing something for "the public interest" is to claim a lie since only individuals have rights and only an individual has "interests." The interests of

each individual are unique, therefore politicians using this term are using it dishonestly, knowingly and willingly with the only purpose being to deceive the naïve and poorly educated. When a politician says that she/he has the interest of the people/public in mind the politician is using a smoke screen to lie to people's faces without them realizing in order to gain support or votes. Such politicians are to be exterminated. The only proper function for an official of the government is the protection of the individual, of the securing and protection of justice. Justice "for all" cannot exist; only justice for an individual can.

42. An Illuminati must never claim a theory as truth. Every theory must withstand the test of the scientific method. This includes the field of Psychology.

43. An Illuminati who owns a business of any kind must never set a company policy which ignore or infringes on the rights of the individual. To do so is to subvert justice. The individual cannot loose her/his rights as soon as she/he steps on the company' property. A proper company policy is one, which is just in every sense of the word. A reasonable policy is a just policy and an unreasonable policy is an irrational one.

44. Pride is an essential essence for mental health. It is healthy to be proud and it is honorable to show pride in yourself, but only as long as the thing you are proud of is your own achievement through honest means. In order for one to understand the meaning and value of pride one must educate oneself and seek to develop a character worthy of being proud. The fool also feels

pride, but he neither knows what it means or how to express pride.

45. The Law of Logic is absolute. Any person who does not recognize this does not belong amongst us. Without Logic reason is reduced to whim worship. Every Illuminati must learn the Law of Logic and be prepared to think logically at all times. Emotions are inherent and for this reason Logic is an essential absolute if one is to function properly. Man is not born with logic; he is born with emotions. Therefore Illuminati must master the Laws of Logic and teach their children how to think logically.

46. Illuminati must never utilize pity or mercy; to have mercy or pity on the guilty is to commit treason, to betray logic and to inflict injustice upon the victim or the innocent. Justice and mercy/pity are 100% diametrically opposed. To be merciful means to be unjust, to compromise justice for emotions and irrationality.

47. Illuminati may never seek revenge; to seek revenge is to reduce your self to a subhuman level, to give in to irrationality and the passion of unreason.

48. Illuminati must never seek peace with the enemy; to do so is to compromise on everything we stand for. Those who seek peace without establishing justice first have no right to live. Either we

have justice or we have death. "Give us freedom and justice or we will give you death," that is all there is to it.

49. Every Illuminati must always vote and must always vote for a candidate belonging to the Libertarian Party. All those who do not vote and do not vote Libertarian, their bloodline will be wiped off the face of this planet. If there is no Libertarian Party where you live then you must form one.

50. An Illuminati knows what it means to have an "open mind" or to be open-minded. Be careful, however, because altruists have hijacked this concept and abuse it all the time. To have an open mind does NOT mean to compromise on your philosophy and principles. When an altruist accuses an Illuminist of not having an open mind, what he really means that the Illuminist has refused to accept or embrace his whims and irrationality. Altruists are not willing to be objective because they lack the intellectual ability to reason. Being an open minded person means to be a person with an analytical and active mind; this means that you consider and analyze new ideas and does not mean you ignore nor embrace ideas and concepts which you have not had ample time to consider. Furthermore, being an open-minded person does not mean that you grant equal status to falsehood and new concepts and ideas, you will not equate such as equal in status to factual and existing knowledge. When someone comes up with a new concept or an idea they expect it to be treated as truth; this is not so. Illuminati are Practical Objectivists and not pseudo-Objectivists who, like the altruists, engage in useless discussions and intellectual masturbation but never put forth-practical applications to Objectivism.

51. Illuminati never accept truths, we only recognize one truth; there is only one true answer to every question or situation. Truth is absolute and we only deal in absolutes. Those who claim that there are no absolutes have no concept of reality; they live in a dreamland; their lives are meaningless, empty and shallow. Such people are cowards.

52. To be Illuminati means to exercise the application of the scientific method to every aspect of reality, to ideas, thoughts, concepts and philosophy. Never loose sight of this.

53. To Illuminati "evil" is any act, which infringes on the individual rights of any individual. Such people who either knowingly and willingly or irresponsibly infringe or violate the individual rights are evil.

54. Our morals are based on the only moral standard ever defined and written down. The Illuminati moral standard is this: **The acts to protect and the respect of the rights of the individual as outlined in The Declaration of Individual Rights.**

55. Justice is the application of Objective Law to protect and maintain the Individual Rights as absolute; to execute Objective Law in the event of a violation of the Individual Rights and the Law. All Laws, therefore, must also be Objective.

The remaining 45 Illuminati Protocols cannot be made public or published for the public consumption at this time.

****

The main body of text for The Illuminati Manifesto has been simplified somewhat for the general-not so educated reader. Moreover, those interested in knowing the full context in which the secrets are presented must carefully read all of the words and paragraphs of this Manifesto, as much of the reasoning behind publishing it is to transmit messages to our 31 million members world wide.

The Goal and Purpose of The Illuminati
The goal of The Illuminati is to cure the interwoven disease of irrationality and dishonesty imbedded within our world's population and to establish just government(s) and not to hold power over the people but to free the world from those who enslave it.

The purpose of publishing The Illuminati Manifesto is to have conscious individuals think about and see everything in different ways—different from the altruistic ways in which everyone on this planet has been enslaved for thousands of years. Indeed, Objectivism, our core philosophy is a new way of thinking, a new way of seeing everything, a new but natural effect of the power of reason, which calls for action that leads to limitless, beneficent power over nature and existence itself.

The Illuminati Manifesto is a treatise on physics, objectivity and reality in a sense, made possible by our philosophy. Physics and philosophy are used as metaphors to explain the omnipotent paradigm called reason, which demands, integrated thinking and honesty at all levels in order for it to be realized and utilized and mastered. Since fully integrated objectivity will increasingly rule the future, The Illuminati will increasingly fight to banish biases and unjust authorities from government, business, science, education, politics, philosophy, communication, and the arts. The Illuminati has no leaders or followers in that we all share a common goal and philosophy; and as such, we all act accordingly. The Illuminati Council does not rule as dictators, but act in accordance with our goals, taking action needed to accomplish our objectives, and it is the duty of all Illuminati to act likewise in their capacity. As an Illuminati, every conscious individual must become an individual self made leader the sole ruler of his fate, destiny and future, prepared to live in an Enlightened society.

In this altruistic civilization, we each are alone in our struggle to live rationally and to fight the most noble fight; the fight for freedom and security for our civilization. Our honesty is our only unconquerable strength in this altruistic civilization. For, we are trapped in a civilization based on dishonesty, altruism and tyranny. In the end, that dishonesty and the altruistic philosophy cheat us of our earned rewards as we each die unnecessarily tragically unfulfilled, having lived dull and meaningless lives

By contrast, in an enlightened civilization, no such struggle or dishonesty exists; the very nature of our philosophy makes it very hard to live as a dishonest person. In an honest culture of certainty and rationality, everyone is free, prosperous, fulfilled to the very extent of one's own efforts and ability.

New knowledge is needed to deliver prosperity and continuous advancement, both now and into the future, but minds trapped in mysticism can no longer evolve; the motivation factor disappears in an altruistic society due to the stagnation persons are forced to live in.

In this socialist environment with socialistic/communist and theocratic governments enslaving people, the most brilliant conscious minds can no longer develop breakthrough knowledge and scientists become endangered species mostly because interest in science amongst the young disappear when one's life becomes so hard and no end is in sight to the slavery; intelligent people get depressed quickly when they see what tyrants are in government and their own freedoms are infringed upon.

Restrictive governments forcing them to focus on limited, narrow, specialized areas permitted and sanctioned by governments enslave the brilliant minds of today and many are trapped in mysticism. Other brilliant minds, which have great potential, are weakened and limited by mysticism. Because of their enslavement to mysticism, geniuses today are thinking and living with increasing impotence, thus impeding the very important genetic evolution, which is taking place. So, what lies ahead into the future? The future lies in the Enlightenment, in the discovery of Objectivism; which we must work hard to help those with potential, to discover it.

Objectivism, through the power of reason delivers boundless knowledge and riches and values to any conscious individual. For, Objectivism frees reality from irrational illusions; forces man's mind to use reason to unlimited ends.

Illuminism provides an entirely different way to view yourself, the world, and all existence; it sheds light on your mind and makes you feel almost omnipotent in your mental abilities. The important part of Illuminism is the development of one's telepathic abilities, one of our most basic senses, yet also one which few have known of and put into practical uses. More on this later.

What are parasites?

A parasites exist in many forms:

1. The class consisting of political entrepreneurs; politicians whom are only interested in a job which allows them to fulfill their thirst for unearned nobility or grandeur, and/or financial compensation which he/she does not deserve.

2. Government-subsidized university professors whom commit intellectual treason by spreading propaganda in order to maintain their comfortable jobs and enjoy a high status

3. The big business owners whom profit from government-subsidies because they are incompetent and dishonest which in turn makes them dependant on bribery, the bribing of government politicians in order to milk the government of unearned profits.

4. Those whom live off of welfare and government funded public aid programs, who multiply like roaches at the expense of the public' money, never producing anything, never educating themselves and have no purpose in life aside from their own happiness at the expense of others.

5. The religious leaders, the bastards which spread the seeds of altruism-socialism and communism; the bastards whom infect the minds of the people and the young innocent children with garbage.

6. The types whom love to run a dishonest business, whom sell garbage products, and defective products cheaply designed so that they break down as soon as the warranty expire; these types also use deceptive advertising and make use of unethical and immoral tactics; their products fill the planet with garbage and waste, depriving others of a safe and clean environment..

7. The lazy, whom seek to gain power by violating even the most basic principles of logic and reason; whom care not for the rights of others and hide themselves in cloaks of righteousness

and good deeds to accomplish their deceptive agendas; to reach positions of power and authority which they do not deserve or are qualified to be in.

8. A perfect example of parasites are the American Republicans and Democrats and "Moderates"; both hypocrites, different kinds but no less hypocrites and parasites, none of them have any standard of values or logical and objective principles; they thrive because the population is uneducated, lazy or too busy striving to make a living-because the Republicans and Democrats both committed constitutional treason and have destroyed and are destroying the free nation we have designed and founded; they have stuck their nose in economics and formed a dictatorial form of government, one ruled not by the constitution we established but by the whims of every sweet talking politician with enough parasites to back them off with bribes.

Stagnation: The Way Things Are in America in 2002

An old man is dying; his one-and-only life is reaching its end. All his adult life he worked hard to produce values for others. Sometimes he complained perhaps even questioned, but never more. He always accepted what the ruling elite—the politicians, bureaucrats, journalists, lawyers, university professors dictated to him. In exchange for his cooperation, he collected social security, food stamps, and other handouts for which he paid hundreds of times over with shrinking happiness, security, savings, and standard of living. Threats from crime, drugs, racism, and poverty kept growing, those living on welfare have 2-7 babies who grow up to be criminals and parasites compared to the educated and the rational people. The cost of public aid too is forced to increase; as the government has created a parasite factory.

His wife died years ago; he is alone waiting to die; unaccomplished and unhappy. Some people devoted their life to following the mystic path from the church, to astrology, to theosophy. Their life path is for nothing—a sadly wasted life. Yet, others take a different path not much different? At times you are feeling an indescribable anger boiling deep within your soul; at times it almost overpowers your mind and brings so much pain. What is the cause of that rising anger? Is it caused by the same source discovered by those who follow mysticism; by the uncertainty of your beliefs, by that feeling of uncertainty and helplessness; the beliefs which guided your life into submission against your desires and wishes?

The anger begins when you start to realize that the mystic path, which consumed your entire adult life, was a terrible hoax—was nothing real; no guarantees, nothing but a life lived in the slavery of altruism. Your life was wasted on an illusion—a vast hoax perpetuated and manipulated by those who used deceit to advance their own livelihoods, self-importance and undeserved power; the truly heartless and careless religious leaders and the socialists they bribed uneducated into submission; the governments they established, all designed with the well being of their own lives in mind not yours.

You live in a society which offers no freedom, no happiness and prevents you from being happy by forcing you to conform your life and life style according to the unjust laws put forth by those socialists and mystics. There is nowhere you can hide. You try to convince yourself that things will change, that you will make things better, that you will do this and that; only to find more barriers in the way, more red tape, more costly overtures.

Time and time again you feel anger rising deep from within. You wonder what would happen if that anger ever discovered its undefined targets. But, which targets? The mystic-leader? The mystic leaders deprive everyone's entire adult life of love, happiness, and excitement; everyone whom they manage to infect with their crap. But you are not one of those whom was tricked by those exploiters of ignorance and illusions; you were a secularist, they did not prevail in infecting you, only many others. Then, who are the targets, whom are those whom caused so much anger to accumulate within you; that caused your life to be so empty and miserable?

You feel life lacked the growth, prosperity, and accomplishment that belong to you; those things, which you could have achieved had things been different; had you had the freedom, the rights you inherited at birth. You missed out on happiness and did not get the chance to experience the things you dreamed of; the things you could have earned but were denied an opportunity to. Who then achieved those things? Did the leaders of government practice everything you were forbidden; did the mystic leaders practice things they preached against; did those in power live a life far better than yours at YOUR expense; while providing you with nothing more than crumbs? How is it that those in power have a much better life than you; where do they get the money; how do they achieve success but you don't; how is it that the mystic lives well without working a single day, but you, your life is chaotic; you are forced to seek refuge in self deception; in alcohol, or a sport, or anything which helps you take your mind off of the cruel reality of making a living. Your life is a lie, you are prevented from being happy, and you are told that the things, which make you happy, are horrible, immoral, and worthy of eternal torture. No, you may only do what the mystics and the parasites tell you that you can.

What happens to your one-and-only life? You grow old, time goes by fast and you wonder time and time again, where has time gone; when will you get to enjoy any of it; when will you be free and safe to undertake adventures which bring pleasures to your soul? What happened to the promise of your youth? Why has your life turned out the way it did; what could you have done different; what should you have done different? The answer lies in determinism; a process of being able to predict what any person would do given certain circumstances and/or environments. When you learn what determinism is and how it works and that it does work, you will realize that how you were raised as a child, that what you are taught as a child was what brought about the results and sum of your life.

Indeed, almost every human life is drained or used up until each one of us dries up and essentially die. Your life is drained of happiness and prohibited from achieving your goals by someone or something. How is it that so many people end up in pretty much the same situation as yours, with the same amount of unhappiness and as unaccomplished as you? How is it that almost everyone has the same fate? Almost everyone seems to lose his or her life to nothing, for nothing; having achieved nothing lasting, nor any meaningful happiness; but a small minority end up achieving great things and enjoying a great deal of their lives. Who is responsible for your misery, who is to blame for the stagnation of your environment, what should have been done different?

Nobody today is *really* happy! Happiness, the very concept of happiness is meaningless today, the word and concept itself has been bastardized; most words have lost their meaning, language has lost its value; everything is subject to interpretation because the educators have become cowards and traitors to the very thing they are supposed to be. Many people are overweight; they have no self respect; no desire to improve themselves; no will to accomplish much of anything; why should they, hope is but fantasy; this is the result of altruism; the socialism and communism the mystic has created by getting in bed with the other parasites whom are equally power hungry, greed driven, at other's expense and freedoms. People are drained of self-respect, of self-esteem, of morals and value; they walk around like zombies; like purposeless robots. Some are harassed by their children, others are unhappy with their spouses; people are irrational and irresponsible;

why should they be responsible, they are helpless, they have no values, no moral standard; no guidelines of any meaning. Nobody has enough money because everyone spits out babies like roaches and thus create poverty. Many dislike their jobs because they have no intellectual integrity; they seek happiness in fields others are making a good living in because they are qualified; and the unqualified strive for the same jobs, only to find that they are miserable; they sought jobs for the wrong reason. The more babies people spit out the more poverty they create which in turn ruins the quality of life of everyone including themselves. People have no concept of economics, how wealth is created and ironically how POVERTY is created. People create poverty; every time a poor person has children she creates poverty. Others are worried about losing their jobs, or have already lost their jobs. Others are bored, anxious, or empty. Almost everyone had abandoned their youthful dreams of success, glamour, and prosperity; because altruism had set in, the mystics brainwashed them; they told them that materialism is wrong and bad, that sacrifice is a virtue but selfishness is evil when the exact opposite is true. Almost everyone's life seems wasted. There are few people of value, most have no value, not worth the air they breath; the planet is filled with losers, with lazy persons; lazy to think, to use their most powerful tool; their mind their reason their faculty. Some are lazy while many are both lazy and brainwashed.

To have so many losses and problems, someone must be guilty of something. The problems facing society did not appear out of thin air, someone or some groups of people, some types of people are guilty of creating all these problems directly or indirectly. Some people are guilty of all kinds of faults, failures, and mediocrity. The mystics shift their own blame on imaginary demons and ghosts; this way they avert taking responsibility; others shift the blame on original sin crap; while others find ways to justify or shift the blame on things that are beyond the reach of accountability. Nevertheless, we cause our own problems and limitations; not some mystical beings or some theory that can never be proven.

Everyone will discover that the deeply hidden causes of human suffering and death emanate from the parasites, the irrational and the mystics; those whom shun reason and ignore logic; those whom produce nothing but demand the wealth of others; those whom neither seek happiness in this life and prevent others from achieving happiness in this life; those whom set goals for themselves but refuse to take the needed actions to achieve those goals honestly through their own efforts; those whom dream but do not think. They are the root and cause of all evil.

The Government Too Is To Blame

Let's consider some of the most parasitical governmental bureaucracies in America today: the BATF, DEA, EPA, IRS, INS, FDA, FTC, SEC and all "Public Aid" agencies. Such organizations use guns, jails, and brute force to impose altruistic and unjust rules, which have nothing to do with justice or freedom. Those organizations breed legions of professional murderous ego driven monsters, destroyers who are responsible for mass property rights violations and unjust confiscation of property and trample on the rights of all people and are the main cause of economic and social devastation. But, most ironical, those organizations are the main cause of bringing *everyone* toward life-wasting stagnation, unhappiness, and death.

On a daily basis, those organizations violate and pervert justice by committing the real crimes through force and fraud. These organizations are not only harming the economy, but are destroying society and everyone's freedoms by violating the constitution of the United Sates thus trampling under foot the rights of the citizens. These organizations are dependent on a legal system corrupted with the subjective laws of altruists, a pervert form of justice used to advance the harmful political agendas of the socialists and communists alike, (there is little difference between socialists and communists).

The DEA

Almost any destructive end, even destruction of entire economies and genocide, can be made to appear beneficial to the public, with conventional accounting within arbitrary or closed boundaries, as demonstrated by Lenin, Hitler, and Mao. However, wide-scope accounting and an objective look at this organization immediately reveal the destructive nature of those men and women of the DEA and their organization. First of all, the DEA exists entirely through gun-backed policies created by self-serving socialists whom have no idea what justice and individual rights are or are simply ignoring that facts of justice in order to keep their boys and girls in good paying jobs, while they test out the waters to see how much more infringements of people's rights they can get away with. The public needs to see that the armed divisions of the DEA are the engines that support and expand the drug problem, crimes, death, and loss of constitutional rights for every American citizen; the DEA' very existence drives up drug prices which in turn causes drug users to resolve to crimes to obtain the money needed to feed their addiction.

The DEA divisions continuously expand the market for drugs by providing the super-high price that make possible the flourishing of organized crime and drug cartels. Such government-forced economics necessitate pushing even more powerful drugs onto others, especially onto vulnerable young people. The end results of the DEA' actions keep escalating the crimes and deaths related to drugs.

Forced submission through armed organizations like the DEA serve but one purpose—the expansion of costly livelihoods that let politicians and bureaucrats drain the economy and damage society by creating ever expanding drug problems and ever growing bureaucracies. From a constitutional and moral standpoint, the government does not have the right or authority to impose the wishes of a few socialists onto the people they are supposed to be protecting. It is not the duty of government to dictate to people what they can or cannot put into their body, or to protect people from harming themselves. The idea that people do not have a right to use drugs is a draconian one, and it is used as a propaganda to infringe on just about every aspect of people's lives. Such laws and agencies as the DEA helps nobody and harms everyone with no benefits to anyone other than the highly paid criminals called "DEA Agents."

The IRS

Likewise, the brute force divisions of the Internal Revenue Service work with tyrant-type politicians in expanding destructive political agendas that enhance their jobs and power. The activities of the IRS are criminal in nature a violation of one of the most basic right of any individual; the right to own property. The armed thugs of the IRS diminish everyone's future by crippling or breaking the daring entrepreneur and aggressive businessperson.

In the first place, in America today NOBODY owns any property-no one! When a person buys a house and finishes paying for it, the only thing that person has accomplished is paying for the **right to rent** that property from the government; as soon as one stops paying property tax, the government "by the people for the people" comes and confiscates the property. Therefore, the American government is not a constitutional government, not the government we intended when we put together the US constitution, but a government of the tyrants for the tyrants by the tyrants hidden behind cloaks of "good will towards men."

Every large corporation today started with the daring courage, hard work, and precious seed capital of heroically aggressive entrepreneurs. The IRS on the other hand drives up the costs of all goods and infringes on the rights of the individual and uses intimidation techniques in order to collect taxes. Today, the IRS is no longer needed; all employers can automatically withdraw and transfer taxes to the government automatically; all is needed is a uniform tax; and with the technology of today, we can have a cash-less society which makes it impossible or at least impractical to cheat the government. Therefore, the IRS needs to be abolished and the automated electronic system can be put in place for the cost of the salaries of all the IRS employees of one single year. The computer systems are cheap; the technology is more than mature and the infrastructure is already in place. Furthermore, property tax MUST be abolished; it is unconstitutional and tyrannical, cruel and unusual punishment, a direct violation of all the rights of an individual.

The "culture of government" in other words the division between government and people existent today in the US is like a relationship between a slave owner and the slave; the owner having all authority and the slave must conform or suffer the wrath of the owner. The armed divisions of the IRS are criminally destroying the essence of our economy, society, and freedoms not only for the generation of today, but for all future generations. The US is no longer the "home of the free" but the home of the enslaved; the US is only a few steps away from full communism.

A bureaucracy protected by armed thugs can never be justified in a civilized society where people are to live free and who are supposed to have "rights" which are inalienable. Local police and courts guided by Objective laws, not armed bureaucratic thugs, can competently and constitutionally protect the individuals, their property, and organizations, including physically protecting government officials.

The INS

There are over 13 million illegal aliens in the US each year, yet the INS is a conglomerate bureaucracy whose employees are incompetent as well as corrupt parasites. Take for example the foreign US agents responsible for approving visas and immigration papers oversees; they take huge bribes from people in other countries to get their paperwork approved; such a case can be seen in Romania and many other nation. Who investigates those employees and why is it that not even one has ever been convicted of their crimes or even fired? The INS is a self serving legalized Mafia, accountable to nobody and doing a poor and certainly inefficient job. Furthermore, it is not their job to protect our borders from illegal aliens; such is the job of the Army and nobody else.

The FDA

What about the FDA? What bad things can be said about such a prestigious agency? The FDA is one of the most evil of all governmental institutions ever concocted by the socialists. The army of the FDA serves nobody but the lobbyists and the self-serving so-called government scientists turned political puppets. By enforcing increasingly cost-prohibitive compliance to irrational regulations, the FDA blocks scientific and medical progress; and infringe on the rights of the individuals; it is directly responsible for the high prices of drugs and other medicines.

Had the FDA and its armed thugs not existed, today we would have cures for cancer, heart disease, AIDS muscular dystrophy, and essentially all other serious diseases. Moreover, biomedical advances, especially genetic research would have the human race moving toward non-aging longer and happier lives. The government has no business impeding science and scientific research; it is not its job to protect anyone from possible harm caused by experimental drugs and research, as long as the participants are willing participants, with full knowledge that there are dangers involved. Not only is the FDA unconstitutional but it is a major stumbling block for advancement of both, science and healthcare, as well as a very costly and wasteful institution.

The Illuminati Wedge

All Illuminati within their capacity must find people in government, business, and the professions and make them targets for personal ostracism or job termination. Those whom are candidates from which we can benefit economically, professionally, and personally and can be brought into the honest side should be initiated as soon as possible.

Armed bureaucrats serve to harm life and property and must be neutralized at all costs. Politicians which live through armed bureaucracies exists not to produce values but to destroy them, not to bring social harmony but to disrupt it; those are legitimate targets and must be eliminated from all facets of society and government. The conflict between Illuminati and politicized-armed bureaucracies evolves from the deepest issues of right versus wrong, honesty versus dishonesty, and protective government versus destructive and tyrannical dictatorship type government. The Illuminati will take back and bring *peace to* America as well as the world and establish the form of government we had intended from the beginning, a constitutional government in which people can *trust;* a government which has no power over the people, and only has authority and duty to protect each individual from the brute force of others.

The Illuminati represents and is a unstoppable force that terminates *all* destructive forces; unstoppable because we are driven by true justice not smoke screens and propaganda, by real morals and values not lies and deception; those who join us know why they do so and are devoted to taking necessary action for change; for the security of our civilization for all time.

Today, right now, you hold a power in your hands—a power to eliminate all forces that harm you, your family, your future. Your power comes alive when you join us to deliver unending happiness and prosperity; your power comes from you by joining us to take whatever action is needed; and the power lies in your secret identity as an Illuminati; the power of continuous surprise, fighting our enemies without them knowing whom is doing the liquidation, whom is behind any given event; your secret identity as an Illuminati along with your action is the most powerful weapon.

To be Illuminati means to deliver limitless prosperity by terminating all life-depriving forces, large or small; to fight the only noble cause in existence, the cause of freedom, justice and prosperity; to live by your principles, to take action; to never compromise on your principles, to never sell out or compromise under any circumstances, to be boldly honest.

The parasites are unnatural beings; they replace their productive human nature with an inhuman one and take actions which purposely harm others, the economy, and society; the programs derived from altruism mentality, from dishonest and predatory greed. They are unnatural in that they live against their own nature, they refuse to use their reason, to be honest and just; they are infected by religious doctrines or altruism in various forms; thus, they are not human beings, they have given up that rights to life when they have chosen to abandon logic and reason. They are subhuman and must be treated as such. For, each parasite has removed from his or her thinking process the essence of a human being and seek to infect and reduce others to their level. Reason is the tool by which we establish morals and competitive production of economic and societal values needed for human survival, prosperity and happiness.

Those parasites increasingly drain everyone and society through dishonesty backed by the deception and brute force; the only way parasites know how to survive. Those parasites live by covertly draining values produced by others rather than by competitively producing values for others and society; they have no values or moral standards;

they have no conscience not a single drop of integrity. A civilization ruled by parasites must end and we must use whatever force needed to eliminate the threat of destruction once and for all.

Today, we are witnessing the economic deterioration of world economies and while the socialists are attempting to patch them they lack the proper tool; economic freedom, so the failure of economies will continue to accelerate. We will help this decline, so that socialism will be shown for its true nature, for the incompetent fantasy they preach; the stagnation socialism will create will undoubtedly wake up society once and for all and history will record these events in our favor. Once we destroy all forms of socialism mankind will finally experience the unlimited prosperity, which a modern civilization deserves.

The Noble Revolution

We hope to start a new revolution, to recruit more persons whom desire freedom and prosperity, to rid the world of trash humans once and for all. This revolution is a revolution for prosperity and freedom and we must be relentless and uncompromising, overthrowing the entire elite parasite class and all parasites regardless of their social status; parasites are parasites are parasites. Join us and march forward; march to the overthrow of stagnation and establish unlimited prosperity!

All revolutions of the past required inconsistencies, illegalities, *and destruction* and the **cause** was always hidden behind carefully chosen words and propaganda buzz words; the leaders of those revolutions were almost always worst tyrants than the tyrants they sought to overthrow. None of the previous revolutions were for a good and just cause; they were sold as such, they were sugar coated, but none of them were revolutions for FREEDOM. No, not limited freedom, not socialist freedom, not communist freedom not American Democracy freedom, but Republican freedom, (not to be confused with the parasitical

Republican Party in the US), a republican freedom is one which is guided by a constitution which IS the SUPREME LAW of the land. This revolution is unique. It is based on the principles of Enlightenment on the Objectivist philosophy founded by man's reason not irrationality, by logical approach to reality, not religious doctrines and vague artificial morals. Objectivism requires logical consistency, objective law, and honest productivity; it demands honesty and integrity; it holds the **Rights of the Individual** as absolutes, unshakable and absolutely inalienable. The Illuminati upholds objective law by terminating all subjective political policies that harm you, society, and the economy. This is your revolution; the men and women of the mind; this revolution will bring humanity unlimited prosperity; permanent security to our civilization and its future.

Former revolutions were fomented so that one group of parasites could take power from another; all were fomented from false or artificial class conflicts of nationalities, races, religions, political issues, economic levels, or social levels. .

The Noble Revolution is the first of its kind and the only legitimate class overthrow possible among human beings; the honest moral class ranging from ditch digger to billionaire entrepreneur; who all work to overthrow the religious leaders and the status of religion and its altruistic values; the parasitical-elite class; a criminal class comprised of the devious from the poor thief and violent criminal to the destructive politicians and their legions of harmful bureaucrats, armed political-policy enforcers, unjust judges, politico prosecutors, corrupt lawyers, dishonest journalists, evil and dishonest academics, and white-collar-hoax business quislings which rely on government subsidies.

Evolutionary Crossroads
Our civilization has entered a new era, a time for the greatest event in human history is about to break across our planet. Humanity will

give birth to a super civilization; a New World Order. Indeed, the whole world is shimmering, ready to reveal a new, previously unknown world. Today, in this new era the raw power of the Illuminati is bubbling from beneath the seams; the organization which the church attempted to destroy is circling the globe. We are at an evolutionary crossroad in our civilization where decisive action is needed to secure the safety and future of our very existence. To do so means doing whatever is needed to accomplish this, and Objectivism is the guiding light and the Illuminati Order is the lamp barer. You need to read with great care the writings of other former Illuminati in history, especially those of Ayn Rand and the "founding fathers" whom used 78-98 million dollars to bribe key members of society in order to get away with passing the US constitution, of Pike, Paine and many others. Just as those brave men risked everything in order to shape the future of civilization, we must once again; once and for all strike the deathblow to parasites.

The Financiers of The Parasites

Who pays for the economic and social deficits created by the parasite class; who is responsible for the stagnation and the spreading of parasitism? His or her well being has to be assured by someone. Who is that someone? Let's concentrate on the United Sates, the nation we fashioned, the nation the parasites are seeking to destroy, to turn it into just another socialist theocracy. First, we must point out that if we cannot save this nation, if we fail, we will destroy it completely; we will not let the worthless garbage savages, the republicans and the democrats and the religious barbaric have it; we have set in place mechanisms for its destruction. We have spend 13 trillion dollars trying to maintain hold of it and to restore it to a republic; and we would rather wipe it off the face of the earth than to let bastards, intellectually bankrupt parasites take possession of our hard work. Now, let's give a good analytical insight into what has and is taking place not only in the west, but also in the US especially.

The root cause of all evil is religion and mysticism. The religious have principles and morals as well as so called virtues directly rooted in their doctrines. This in turn guides their political and social views and values. This is what is wrong with the world; this is the root cause of all evil: Religion is directly opposed to reason and logic, religion deals with the after life, and therefore it holds no absolute values for this life. Because the religious do not value this life and the individual rights to life and pursuit of happiness in this life, it has no right to exist on this planet. It must be eradicated with all force with whatever means at our disposal, and the time has come where we are faced with do or die.

The religious people, along with the liberal mystic, the voters who have been entrusted with the power to vote for their elected officials, they are the parasites, they are the ones whom produce other parasites and it is from them that all sorts of venomous snakes are born, whom hide behind good deeds and false virtues and self righteousness. Then there are the mystics, not just the religious mystics, but the atheist parasites whom have infected the minds of many with the idea of anarchism and communism; forms of philosophy which are contrary to individualism and the rights of the individual. Although these parasites pretend to be pro-individual rights, they deceive people with an irrational and impractical philosophy, which has the exact opposite effects of Objectivism. Some of these atheist parasites are republicans some democrats some moderates, but they are all one and the same in goal and scope; in that the result of all of their philosophies leads to depravation of rights and to stagnation.

Their politics is the politics of unreason a.k.a. statism. Let's take a look and see what these republicans and democrats really stand for, and for the sake of simplicity we shall refer to these types using one word-traitors. Traitors in that they represent everything the constitution of the United States we have established is against. Some of these traitors seek to delegate and concentrate more power in the state, and so far they have been very successful, and this power is delegated to the state by each parasite each time they vote for traitors; and this is done at the expense of individual freedom. These parasites are the type which seek to oversee and dictate the life of everyone else; they do not value individualism or individual rights, they have no standard by which their morals are guided, they have no values which hold absolute authority over their principles, they change their minds like the wind changes direction and as often as the weather changes; they are intellectually and mentally defective to say the least.

These traitors wage war against man and his mind, against his property and body, they seek to control even what people think, what they should eat or not eat, watch on television and what people should say and do. The result of these traitors' handy work is evident and becoming more and more evident every day. They manufacture zombies, worthless people, children brainwashed through regulated education, and persons whom have lost all sense of responsibility. In the US, people do not even consider that they must be responsible for much of anything. When something they do not like comes up, they protest and call for more laws, more restrictions, and more intrusion on the lives of others. They do not educate their children with values and moral principles, because they themselves are immoral and poorly educated. The children of many Americans are walking demons, evil little bastards disrespectful and destructive to everything and everyone they come in contact with; they lack even the basic respect for others. While the actions of the children are not 100% reflective of their parents, it is in a major way a reflection of their parents. But how can these parasites teach their children values and morals when they themselves are intellectually bankrupt? The average person here thinks that a mere high school education and a college degree has qualified them to be good and moral persons, they no longer need to educate themselves, they already have an education. They ignore philosophy, the engine that drives the minds of men towards principles and values and morals. They don't need philosophy, because they are not interested in being intellectuals. This mentality is due in part to the stagnation they have brought into this country. People are too busy making a living, because everything is expensive and getting worse, because they kept voting for morally and intellectually bankrupt politicians whom have inflated the government into a huge bureaucracy, costing more and more, and taxes going up up up, and these morons in government have restricted the economy and the private sector to such an extent that producers have no choice but to raise prices on all goods and services. Not only is the current Government unconstitutional as far as its actions and laws, but it is way out of control and it is grossly inefficient. It is no longer a government by the people for the people but a government by the special interest groups and lobbyists for the special interest groups and lobbyists. It is corrupt to the core. The political spectrum of the US government is in the hands of a special high society in which only those whom are ready to be cut-throats can join, only those whom have learned to play the game of politics can rule and hold positions of power. The next time you hear someone speak of the "American Culture" you need to know that 1. There is no "American culture" there never was, and 2. If you must identify a culture in America, you need to consider naming the political circle a super-culture; not an American Culture, but a culture of vipers and vultures; you know the type that has always existed in human history in many forms.

Individualism cannot exist without reason, it demands reason, while the traitors' philosophy demands unreason. The system of government we designed and sought to establish is a free system, one which promotes and protects freedom; the freedom **not of the people** but of the individual, a system which protects the rights of the individual **not** of society. We do not recognize society as the term is used in the classical sense. The word and concept of "society" in the classical sense, to us it does not exist, it is meaningless, it is a buzzword used by tyrants who use it to deceive and brainwash the naïve and the neurotics. People who use such language as "the good of the people" or "for the common good" are most likely snakes and wolves in sheep' clothing. There is no such thing as "the common good" or "the people" as long as the inalienable rights of the individual are trampled under foot, there is only slavery.

The system of government we designed and the government of the US we had established was to be a government which is guided by a constitution which accepts reality and upholds principles which derive from the very idea of inalienable-rights. An individual whom has inalienable-rights is sovereign over his/her person. Neither the Democrats nor Republicans nor the new worthless cowards called "moderates" respect the rights of the individual; the constitution has become a buzz word, but it has no value to any of them. The very existence of republicans, democrats and moderates is an insult to the constitution; everything those scumbags stand for is nothing but tyranny clothed in kindness and so called "good deeds" but to the intelligent open minded person the end results are clear and obvious.

These traitors are:
1. Anti science and logic; they only support and protect the scientists who have committed treason and are now dependant on government perks, bribes and subsidies.
2. They are pro mysticism, religious revivals and other neurotic practices.
3. They all promise the "pie in the sky" by claiming to be concerned with man's well being.

4. They oppose the conquest of nature, advancement of science and technology, and oppose economic growth, and do not respect the achievements of men and women whom, through the unlimited powers of reason, have developed scientific and technological advances in all areas including the arts.

5. They do not have ANY ideology, no calculated long-range answer to any social problems.

6. They oppose a government of law and promote a government of pressure groups, the use of brute force at any cost; they can justify anything since they have no standard of values to be held accountable by. Everything is open to interpretation in their systems, because nothing is concrete, nothing is of any value, honor and respect.

7. They are pro "fairness" government forced "equality of opportunity" (such as welfare, public aid, infringement upon the rights of private business) thus dictating to every sector of society whatever mandates their emotions inspire in them. Some argue for "equality of results" i.e. egalitarianism.

8. They have brought America to the bottom of the bottom of political chaos; America no longer stands for anything but socialism, it is crying out "communism we are almost ready for you."

The Right To Self Defense

Let's look at the dynamics of a valid and justifiable revolution: What takes place when totalitarian oppression and censorship occur? Thomas Jefferson said it best two centuries ago; "overthrow becomes the only *moral* self-defense against the resulting rise of totalitarian politicians and government. This is why the government should never be allowed to disarm its citizens. The only way citizens can successfully revolt is if they have the means to impose force in response to force and injustice."

However, the opportunity for a peaceful overthrow must not be lost. With unfettered free press the message of the revolution will spread and through decisive action, the Noble Revolution will eliminate the parasites and their elite class without a single incident of physical harm or violence, as long as the people start taking responsibility for change; in this case, by voting for The Libertarian Party and their candidates. Objectivism is the natural essence of conscious beings that are guided by reason and logic as demonstrated in *every* young child still uncorrupted by dishonesty and irrationality. Through integrated thinking and rational exuberance, every child learns to perceive, talk, and then conceptualize. Every child learns with the certainty of integrated honesty present within our nature. Children lose that certainty through the diseases of dishonesty, irrationality, and mysticism, which is infected into them by irresponsible and irrational parents. The end result of such brainwashing is a people, which breed irrational and tyrannical politicians and leaders. In the end, the intelligent become and endangered species and entrapped in a society of stagnation and suffering. For this reason, people must always have the means of self-defense as a counter balance to government oppression. The only type of government which seeks to disarm their people is one which is ruled by tyrants with a totalitarian agenda.

The dynamics of Objectivism brings back that certainty of fully integrated honesty; Objectivism demands honesty and objective laws. Objectivism helps to bring everyone back to his or her nature; that is to our natural reason ability, to our rational state in which we were born. Therefore, self-defense and force must be used whenever tyranny sets in an otherwise civilized (or uncivilized) society, and the tyrants and the root cause of the parasites must be eliminated, at all costs.

What is Illuminism?

Illuminism a process of fully integrated honesty and wide-scope accounting, one which begins by refusing to be irrational, by self examining the self and discarding all irrational, illogical and unreasonable tendencies and practices. From that process comes a certainty about the most effective way to live every aspect of conscious life; thus Objectivism is the logical choice, it is a product of reason. Each human being has sought that certainty; and has always felt incomplete, as if something is missing from one's inner being, a sort of emptiness which causes one to experience loneliness. Once man is introduced to reason, to Objectivism, his whole life changes in a most profound and positive way.

Every human being is born an atheist, and it is after birth that the process of brainwashing and indoctrination takes place, that is when parents destroy the life and happiness of their children, by teaching them things which are not real, virtues based on irrationality, morals based on emotionalism not logic and reason. The values of religious thought have their foundation in savagery and barbarism. Illuminism is the *natural* certainty residing in every conscious being; every human being has this fire this inner strength which is fighting to come out to be realized, to be acknowledged, but cannot because people have been taught the wrong kinds of morals, the wrong kinds of virtues the wrong way to think, to feel guilty for things they have not done, to feel guilty for things that are not wrong, to feel guilty even for thinking certain otherwise natural thoughts, to feel guilty for being a natural human being; to deny reason and logic and to embrace fairy tales, to believe that myths are true and facts are not facts.

It is the religious leaders whom have hidden the objective process of honesty for centuries by manipulating subjective assertions of truth. By using the arbitrariness of truths to turn reality upside-down, masking a sea of lies behind false nobility, illusions, deceptions, shadows, doubts, and uncertainties, the religious leaders have managed to convince the naïve and the uneducated that their lies are virtues; that their barbaric and illogical doctrines are the truth and noble, and that anything natural and material is evil; that faith is superior to reason, that circular logic is the guiding light of man and not pure logic, that some devine being told them what to teach and say.

By contrast, Objectivism and Illuminism eliminates manipulated truths, doubts, uncertainties, out-of-context facts, deceptions, illusions, and sets the foundation and groundwork for a new civilization, a real civilization of enlightenment, of order and happiness. Objectivism is simple and easy to grasp, it needs no complicated unintelligible rhetoric.

Putting An End To Tyranny

The world today is a world of cruel masters binding to a stake every puppy born—binding every dog for every moment of its life from birth to death to a stake with a short chain; that puppy is you. You, during your entire life know nothing except a totally bleak, constantly chained life. Thus, you would and do accept your one-and-only life being used up and wasted without ever experiencing the joys and well-being possible for all humans, but experienced only by few. You have been conditioned what to think how to think your freedoms are being dictated to you by the parasites you voted for. You are led by the nose like an animal, you have been deprived of your own mind, you know not what logic and reason is, you have abandoned your humanity in exchange for a few comforts, because you have lost hope. You have lost hope because you have been turned into a mindless pet, a slave to your own stupidity, you have done this to yourself because you refused to think. You naively swallowed every chunk of shit those tyrants taught you, you voted for those whom used sweet words which appealed to your emotions, even against your better judgement. This is the world you live in, this is the world you have created; yes you, every one of you, you "the people" the cowards.

In your world, in the world you created not a single human would ever experience natural happiness, playfulness, or the happy companionship of a loving friend. But, imagine if you had the ability to become aware of your chained life. What if you were to accept the fact of truth, that you are a slave, that your government is your enemy, that the way things are do not have to be so, what if you, for once were to decide NOT to vote with the crowds, to try something new, like a Libertarian party platform, just to see what happens. What if you gave a new concept a chance; consider the possibilities.

Imagine a society where it is not immoral to have sex with as many people as you like, simply because you like it and it does not harm anyone, a society where that was not wrong. Imagine a society where you don't have to conform to false virtues, where morals are absolutes and founded in a moral standard and not in emotionalism, in logical approaches to reality, not in mystical legends. Imagine a world where you don't have to feel pressured to be married, where marriage is not a sacred institution, where nobody is labeled with such labels such as whores, or a murderer because you have an abortion, or a tyrant because you refuse to give your hard earned money to the lazy, where nobody can tell you how to run your own business or company, as long as you do not harm anyone by violating their rights, where you have the right to be greedy and selfish because it is our nature and a virtue to be selfish; where honesty is a virtue not sacrifices, where wealth is a sign of nobility not of tyranny, where nobody tells you that you must give your money to lazy preachers, mullahs and rabbis, where nobody can take away your home and property because you refused to pay property tax every year, where government is not your dictator but your body guard.

Reason and creativity, demand that individuals pay close attention to reality, discover its physical principles, and commit themselves to the rigorous work of conquering nature. Enlightened human beings must not daydream about the world but instead must use their ability to change the world and not to ignore it, and to expect something for nothing. Only parasites try to evade reality in these ways and unfortunately they do not just die off from sheer stupidity, but instead multiply like rats. They have loads of children who like their parents **become poverty** and a burden on others; they are the seeds of the criminal element in societies for the most part. Through force and fraud, they devour the products of those that create and manufacture; they vote into power politicians whom sing their songs, whom will support anti-freedom legislation, legislation, which creates welfare and public aid.

Those who take responsibility for their own lives—through a sustained and conscious commitment to developing their abilities to learn and to produce—are in effect the only real human beings, the only ones worthy of life liberty and pursuit of happiness. Free trade is the natural expression of mutual respect among productive individuals. The only valid role of the state is to prevent violence, especially that of "parasites" and "looters" against the inventors and producers. Unfortunately, the state has always been a major instrument of the reality evaders; the parasites only voted for those who made promises to change things in their favor, in taking from the rich to give to the poor-the parasites.

We urge all enlightened individuals whom heed this call to direct every thought, every discipline and every effort toward the overthrow of the altruists, socialists and all forms of parasites. Toward the eradication of every livelihood that harms the value producers, the economy, and the liberties of man kind; only then will the world be a much better place, a place of beauty and joy and not of stagnation and pain.

Basic guidelines to help you achieve Illuminism and results in the fight for freedom and justice:

1. The Noble Revolution that eradicates the parasites will permanently empower the individual, so fight the good fight, join us and fight alongside with us.

2. Be the individual you were born, do not conform to stagnation. Read Atlas Shrugged, and Rand's other books and learn to be an enlightened individual.

3. Be your own authority over your life and happiness, take responsibility for achieving your own happiness and eliminate all obstacles, which prevent you from being free. Vote Libertarian and promote Objectivism and enlightenment. Use your brain to guide your life, not your emotions.

4. Be a leader in the Noble Revolution (The Forth Revolution) and take charge of your environment within your capacity and ability. The sole task of the Noble Revolution is to eradicate the parasites by eliminating their dishonest illusions, hoaxes, and mysticism; by exposing their fraudulent nature, by standing up to tyranny on ALL fronts using what ever means available or necessary.

5. The Illuminati dedicates his or her life toward the uncompromising eradication of the parasitical-elite class, and it is our duty to secure the freedom of our race from the hands of the barbaric once and for all. Your life is meaningless as long as the world is in the hands of evil parasites and idiots. Take a stand and do not compromise. When you compromise you have already lost.

6. Break all bonds with the world controlled by parasitical elite. Infiltrate the organizations, which are the enemies of peace and cause them destruction from within.

7. Rejects public opinion and the existing social morality, ignore anything, which stands against reason, logic and objectivity. Give your life meaning by being a person of integrity, morality and honor.

8. The Illuminati has but one thought, one aim—the merciless overthrow of the parasites. Have no mercy on parasites. Mercy is a gift, and giving gifts to persons whom are worthless and destructive is to sanction their existence and activities and everything they represent. Do not show mercy to them, they do not posses integrity and honor therefore they do not qualify to be granted mercy. Mercy is a gift to be granted to the innocent only. In fact there is no use for mercy amongst civilized honest beings.

9. Your degree of friendship, devotion, and obligation toward others should be that determined solely by the degree they are useful in terminating the parasites and the stagnation they have inflicted on the world. Chose your friends carefully; it is better to have few or no friends than to compromise on your principles and values. But when you are one of us you have millions of friends; true friends.

10. The Enlightened is proven not only by his or her words but also **by the deeds** toward advancing the overthrow of injustice and by living a life of honor and respect.

11. The Illuminati has no sympathy for the parasites and does not hesitate to undermine their every position. We frequently penetrate their organizations and live among their world in order to hasten their eradication and use their knowledge and information towards their destruction.

Parasitical elite can be split into several categories. The first category consists of those who are condemned to termination as soon as possible. The second category consists of those who are spared temporarily as being useful for provoking the public into revolution. The third category consists of those liberals and conservatives in high positions of unearned power and influence, various dishonest politicians, and certain harmful bureaucrats, lawyers, and judges. Those parasites can be useful—they can be exploited for advancing the revolution. The fourth category consists of pseudo-leaders who can be useful for a while. But, eventually, parasitical elite in all categories must be terminated.

Independent Illuminati Agents

Independent Illuminati Agents are members of the Illuminati whom are not associated with any Illuminati clubs or lodges but instead act on their own for the interest of our goals. They are people who will increasingly carry out missions of subversion against the parasites and the corrupt bureaucrats. Some of them have infiltrated charity organizations and missionary groups in order to help spread HIV throughout the world among the parasites.

So long as Independent Agents have no lodge connections, they will steadily multiply and never stop moving forward while maintaining a high level of personal security. We urge you to become one of them. In order to break the hoax of professional parasitism, Independent Agents are needed to act personally against each parasite who harms or drains society; to take actions which cannot be connected directly or indirectly against any other member of the Order of the Illuminati. By acting on their own, they are the most effective weapon, one which is transparent, coming out of nowhere, nobody knows whom they are because they wear no uniform, they do not sound alarms, they have nobody whom they can give up in case of torture under interrogation. On their own, in their own ways, they will increasingly subvert the entire parasite class; while the higher members of the Order maintain powers and pull strings in the governmental levels of various governments and economies. Join the Illuminati Order as an Independent Agent and work to subvert the leeches one by one, relentlessly, until each is driven from his or her bogus career, homes and existence.

For the past two centuries we have been condemned by nationalistic governments and mystical religions; lies and false accusations were spread against us; now let us give them what they accused us of wrongfully, let us pay them for the lies they spread for the destruction they have caused to every society throughout history

We have semi-secret organizations that for the past several decades have been working hard to prepare and put into place pieces of the puzzle for what is to come. We have been hysterically attacked as the epitome of evil by the ultra-conservative media, the nationalistic-populist media, and the religious-right media, yet, we are the ones who made this country great, we are the ones whom have taught the world about capitalism, about freedom, we are the ones whom established the US as a free country, we are among the world's most moral, clear-thinking, responsible organizations.

On The Illuminati Protocols

Our protocols—the master plan for worldwide government (not control) first formulated by the founding fathers after the passing of the US Constitution, with the help of leading European bankers and businessmen, calls for a free world not world communism. It calls for a world federation due in part because religion must be eradicated on a global scale and the world itself needs salvation from parasites, not just one nation. Anyone reading the protocols alone and out of context would view them as one of the most evil plots ever devised. But if you read those very same protocols in the context of wide-scope accountability, one will realize the men responsible for those protocols were among the most moral, clear-thinking, responsible people who ever lived on this planet. The reason we were and are vilified, and the people whom have been and are doing the vilification are the very people we seek to destroy—the religious, the socialists and the communists. Yes we seek their destruction and we will exterminate every one of them, we will squash them like a bug, like the parasites, which they are. Yes, to them we are evil-if fighting for the ONLY noble cause in all existence is evil, then so be it, if that is the standard of evil, if fighting for freedom, justice and honesty is a standard of being evil, then yes, we are evil. We are evil to the core, we will eradicate all the good and save only the evil. Only the evil desire freedom and only they will be left standing.

Master Plans

The Illuminati, protocols forged in 1701 by the Illuminati Council and amended and ratified by some of the "founding fathers" later entrusted to Adam Weishaupt along with the World Federation protocols established by the founding fathers and carried forward in the 19th century by Albert Pike, are about to begin their noble goal of undermining and eliminating the twin instruments of irrationality and destruction on this planet. We are approaching a phase where the destruction of forced-backed nationalist and theocratic governments is about to begin, and the destruction and eradication of all religions. Now, after two centuries, that goal will not only be achieved but also far surpassed.

Since the late 1700s, essentially all public reports about and exposés of our secretive Illuminati Order have been grossly negative. Most such reports and exposés emanate from paranoid conspiracy theories presented in populist, nationalistic, or right-wing religious publications with the backing of the Catholic Church. All such reports and exposés present the Illuminati and our protocols as diabolically evil. Modern-day exposés especially rail at the Illuminati's tools used to undermine public respect for anti-liberty laws, irrational traditions, and predatory institutions. The Illuminati Order works to undermine public support of the elite-parasites—a destructive class that survives through politically and religiously ruled governments.

The Most Moral Men And Women on Earth

Without the full understanding of Practical Objectivism combined with the use of reason and open mindedness, anyone who reads the Illuminati protocols will come to the same conclusion: Those protocols are the epitome of evil. But on understanding Objectivism and the concepts of justice, one comes to the exact opposite conclusion. The Illuminati protocols reflect the most responsible and moral forces on Earth. Forces designed to bring wealth and happiness to our world by breaking the institutions and racism that support this parasite infested altruistic system, which has plagued humanity for time immemorial.

The Illuminati hold true that honest business dynamics are what sustain and advance conscious life, it is the engine, which drives the growth of prosperity. Therefore, capitalist business dynamics are the only source of genuine, life-enhancing power among conscious beings, and without a free society without the freedom to roam unhindered the engine of prosperity, business, without a purely free capitalistic society will die off, and the minds of innovation, their light is slowly extinguished. Indeed, only competitive value-and-job producers hold real power – they are the driving force of the engine of prosperity, they are the fuel of the prosperity engine; the ultimate power and driving force which determines not only current events but future events on our planet.

Until the Illuminati instituted America with a solid constitution, with a foundation of freedom, no value-and-job producer understood the draining hoaxes and illusions of the parasites. Since the time of Plato, a ruling leech class has built and propagated altruism and the system of stagnation which boosted the rise of parasites with the single purpose-sustaining their own harmful livelihoods by draining the productive class.

The Illuminati Council had made plans to free the world from stagnation once and for all. The power of kings, popes, tyrants, sultans, or other parasitical elite must be taken away, their legs must be cut off from under them, and let the people hold the power to control and direct the future of our civilization. On that realization, the Illuminati had to recruit powerful businessmen and bankers, open minded politician, professors and anyone whom had power or connections and bring them into our fold to eliminate the parasitical elite by relentlessly pitting those leeches and their institutions against each other.

The Illuminati comprise the most efficacious businessmen throughout the world, as well as persons from all walks of life whom share our vision and uphold our philosophy. We reject parasites holding false or life-draining power, from joining our organization. The Illuminati's relentless work has always been and is directed toward saving the future generations of conscious beings from destruction by the institutionalized irrationality woven throughout every fabric of society. Our goal has been and is to free conscious beings from the tribal mentalities that make possible criminal societies: parasitical governments, socialism, fascism, the welfare state and mystical religions.

The Illuminati envision a world in which its citizens are valued not only by social status and wealth, but by their integrity and honor, by the standard of individual rights; by the moral standard, by how they live in regards to each other, by the respect and honor they hold for the individual rights of others.

For The New Illuminati
Reason

You must boldly apply reason to the business of living-to every day life. You must strive for constant control and discipline of your mind, until reason is once again the dominant light of your brain-your thought process. You must act in harmony with its nature and Objective reality. Reason is your epistemological relationship with yur mind, which begins with facts. It organizes the sensory data in accordance with facts and is guided at each step by rules that rest on the fundamental; the law of identity, a.k.a. fact.

Individualism: Your primary orientation must be to objective reality, not to the well being of neither others nor their philosophies. You must accept the profound moral responsibility of forming your own judgments and of living through the work of your own mind and efforts in a proactive fashion. As an individual in principle, you are alone in society and as such you must hold the primacy of existence as absolute.

Integrity: You must learn the proper principles of living, then uphold and live by them regardless of unwarranted protests from either your own or others' emotions, or outside influence which is contrary to objective reality. Only through practicing integrity based on rational principle will you achieve self-preservation and honor. Attempting to practice integrity based on mystical philosophies and altruistic principle leads to self-destruction and direct and indirect harm to others.

Honesty: You must never fake reality or pretend that facts are other than what they are, and you must recognize that pretense can neither erase an established fact nor lead to positive and objective results. You must apply fully integrated honesty based on the facts of reality to search the depths of your mind for bits of mysticism, then tear that mysticism mercilessly apart and never allow mysticism to infect your mind again. Individual human life is the ultimate standard of value and because of this fact all moral principles, within their proper context, are absolute. To obtain money or values from an honest and productive person through deceit is morally wrong and such action or behavior of this nature may never and must never be justified. You may lie in order to protect your own selfish interests values and property, but never to deprive others of theirs, nor to acquire what is not yours or to violate the rights of others, or deprive them of such.

Justice: As an Illuminatus you must judge people's character and conduct objectively and act accordingly, granting to each person that which he/she earns. You must adhere to the *trader principle*, sanctioning people's virtues while condemning their vices, thus encouraging good (life-enhancing) behavior and discouraging evil (life-diminishing) behavior. Moral judgment can only be passed on observable behavior, not psychological problems. You must identify individual human life as the standard of value and the individual's own volitional reasoning and property as his/her proper method of sustaining that value. An Illuminati must use reason to reach moral estimates through two steps: first, identification of the relevant facts; second, evaluation of those facts by reference to the following four objective ethical-political principles:

1. Any chosen action that purposely benefits humans or society is morally good and right.
2. Any chosen action that purposely harms mankind or society is morally bad and wrong.
3. The initiation of physical force, threat of physical force, or fraud against other human beings or their property is the fundamental of morally wrong and evil.

4. The commensurate use of retaliatory physical force against those who violate principle 3 is morally justified.

Purpose Of Life

The moral purpose in life of an Illuminati, like that of every rational human being, is to *prosper* and to *live happily*. Fulfilling this purpose requires a social or businesslike interaction with one's surroundings. This consciously chosen central **purpose** explicitly defines the abstract values and the associated concrete goals and action plans of an Illuminatus, allowing one to integrate smoothly all one' actions into a rational whole. *Reality* must be your only metaphysical relationship with the universe at large, while the Illuminati' political relationship with one's fellow human beings is *Capitalism*.

Productiveness: An Illuminatus conquers or adjusts nature to suit his/her needs, always *beginning with the end in mind* and *putting one's own selfish interests first*. An Illuminatus must constantly acquire knowledge and shape matter to fit his/her purpose, translating one's ideas into physical form and remaking the earth into the image of one's values. Through thought and action, one can rearrange entities to suit one's purpose, but in all cases, the metaphysically given **laws of nature** cannot be broken. When dealing with others of known or potential value, you must think *win-win*, seek first to understand and then to be understood, and, wherever possible combine your efforts with those of others. However, you must not suffer fools gladly; instead, you must dismiss their false, arbitrary or irrelevant assertions clearly and boldly, thus optimizing the use of your most precious commodity, *time*.

SELF-ESTEEM

Only when an Illuminatus is able to reason and to produce values, does one know that one is able to live, and that one is worthy of living.

Your ethical relationship with yourself is and must always be *self-interest*. Romantic Realism is the aesthetic relationship with the functional beauty of the products of your own and others' efforts.

Pride: You must be committed to achieving your own moral perfection by shaping yourself into the image of your own chosen values, *sharpening the blade* in all areas of life. Your commitment to follow reason must be the driving force behind your commitment to achieve moral perfection.

****

Illuminati Perspectives

The following are perspectives extracted from various documents and essays from the Illuminati Archives which is privately held and protected from outsiders and new Illuminati members who have yet to prove themselves. The names of the authors will not be published in order to protect them and their living relatives.

1. We must watch out for parasitical intellectuals. There are only two types of intellectuals; those who achieve great degrees of education for the purpose of enlightenment and justice and those who become intellectuals in order to climb up the ladder within a private club or organization for the purpose of obtaining power to control, manipulate and exploit the less educated. The reason we must keep an eye on all intellectuals is because they are the buffer between the elite of the world and the people; they influence politicians, businessmen and the media; it is the intellectuals who maintain control of education and the direction of the future generations. If you want to

predict the future of a nation, peoples or a region with a high degree of accuracy read the materials written by the intellectuals; read their books, magazines and their editorials. The intellectuals are the most powerful group of all the people regardless of their material wealth. The intellectual does not need much material wealth; the intellectual thirsts for knowledge and education; he is a person who reads many books and writes his/her own; they are the teachers, the professors the advisors of corporations, the assistants of other leaders or powerful figures; they come in many forms, they are on the radio, the movie script writers, newspaper owners, the producers and the politicians.

2. We must encourage each one of our members to become intellectuals. A university or college education is essential for obtaining a honorable job or advancement in life but to become an intellectual what is needed is continuous self-education. All it takes is to read one book per month or every 2-3 months over a period of several years. The most important education an Illuminist can obtain is a strong foundation in our philosophy, Objectivism. This we must teach our children while they are in school, especially in High School. The Declaration of Individual Rights must be embedded into the mind of children from the age of 7 years old and up. They should memorize it and whenever they do something contrary to it the parents or teachers must bring it to their attention and explain with kind words why what they have done or said is a violation of it, and thus it is an immoral act. The future will always be in the hands of our children, for this reason it is of out-most importance to indoctrinate them with the proper and sacred values becoming of a moral person.

3. Intelligence is an essential component of a healthy mind, which helps one be successful as well as happy. Intelligence can be

acquired through a solid foundation in philosophy and a good education. Such people who value education as the most sacred goal for their children (as our Jewish friends do) will develop the ability to deal with a wide range of abstractions. Children must never be forced to learn what the parents want; they need to be taught that there will be a reward for every requirement of the parent, the reward must be of such nature as to convince the child to accept the challenge. If a child is not allowed to choose to undertake an effort her/his mind will eventually reject and rebel against that which is forced upon her/his brain. The use of force, fear and threat will never produce positive results and will cause mental disorders and defects. Never fail to praise a child for even the smallest achievements; children require motivation and sometimes/many times praise is enough of a reward or the icing on the cake, if you will, to give the child self-esteem. If a child has no self esteem he/she will never become a proper person.

4.   Illuminati are people of integrity; your word should be as valuable as gold. For this reason do not ever make promises; to do so is to acknowledge that your word is not good enough without extra assurance. Even if you are 100% certain you can keep a promise, do not make one and do not offer one. Never ask someone to make a promise either.

5.   People whom cannot provide for their children and still have them, those are people whom have violated their own right to live, by infringing on the rights of others, the right of others to pursuit of happiness, life and liberty. The children of the poor are a burden on everyone else, also a danger and a threat to others and their property, so those parasites MUST be sterilized by force, plain and simple. ONLY people who respect the individual rights of others as well as their own are people whom have rights. Those whom do not respect and honor the

individual rights are worthless scum, complete trash, and absolute garbage. Is this clear enough for you?

People whom would dare have children before they can provide for them are people who violate the rights of the very child they bring into the world, by subjecting a new person, a new individual to pain and suffering.

This is not hard to understand it is very simple, because it is absolutely logical, so if you cannot understand this. People whom do not have the means to provide for their children, for all aspects of their needs until the children can make on their own, those people have no right to have children.

The children of those types of people would be a burden on everyone else and trouble makers and thugs and criminals...

31 million people born to people on public aid in the United States, 93% of them have been arrested for violent crimes.

31 million children born to middle class people and only 13% of them have been convicted of violent crimes...
There is an inflation of people in the world; what this means that people are multiplying faster than wealth can be created. In other words poverty manufactures poverty; by poverty we mean "the poor" they are the poverty factories. Those who want to feed the poor should be eliminated along with the parasites; they are the ones contributing fuel to the poverty factories. It is basic math and economics, any 12 year old should be able to understand this.
End of discussion.

6.   Religion, (and we are mostly concerned with the most evil ones such as Christianity, Islam and Judaism) seeks to control every aspect of a person's life; in fact all three of the big religions even dictate what thoughts are permitted to entertain and what are not. Those who embrace these religions are people who have denounced reason; we cannot educate them because they refuse to be educated and actively fight to destroy what we accomplish. Therefore it is of out-most importance to fight back and destroy these parasites.

7.   We must return the Gold standard or another system of value, which must have absolute value. The reason there is such a thing as inflation is because corrupt government has forced itself over the people and the economy. It is ONLY government, which can and does create inflation; it is simply not possible for a private citizen to create inflation. For this and many other reasons government must never be permitted to interfere or infringe upon the economy. He United Sates is a nation in the process of committing suicide; this process had begun as soon as the government started to take control of the private sector through myriad of laws and regulations. A nation, which does not practice pure Laissez-faire capitalism, can never have freedom and will never have peace and prosperity.

8.   One of the cancers of an economy is the concept and the practice of pay-raises. To give someone a pay raise as a reward for doing the same job he/she has always done is to create a run-away train and contribute to the destruction of value. In such a system everything always gets more expensive because pay raises keep going up. This is especially detrimental to taxation systems which forces taxes to keep going up to pay for all the pay raises of the officials who are supposed to be paid a certain fixed value for performing their job. Furthermore, this also helps deprive people of the motivation to seek a higher education to improve

oneself. Seniority does not justify an increase in pay. Instead of having pay-raises we should seek to establish a standard for each job or position and require a new degree of education to advance to a higher position. To promote someone to a new position is a form of economic suicide in that the employer exchanging tangible value for sentimental value; sentimental value is determined by whims not intelligence. Let's hope our people understand this.

9. Many amongst us are of the opinion that women are superior to men in certain respects. It has been said that the only reason Mother Nature advanced the male's physical abilities is to protect the female who when pregnant or nurturing the young cannot properly defend herself. Some of the arguments used to show that females are indeed superior to men is the recent advancement in science which has developed a technique for women to have children without the use of any male or male sperm; in fact without the use of even one single male atom. In this respect, the logical conclusion is that women can now survive without the need of men. A second argument is that since women have a smaller brain than men yet can perform very complex mental exercises as well as men and in many cases better; this, it is said, is ample proof that women can be considered superior to men. However, the Illuminati Order (the majority of the ruling body is women) forbids the discrimination of anyone based on gender and we recognize all individuals as having equal rights absolutely. Furthermore, we abhor and apologize for the way men have treated women throughout the ages. We shall do everything in our power to see that this never happens again as well as to see that in the future women do not seek revenge on the innocent and enlightened men of the future who will respect them as equals amongst the Illuminati.

10. Humility is something Illuminati must never practice or teach as a virtue. Humility is practiced only by the most despicable of parasites. Civilized people can not and must not respect the humble; to be humble means to be a coward, to seek to please others at the expense of betraying your self-esteem and values.

11. Many of us practice an ancient way, which we call "Parental Intimacy" which has been practiced by the enlightened throughout the ages. Parental Intimacy means tearing down a wall of destruction which has been created and instilled in mankind by the mystics through their irrational doctrines. One of the most essential elements of proper parenting which nourishes the child and fuels a most healthy mind is the practice of being nude with the child from birth to puberty. This is not to be interpreted as being sexually intimate with the child at all. The child feels a perfect sense of security and comfort at the touch of its naked skin with the warm body of the mother and father. Furthermore, kind and very soft spoken words of comfort with the child together with the warmth of the touch of the parent's body instills a deep sense of security into the child's mind. As the child grows older both parents must take turns in bathing the child and not just bathing but doing it together with the parent being nude in the bath tub with the child. At age 5 and up let the child share the bed with you, (both parents if possible) while all of you sleep in the nude. It is of out-most importance that the child becomes comfortable and knowledgeable with and of the adult nude body as well as its own anatomy and inner workings. It is also essential that the parent answer any and all questions the child may have (not just about anatomy) because when children ask questions their mind is in need of essential information. A brain deprived of the proper knowledge when it seeks it is a brain that will always lack intellectual ability. Out of the 10 million Illuminati who have

practiced Parental Intimacy, none of their children have become aggressive and none of them have ever been convicted of any violent crimes. In fact all of them have grown up to be very healthy and successful. Furthermore, the family bond created by this practice is so powerful it would take volumes to explain. We never argue, use loud tones of voice or scream at the children and we never discipline them physically. In addition, we never discipline them in front of strangers. This way they never have to deal with being subjected to psychological trauma.

12. It is of our most importance that we revolutionize the education system and that we apply the scientific method to every aspect of the nature of education. The first step must be the acknowledgement that teachers are to be held as one of the most sacred component of a proper civilized society. In our view, the way teachers are treated (or better said mistreated) is nothing short of despicable. Because teachers are not honored and respected and are amongst the worst paid intellectuals many very high quality people have turned away from joining the profession. The best and most noble profession is that of a schoolteacher and humanity must be made to understand this issue if we are to advance as a civilization. Amongst the very best salaries must be those of the teachers, period. It is absolutely heart breaking to see teachers being abused and disrespected; to see them having to beg for proper pay and recognition. When you see teachers on strike you must know that you are witnessing the failure of a society, a breakdown in responsibility upon the part of every parent and political leader. It is from the teacher that the young people obtain the most essential tools needed for a person to become a civilized human being. It is the teachers who are the engine, which fuels the minds of the young; the teachers are the scientists of the mind, they are the gods of of knowledge, the schools are the temples of wisdom

and civilization. It is in the schools that the mind of the young people that the mind is equipped to deal with reality. It is the teachers who hold the very future of our race in their hands, it is on their shoulders that the responsibility of success rests. It is the teachers who should be paid the highest salaries and not the bureaucrats and the legislators or the so-called "presidents" of our nations. Fifty percent of the problems in the world are due to the lack of a good education; the responsibility for the many problems and hardships in the world must be placed on every parent who ignores this most important issue. Furthermore, schools must be state of the art, must be beautiful and designed and built in such fashion as to be the most beautiful architectural successes of our civilization. The schools must be a place the young must long to be in; they must be the central centers of every town and city. The ONLY reason we do not have top-notch teachers is because the motivation factors for the real noble people who would love to be teachers has been absent; Quality salaries and prestige; these are the two motivation factors missing, these are the essentials. People want good education for their children but are not willing to pay for it. Therefore, irresponsible people must never be permitted to have children. End of discussion.

13. The Declaration of Individual Rights and the Constitution are absolute in authority limiting the power of the government not of the individual/citizen. The are intended to secure the freedoms and powers of the people (private individuals) not of the government. The constitution is a prescription of how government is to conduct itself not the citizens; it is not an authority for the government to maintain power over the people but a set of basic law to protect the people from the government. A government, which seeks to control every detail of a person's life, is a dictatorship in the making; it is a tyranny;

such a government is a monster. The United States of America is becoming a police state right under the nose of the lazy people who are too lazy to fight it; the US Government is out of control; it has fallen in the hands of the religious leaders and the Vatican which manipulates the world through their army of Jesuit priests. This Illuminati Manifesto is to serve as the last warning and the only chance humanity will have to fight for freedom; if you do not join the fight for true freedom as we had intended from the beginning when we created and fashioned the US and France, you and your bloodline will be tormented by what is to come. If you don't start voting Libertarian and vote every chance you have, especially for the next 100 years, we will wipe out two thirds of the world population; only our own and a few will be left standing.

14. **For the New Illuminati.** All those of you who wish to join us in the struggle for freedom now have a chance to establish your bloodline. Objectivism as set forth by our beloved Ayn Rand is the springboard. She was raised and educated by our best minds in order to establish and put forth our philosophy. There are a few issues she included in her works, which are her personal opinions, such as her views on women, sex and marriage etc. This is fine, we gave her liberty to put a personal touch on our philosophy in order that it may be accepted. For this reason her books are the second most read books on the planet. You should also understand that she was one of us, one of our greatest investments, we fashioned her for a special purpose and task; she was chosen because she had the mind and intelligence needed. Now it is time to set forth Practical Objectivism, meaning putting our philosophy into action. The senior members of the Order shall remain underground due to the sensitive nature of our organization and the nature of our actions and tactics. The new members must prove themselves

for 7-15 years before we reach out and pull them into the underground; but we will keep an eye on all those most active of the new Illuminati, we will watch over them like an Eagle watches over its young; we take care of our own. We are publishing this very abridged version of our Manifesto in order to give a chance to every person who are fed up with stagnation to join us and make a statement to the masses that we will not suffer or tolerate stagnation brought about by religion, socialism, communism and social democrats or religious republicans. You have the authority and moral right to take whatever action you deem appropriate to reach our Objective. Let this Manifesto serve as the absolute authority over every question you may have.

15.   **To the Young Illuminati.** All those of you who are young and wish to show your solidarity with us should have their left arm tattooed with the Illuminati Symbol, the Pyramid and the All Seeing Eye as is found on the dollar Bills, but have it made in color with the eye being blue and golden rays shining from the eye; the Pyramid itself should be of blue stones or golden ones. Let this symbol represent the fact that you accept and honor the Declaration of Individual Rights. In doing so you are recognized as a 1st ° (degree) Illuminati. All those who sympathize with us should do this as well. The tattoo should be made on the left arm, shoulder of just bellow the belly button. Also try to have Jewelry made with our symbols and make both the tattoo and Jewelry visible. Start your own Illuminati Club or activist cell and do what you must to help us further our cause in this Illuminist Revolution. Become a cell of the IRA, (Illuminati Liberation Army) and fight for freedom, for true freedom and justice.

16.   Illuminati are required and expected to be compassionate at all times towards those who are innocent victims. However, we

must never show compassion towards the immoral. For example, people who are oppressed and enslaved by tyrannical government are victims which we must try to help both in saving them from oppression and then to enlighten them philosophically. An Illuminist must never show compassion towards a tyrant of any kind; to do so is to commit moral treason. On moral issues and philosophical principles we can never compromise; our moral standard and our philosophy is absolute, pure and simple.

17. One of the new religions invented by Psychologists (possibly unknowingly) is the "humanitarian" ideal, the idea that being a humanitarian is good and honorable. This is a destructive force, which must be fought. Psychologists are not scientists and are not worthy of prestige; not until they start to apply the proven scientific method to the field of Psychology. Until such time Psychology and Psychologists must be ignored and stripped of authority. They set themselves up as gods, as experts on behaviorism without being able to prove any of their theories; they have become like the socialists of the world (like the Republicans and Democrats of America and Europe), they invent all sorts of theories which they cannot prove and when they are proven wrong they invent yet a new theory and so on and so forth. They are no different than religionists who keep inventing and re-inventing all kinds of doctrines. Psychologists have become amongst the worst of parasites within the intellectual realm.

18. There are thousands of people under the age of 15 whom are already in college.
Studies show that all these children come from very intelligent and genetically unique parents.

Sho Yano is such an example.

We urge intelligent mothers, whom have daughters whom do well in school, to seek out and keep track of these advanced people, and encourage them, as they grow older, to acquire sperm from one of such, and produce highly advanced offspring.

Sho Yano:

1. His score on the college-entrance SATs was 1,500 out of 1,600.

2. At age 9 he started college.

3. "Last fall, at Loyola University in Chicago, Sho, some 4 feet 4 inches tall, became the smallest man on campus with arguably the biggest IQ." CBS Correspondent Carol Marin

4. His IQ test scores—200—far above average, and that of a genius. His IQ was "off the chart"

5. Sho studies biology, music and composes astounding classical music.

6. "His grade on his first college composition was an A-. On his first chemistry exam, he scored 106 out of a possible 108."

7. "I think there are genetic factors from my parents. And my parents really brought me up well." Sho Yano

6. By the age of 2 Sho was writing.

7. By the age of 3, he was reading.

8. By the age of 4, he was playing classical music.

9. By the age of 5, he was composing his own music (29 songs). "I like classical music, nearly every composer of classical music. My favorite is Bach. But I don't like heavy metal."

Sho is the youngest in this area, but certainly no the only one.

As time goes by, other things regarding this genetic makeup and DNA structure will be revealed. However, we can only allow the media to reveal a little at a time. The religion factor is a major roadblock to our goals, and much of the data we have would be an absolute shock to most people. So, we have to baby-feed the masses, and when time comes, much of the research will be made public.

Sho is a byproduct of mixed marriage, of two different races. Most advanced children are.
Expect much more of this in the media in the coming future.

19. The Illuminati Order strongly disagrees with the Americans with Disabilities Act of 1990.

Civil rights laws cannot promote equal opportunity for all people by prohibiting discrimination against individuals with disabilities, because this violates the rights of the individual employers and businesses. Furthermore, the rights of the healthy individual are superior to the rights of the disabled. The healthy individual is a functioning member of society, and contributes to the betterment of society, while the disabled, on the other hand, is a burden.

Here is the **Illuminati Response to People's Without Disabilities** Act

Title I
Justice:
Prohibits government from interference with public and private employers from discriminating against qualified individuals with disabilities, because the disabled can never be as qualified as a non-disabled, and an employer has the right to hire the person/he/she/it sees most fit for the job, and the well being of her/his/its business.

Does not restrict questions that employers can ask job applicants about their disabilities;

Does not require employers to make reasonable accommodations to the known physical or mental limitations of otherwise qualified individuals with disabilities.
Government shall not pass laws which impose hardships on business, as long as the environment is not in danger of the actions of the business.

Title II

Does NOT require state and local governments to provide individuals with disabilities an equal opportunity to benefit from all of their programs, services, and activities at its own expense which is the expense of the whole of the people;

Does NOT directs state and local governments to follow specific architectural standards in the construction of new buildings and the alteration of existing ones, as this makes all government and business services and products more expensive, and a burden on society at large. No minority shall benefit at the expense of the majority. It is undemocratic otherwise.

Does NOT prohibit discrimination against individuals with disabilities in public transportation;

Title III

Does not prohibit discrimination against individuals with disabilities in public accommodations (i.e. restaurants, retail stores, hotels, movie theaters), as this violates the individual rights of the healthy and the business owners. The idea that disabled people somehow have a right to impose its needs and burdens on society at large is ridiculous and unjust.

Does NOT require public accommodations to follow specific architectural standards in the construction of new buildings and the alteration of existing ones;

Does NOT require public accommodations to remove barriers in existing buildings at the employer's expense, or the government.

Does not require commercial facilities (i.e. factories and warehouses) to comply with specific architectural standards in the construction of new buildings and the alteration of existing ones; and

Title IV

Does NOT require telephone carriers to enable individuals with hearing and speech disabilities to communicate with each other through third party communications assistants.

Title V

Requires the employers to provide reasonable compensation to a disabled person whom became disabled while performing one's duties as an employee of the employer.

Requires parents who give birth to disabled people to provide for all the needs of the disabled individual for as long as the disabled has the needs.

Requires that government to not provide any financial aids/welfare to the disabled, just because he/she is disabled. Society does not have any obligation to support, raise and feed disabled people.

Requires government to prohibit people from giving birth to severely disabled people if the parent(s) do not have the financial means to support such an individual for the rest of his/her life.

20. **Epicurean Pleasure & Sex Magic.** Many Illuminati practice Epicurean Pleasure. Epicurean pleasure is a lifestyle which many Illuminati have introduced to the public; the people who practice it are also known as "Swingers" a practice which has become more popular among the non-enlightened. Swingers are married couples and singles who seek others to play with sexually. To practice Epicurian Pleasure you must be STD-Free (meaning you must not have any sexually transmitted diseases). The rules for practicing Epicurean pleasure are simple: You start

your own circle of lovers who are either couples or singles and only bring others into your circle with the approval of the other members of the circle. You must also have available documentation proving that you and/or your spouse or lover does not have any STDs. To find other Illuminati or non-Illuminati Swingers visit *www.IlluminatiMatchMaker.Com* or Swingers.Com. (Now you know why President Clinton's wife did not divorce him; he did nothing wrong with Monica, it was perfectly alright and this is always alright amongst the Enlightened who practice Epicurean Pleasure) **Sex Magik.** Sex Magik is sexual intercourse between two or more Illuminati (or telepaths) who have developed their telepathic abilities. When two or more telepaths have intercourse and decide to establish a telepathic link they both reach orgasm simultaneously. However, those who are not in excellent health, because during a Sex Magik session the orgasm is amplified at least 5 times and lasts up to 2-3 minutes in some cases, must not practice Sex Magik. During a session the heartbeat can reach as high as 190 beats per minute. Furthermore, at least one of the participants should be a Master of the Craft (telepathic master) otherwise the sexual experience can lead to a heart attack or permanent mental damage. It is advisable that no less than 3 people are present during a Sex Magik session with the third being the observer to make sure everything is going well. If there are 3 participants there must be a forth as the observer. If at any time the face of one or more of the participants starts to turn blue the observer must have a bucket of ice water to throw over the person's face and break up the session. The best situation for Sex Magik is where at least one of the participants is very young (or both participants be Masters of the Craft). In addition, **never ever initiate Sex Magic while under the influence of any alcohol or any mind-altering substances.** To do so will cause both participants permanent mental damage and may even result in being put in a mental institution. If you train a young person in the Craft (telepathy) you must make sure she/he is mentally healthy, trustworthy and a person of good moral standing. We strongly recommend that you not engage in this practice until you are certain that you can control your emotions well and have advanced in the craft. If you have not practiced the craft at least 3 times a day for a period of no less than 3 years do not engage in Sex Magik at all. Sex Magik is also practiced by many pagans, Catholic priests and those in the leadership, Enlightened Freemasons, Kabbahlists and others belonging to various secret societies.

****

Telepathic Communications

Before we teach you the basics of telepathic Communications I need to address the subject of conscience and "free-will." The conscious mind is as follows. When a fetus is developing it has no conscience. As soon as it develops the senses such as hearing feeling seeing etc. it starts to become self aware. Without these senses the fetus cannot become self-aware and would be nothing but a comatose vegetable. As soon as it is born the senses are all turned on.

All senses are forms of communications and all senses utilize the exchange of energy of one form to another and so on and so forth. Take the light for example. The fetus does not become conscious of light until it experiences it. Our abilities of self-awareness are only possible due to our senses. In other words a blind and deaf person is not as conscious as one who is only blind but not deaf and likewise a deaf person is not as self-conscious as a normal human because it lacks the ability to experience sound, which is one of the components for consciousness. Let's suppose a baby is born blind and deaf and cannot feel, taste or smell anything. This baby would be less conscious than healthier ones (it would be vegetable-like).

What happens to conscious people? Do we have free will? Free will does not exist. A baby learns by trial and becomes more and more conscious as it learns. Free will is a contradiction in terms because one cannot choose anything without first having experienced and learnt by use of the senses. Without the senses one could not choose anything. One could argue that there are 10 roads leading to the same place and one must choose even though he or she has never seen those roads before. The choice cannot be made unless that person has prior knowledge of the Environment around and prior experience in life. So the choice would be a calculated risk knowing that there are possibilities of unknowns. The mind knows that there are unknowns only after the first experience of the use of the senses.

So instead of saying that we have free will we should say that we have an-acquired-free-will (ability to make calculated decisions would be more proper), more knowledge due to experience and experience due to our senses and all of our senses use different types of electrical communications. All chemical interaction is an exchange of information made possible by interaction of different types of matter, energy and compositions there of.

Now here are the basics for telepathic communications

1 Telepathic Communications is the ability to hear and transmit thoughts through quantum energy waves.

2 All beings can hear each other's thoughts.

3 If you can think you can hear your own thoughts.

How to use telepathic Communications

Find a partner who is willing to take this seriously because the first few months are like learning a new language with microscopic ears. Find a very quiet place. One of you and only one of you should speak the same word with your mind over and over and the listener should tell you what you said only when he or she is 1000 percent certain of the word which was heard. The transmitter should think to the listener instead of to oneself. It's like saying a hello to someone with your mind.

The listener will hear the word in a form of thought. It will seem like sporadic thought. These is all there is to it, but remember to concentrate.

Once you both learned you can invite a friend over and you too can practice by repeating the word popcorn? to your friend without telling him or her you are doing it or even mentioning Telepathic Communications. When two or more people repeat the same word or words to a newbie, the newbie will think the word popcorn is his or her own thought which you two, repeated, over and over to your guest. He or she will start to speak out loud about popcorn in one way or another.

Another way to practice is to try to finish the person's sentences with your mind. You will find that the person will eventually begin to finish his or her sentence with the words you transmitted. Another way of looking at telepathic Communications is what humans call this gut feeling. Yes, all telepathics can hear the thoughts of others as long as the thoughts are external, and not to oneself.

If you want to speak in secret with a friend or friends once you master telepathic transmission, turn on a TV or radio to a comfortable level so that the walls in the room vibrate slightly. All music and sound causes the atoms of walls to vibrate. This vibration will distort your transmission when it reaches the walls. Do not turn the TV or radio too loud it does not need to be so. As your telepathic abilities mature, you will be able to communicate over longer and longer distances.

Once you master telepathic Communications you too should be able to hold a conversation with your mouth on a totally different subject than your conversation you have telepathically.

NOTE: If you are having trouble getting started buy a talking board, IGNORE the booklet and instructions it comes with, and simply say out loud," I (or WE) wish to join the Illuminati", and one of the Grandmasters will hear your thoughts and respond.

Then ask a question and use the instruction for using the pointer. You may also place a YES and NO marker on the board for a yes or no answer. Once you have felt the Grandmaster move your hand via your mind telepathically, you are more ready to practice telepathic communications with a friend. By the way, you can also speak to birds and animals, but you may have to repeat the same word or words over and over to animals, until they can learn your intentions. When using telepathic communications, your FEELINGS are also transmitted via other wavelengths, so be honest, otherwise you will upset the grandmasters, and they will not help you. NEVER ever beg a Grandmaster for any favors, and never pray to them. They are people just/almost like you, with long range telepathic abilities. Nothing more.

Psychics and Clergy use telepathic communications to deceive people by invading their minds. A Psychic knows only what you know, and by asking you a question telepathically, you answer it unknowingly and this is how they are able to make you believe they have "psychic" powers. Preachers use a similar method by speaking to people telepathically in order to get them to give money or induce a high-sensation during a special service etc. The Catholic Clergy are the most advanced Telepathic Grandmasters, aside from the Illuminati. The Illuminati is now taking their powers away, because religion has outlived its purpose, and is backfiring on us. So, learn and master this as soon as possible.

Start with a partner of the opposite sex and both of you must be relaxed and sit close facing each other. You might want to begin by placing several objects between you. Then the transmitter should transmit the word or name of one of the objects without telling the receiver which one he or she is transmitting.

The receiver should point out which object he/she heard ONLY when he or she hears it over and over, as the transmitter keeps repeating it.

It is very, very important that both parties are very relaxed and comfortable and there must be no distractions in the room. A group of telepathic able people can control a unsuspecting subject and make him or her do anything if a enough effort is put into it. I cannot recommend you do this unless it is absolutely necessary.

It is imperative that all members learn telepathic communications as soon as possible as it is needed to further our cause, as well as yours happy future (but is is optional, however). Once you are successful, your partner and you will feel a warm sensation mixed in with happy feelings, as well as a chill. Don't freak out, this is normal and natural.

The other form of communication is telepathic imaging and or telekinetic ability. This form of telecommunication is more complicated but also very dangerous to teach someone who may misuse it easily even unknowingly. This one is like placing a cigarette lighter in the hands of a four-year-old and left alone in the House. Once you become a master of telepathic transmission one of the grandmasters will eventually teach you the rest. Don't worry he or she will find you.

You can also communicate with various animals, but only one way, since animals do not share our language and emotions. When you communicate telepathically, both thoughts and emotions get transmitted. The whole thing works at the quantum level, so it would be difficult to explain unless you have knowledge of physics, biology and electronics principles. As soon as scientists come up with measuring devices, which can measure quantum particles and quantum radio waves, telepathy will no longer be a mystery.

Good luck.

Part Two

We have many other websites; mostly secret ones where there are other forms of membership through invitation-only.

If you are not able to take a telepathic journey, go and buy a very HIGH quality "Talking Board" throw away the instructions and simply use the following instructions in order to interact with some of our Grand Masters who spend most of their free time intercepting telepaths who do not know they are telepaths.

Try to do most of you   however, as the
sun interferes with comr   e during the day
(but not always).

We have about 50,000 Grand Masters who do nothing but play with
people's minds; they are just as addicted to the craft as others are to
sports or TV. However, these are very responsible people and of very
high integrity within our organization.

Because many of our people sell their own version of the talking
board we cannot make any recommendations as it would be unkind for
me to harm another member's business or livelihood.

Here is what you do once you obtained your Talking Board:

1. Find a VERY quite place to set up the telepathic session.
2. Make sure you are very relaxed.
3. Do not drink any alcohol before, during or after the session.
4. Make sure the room is dark except for 3-7 candles.
5. Make sure you are in a place where there will be no interruptions.
6. Say in you mind outwardly as if you are talking with your mind to
   someone, "Masters of Light, please hear me!" Repeat this several
   times while you hold your index and middle finger on the pointer
   very gently.
7. The Grandmaster(s) will attempt to establish a mind to mind link
   and will move the pointer through you.
8. Once you have experienced the first telepathic interaction say, "I
   am a new disciple, please enlighten me."

From this point onward, ask whatever you wish but to not expect to
be welcomed right away as the Grandmaster who responds to you will
form a Triad with other telepaths to focus and locate you and they will

probe you through your sessions. If you are dishonest in any way they will see right through it, so don't start any sessions under false pretenses because that will cause you serious problems; we do not take lightly those who are dishonest with us. If you joined us sincerely and wish to be one of us you must know that what we have to offer is something you could never buy with money because it is priceless.

Furthermore, we do not expect anything from anyone other than honesty, but if you make a promise and you do not keep it you will end up paying a very high price for it; so once you develop a relationship with a Grandmaster or a triad, do not make any promises even if you are sure you can keep them.

Once you feel comfortable with telepathic sessions try to recruit others to our philosophy and once you have done so, invite him/her to do a session with you using the talking board.

BTW, the instructions, which come with the taking, board should all be ignored except the ones, which deal with the technical use of the board. All that stuff about fire, wind, water, god(s) or goddesses, all that is a smoke screen so ignore that junk; those are instructions for the general public who wish to play around with us unknowingly.

How far the Grandmasters will take you I cannot say, it is up to them. After you have finished several sessions you will notice that your telepathic abilities have improved and you will notice this as soon as you enter a room where there are a group of people; you will start to sense their thoughts and especially their feelings. Feelings and thoughts are inseparable, in other words nobody will be able to hide their feelings from you and once you know their feelings you will know much of their thoughts. You will start to feel strange so do not think outwardly from this point onward when you are not intentionally speaking to someone telepathically. The reason is, people who are very familiar with your voice may pick up your thoughts so clearly that their minds will interpret the thoughts and cause the person to think they actually heard you say what you only thought.

Telepathic communications are much like a data packet sent via a wire to another computer which the receiving computer will identify by searching a database for the identifying marker which comes with the packet. Once you learn to master telepathy you will start to notice other telepathic abilities. I will not tell you what they are, but I am telling you that you will experience other things simply because I do not want you to think you are loosing your mind or that what you are experiencing is in any way "supernatural."

Later on you should try experimenting with an unsuspecting subject by transmitting a short message telepathically repeating it many times over and over until you see a response. Keep practicing this but be careful not to use offensive messages, because you never know when you are around another Illuminati or a telepathically advanced person. Most women are 70% more telepathic than men, so use a female as a test subject.

Make sure you are well rested and never do a session right after you wake up.

That is all I can give you. If you follow these instructions your life will change for the better, if you become a devoted active member.

Illuminati Lodges

Any person wishing to establish an Illuminati Lodge must follow these instructions.

1. Each Illuminati Lodge and all of its property must be privately owned by one and only one individual. It must not be incorporated nor registered with any governmental body. Furthermore, each lodge should maintained a well-designed website.

2. The Lodge must not have the word Illuminati on it. It must be named something illusive or remain unmarked.

3. Each lodge must have its own charter and rules, and must comply with all the goals of our Philosophy, and agendas.

4. Each lodge must be of high quality facility, comfortable and prepared to have social gatherings only of the Illuminati members, and no outsiders are to ever be allowed inside.

5. Have at least one conference room sound proofed and shielded with sheet metal behind the drywall, or inside wall coatings. This is where all sensitive issues are to be discussed, when there is a need for such meetings, which require secrecy. Play a radio or TV a very low volume inside this room if you engage in telepathic sessions/conversations.

6. Each Lodge must have set goals, and must achieve whatever goals and agendas set forth and all members are required to participate in one form or another. When certain goals are accomplished, new ones must be instated.

7.   Each lodge and its members is responsible for the production of jewelry with the Illuminati symbols, such as the pyramid with the all seeing eye (which represents the Illuminati Order), in the forms of rings, necklaces, bracelets, etc. which must be made available for purchase by Illuminati and sympathizers. Furthermore, Lodges must provide its members with identification symbols for their vehicles, at a price, if such members wish to mark their vehicles so that Illuminati police officers may know them and act accordingly.

8.   Each Lodge member is obligated to contribute financially to the costs of maintaining/establishing a lodge, but the contributions must have no minimum or maximum limit. Furthermore, all costs involved in running and maintaining the lodge must be made available to all members in the lodge.

9.   Each lodge must have certain tests required of new recruits to prove themselves, and upon acceptance into the Order, by means of a Lodge initiation, each new recruit must agree to have the pyramid with the all seeing eye tattooed under his right arm just bellow the arm pit. The lodge Grand Chancellor (which is the official title of any lodge founder) should establish the tests. Initial one time membership fee of no less and no more than $95 US is required.

10. Each lodge owner must have a secret set policy by which to take any action needed to neutralize any traitor who betrays the Order. You know full well what the punishment for treason is…

11. Freemasons should place the Illuminati Symbol on their building so that other Illuminati may know that the particular Masonic lodge belongs to Enlightened Masons, only if it is safe

to do so in your region. Not all Masons are Illuminati, and we do not encourage Illuminati to join the Masonic Order.

12. A group of senior members of the lodge of 13 members or more may bring into question the Grand Chancellor, and vote to remove him from office, and require all of the property be transferred to another chosen Grand Chancellor. Grand Chancellors must be of the highest integrity, but this is required of all Illuminati.

13. The Founder of the Lodge and the first 12 members are to comprise the Lodge Council

14. Each   nati Symbol tattooed under
     his/he   npit in transparent ink. A
     secon   apital) should be tattooed
     behind   r in transparent ink. Each
     membe   ), have the letter i tattooed
     with in   ...y under ultra violet light),
     somewh   ... on his/her body.

****

Illuminati Clubs
How to Start an Illuminati Order Club at Your School
Every school is different in terms of how they handle student-run clubs. Some schools make the process of starting a club very simple, while others have layer upon layer of bureaucratic requirements that must be carefully fulfilled. So, one of the first steps to take is to find out what your school requires in order to set up an officially recognized club. Do you need to have a faculty advisor? A club constitution? A list

of officers? A minimum number of members? Contact the student affairs office at your school and find out what is required.

While it is possible to have a club without official recognition, the one thing you can't do without is club members. Do you know of any others on your campus that has expressed interest in Objectivism and Ayn Rand? It is important that the Club is named The Illuminati Order Club (if possible/safe to do so) and that the charter for the club is the promotion of Objectivism and Illuminism. Do NOT mention any of the agendas in the public charter of the club, or in any public-publications.

Not sure whether to start a club?
Students usually have little difficulty starting a club. However, Objectivism is often misunderstood or distorted by others, and you may occasionally encounter bewilderment and even hostility from other students and university officials. In addition, red-tape procedures and other delays typical of a university/School bureaucracy may impede your progress.

Don't feel that you must be an expert on Illuminism or Objectivism in order to start a club. Students who start Objectivist clubs are in the process of learning about Objectivism themselves. Don't feel that you must be able to answer all questions and objections from other students or from faculty members. Clubs are a forum for learning about Illuminism and Objectivism, not teaching it.

Are you unsure that there is sufficient interest at your school to make an ongoing club possible? One way to "test the waters" is by putting up "teaser" posters, with provocative quotes from Ayn Rand and a copy of "The Declaration of Individual Rights, with your name and contact information at the bottom. This allows you to locate other students who might be interested in a club without having to commit to anything or having to plan an organizational meeting. As an added benefit, you'll be exposing Ayn Rand's name and ideas to students who may not have ever heard of Objectivism. Furthermore, The Illuminati Order organization name has allot of weight, and this too might help get students involved. Try to recruit none-theists only. Do not permit religionists of any kind to join.

Don't feel that you must commit to a full-blown club. Do what you are selfishly motivated to do, given your time and circumstances. Even if you simply establish an informal group of several students who meet somewhat regularly to discuss Objectivism and Illuminism, you will have created a value.

Your club should include some form of initiation rituals, which should be designed by the club owner(s) and the rituals must remain a secret.

Each member should also be given a serious test, to prove their seriousness and willingness to join the club.

Design a Membership Card, which should contain ONLY the Illuminati Order symbol in full color and visible, and obtain some transparent ink which is only visible under Ultra-Violet Light. Have a stamp made at your local office supply store, with the Illuminati Symbol. Use the invisible ink to stamp the back of each membership card with the Illuminati Symbol. Also obtain an alphabetical stamp to write the member's name in invisible ink as well. Then laminate the membership card and give it to the new member.

Each Member is to have a Illuminati Symbol tattooed under his/her left arm just bellow the armpit.

A second tattoo of the letter **i** (not capital) should be tattooed behind the top of the left or right ear in invisible ink.

Each member should, only if they choose to, have the letter i tattooed with invisible ink (**visible only under ultra violet light**), somewhere on his/her body.

****

Take Action-The Duties Of all Illuminati

We seek fervently to establish "the happiness of the human race." Some day the Order of the Illuminati will be seen as a "blessing to the world." However, in order to achieve our objectives we are obligated to do whatever it takes. The Illuminati Order is not for the faint hearted the emotional and the weak. The following are the duties of all Illuminati. All Illuminati are expected to take part and abide by these directives in whole or in part. Clearly they do not apply to all, but to each one to who is able to participate based on their environment and skills.

1. Take any necessary action within your power to eliminate religion, religious leaders, weather it be through character assassination or other means.

2. Recruit, recruit and recruit. Give each person you wish to recruit into the order a copy "The Virtue of Selfishness" by Ayn Rand and/or a copy of The Illuminati Manifesto. This is the test bed, the basic test for any potential candidate to join the Order. If the response is very positive, use whatever means in your best judgement.

3. Give a copy of the above said book(s) to politicians, school teachers, judges, police officers (especially ranking ones), business owners, board of directors of corporations, college

professors, college officials and any person of the media especially those in management.

4. If you are a Judge, recruit those in your field and set up your own secret lodge and circle of Illuminati. Furthermore, until the New World Order is in place, do all within your power to make rulings always in favor of the Illuminati in your courtroom. If your defendant(s) is Illuminati/Freemason, rule in their favor if no technical legal issues stand in the way.

5. If you are a police officer, always let Illuminati off the hook, and seek to establish a circle of Illuminati Officers.

6. If you are a writer, write articles and columns for newspaper and Illuminati websites promoting our philosophy (Objectivism) and Enlightenment. Do not use the word Illuminati in any article, which is written for the main newspapers, but use the words Enlightened and Enlightenment.

7. If you are a business owner, hire Illuminati whenever possible, and recruit other business owners and people in high positions.

8. Use bribery, blackmail and all other means to accomplish goals whenever needed. Remember, none Illuminati (with few exceptions as written in the Illuminati guidelines) are the enemy.

9. If you are a politician in a high position, or position of notoriety, use whatever means you can to promote the Illuminati agenda, our organizations and recruit recruit recruit.

10. Business owners and people in high positions should always seek out and grand favors to Illuminati/Mason-owned businesses, Order members and the like. If you are in position to grant contracts, use that power to favor possible recruit's organizations/companies.

11. If you are a college professor, make it a requirement that all your students read the above said book(s), and other books of AR, such as Atlas Shrugged, and make efforts to recruit students into the Order.

12. If you are in a position of law enforcement, such as the FBI or CIA, Mossad, MI5/6 or any other agency in power, seek to and help destroy our enemies using the powers you have. Seek dirt on leaders of religious organizations, political leaders whom are socialists and/or communists, and use any other means to destroy our enemy. Make sure you too recruit and form a secret circle with and of your peers, and take all needed action to recruit and help other Illuminati.

13. If you are in any other powerful capacity, use whatever powers you have to further the goals and cause of The Illuminati Order.

14. Whatever country you are in, start lodges and/or Illuminati clubs and recruit as much as possible.

15. Support all Libertarian parties, and/or start a party, a Illuminati Republican Party, or a Libertarian Republican party in your state/country and promote it as much as possible.

16. Never admit to any outsider that you are an Illuminist if you hold a high/sensitive position. Don't deny or admit it. Just say something like, may be I am may be I am not.

17. Invite all non-theists to join us and advertise our websites.

18. If you are a high school teacher or person in authority, teach children about Objectivism and make them read the above said book, at the very least and seek to recruit board of education officials as much as possible.

19. **Translate and publish this Illuminati Manifesto your native language.**

20. **Translate and distribute The Declaration of Individual Rights to students at universities and Colleges as well as High Schools.**

****

Illuminati Guidelines

I. Rules/Guidelines of the Illuminati
I.I. Thou shall not endanger the Illuminati by informing, directly or by implication, outsiders of its tactics or plans.

I.II. Thou shall not diminish the power of the Illuminati by affecting the positive work of other members, or by any other means.

I.III. Thou shall not change the Order of the Illuminati guidelines or deviate from agendas.

I.IV. Thou shall not divulge secrets of the Illuminati to outsiders, nor divulge confidential secrets of individual's houses and/or Lodges to any person.

I.V. Thou shall not disobey reasonable, direct orders of the Grand Chancellor if you are a member of the a Lodge.

I.VI. Thou shall not abuse any influence over the lower tiers of the Illuminati, except where this will lead to an increase in the power of the Illuminati as a whole.

The Order of the Illuminati

II. Structure:
The Illuminati is hierarchically structured, and it is expected that Members will try to improve their position within the Illuminati. All Illuminati Organizations are to function as independent Cells worldwide. Nobody shall make any reference to the Areopagites, nor shall anyone inquire of their identity. They have their own special way of contacting and getting the attention of those they wish to communicate with. The Illuminati is divided into six Elements, which are in turn under the sole authority of the Areopagites (The Illuminati Council). Each Element has different duties in function but all must strive hard to accomplish our objectives. The Elements will be revealed to the worthy through secret invitation only.

III. Illuminati Structure:
The Areopagites are the sole authority of the Illuminati Order and until such time as our Vision is set in reality, until our New World Order is set up, the Illuminati Order shall not be devolved. The Areopagites deal only indirectly with world players to accomplish our goals. However, every Illuminati is to work hard in his/her capacity for the advancement and empowerment of our Organization. Keep in mind

that these titles are not gender specific. They are neutral in nature in regards to gender.

Official Illuminati Titles and Functions:

Areopagite(s)-Council (Self explanatory)

Venerable Master-Heads of state/nations. Title is for life, even after the Venerable Master is no longer in the position of government, and Authority of a Venerable Master within the Order is for lifetime as well.

Charter Master-Judges. They may, from time to time, ask Grand Chancellors to make changes to Illuminati Charters and place orders of execution upon a Lodge. The Lodge Council must vote to approve such orders for execution or not.

Master of Light (Owner of The Lamp)- Also known as "Lord of Dominion" (Initiators, such as Adam Weishaupt, Solomon Tulbure, Osiris and Diane of York) These are chosen by the Areopagites and initiated at their request. The duty of the Masters of Light is to insinuate/initiate the Order every 300 years, shall it become dormant, after which the Master of Light is free to seek his/her own goals, and remain an activist and militant Illuminati if she/he chooses to do so.

Grand Chancellor(s)-Lodge Owners
Vice Grand Chancellor-College Club Owners/Presidents (Directly under the authority of Grand Chancellors, and above)

Light Barer-Every other Illuminati

IV. Special Requirements

All Illuminati are required and expected to educate themselves continually, and keep up to date with scientific advancements and political situations worldwide.

****

Telepathic Journey

We realize that new members whom have not yet had a chance to fully explore their telepathic abilities may feel a urgent need to utilize this ability, at least to authenticate a curiosity of a sense which still lays in mystery.

Therefore, we have arranged with some of our members for you to have an opportunity to engage in a telepathic Journey. So, if you are interested, what you need to do is spend a few months in Waukesha, WI, if you are in the US. We have not agreed upon other lodges to undertake new initiates in other parts of the globe, simply because it is very risky, especially with new members whom have yet to prove themselves and their loyalty to the Order. The traditional way to initiate new recruits is through lodges, but since we have an urgency at hand to recruit new members, this site was approved.

In case you are wondering, we have 31-35 million members world wide, and our analysts found that now there are over 700 million new potential candidates.

Now, for those of you whom wish to experience one of the most thrilling experiences of your life and are able to do so, here is what you need to do.

Our Waukesha Masters of the Craft have agreed to receive new initiates under the following conditions:

1. You go to Waukesha, whenever you wish.

2. You will hang out there in the only FEW places to hang out, in the center of Downtown Waukesha. There is a certain Restaurant where you will eat, and a certain club you need to hang out at least 3 hours a day.

3. When you go there, bring very casual clothing, and make use of the library.

4. Do not go there under false pretenses, as our Telepathic Masters are god-like in their abilities, and they will probe you before you ever realize.

5. Do not speak with anyone there about the reasons you are there nor make up false stories. You are there simply to get away for a while, that is all.

6. Once you have been screened, you will be approached by the least likely people, as far as looks and appearance are concerned and in some very unusual ways. Take nothing there for granted and do not underestimate anyone. You are not dealing with amateurs; in fact, you will be shocked to say the least, in a pleasant way.

7. Expect your experience there to be very strange to say the least and know this, while you are there your thoughts will be proved and heard by just about anyone and everyone there in that town. No outsider knows who is one of us and who is not. Let's just say, we own that town.
Waukesha is a very small town, very peaceful, charming has a very nice library and is one of the 72 US Telepathic Journey recruiting areas. Once again, be prepared to spend 3 months there. **It may take much less**, but it may not. Never ever repeat to anyone what you experience there and once you leave there, you will know for sure if you have passed the tests or not, if not, you will have to try another year.

Those of you whom are from another country, you should seek an Illuminati website in your own country. It is up to the Grandmasters there to publish a Journey place for new recruits. We have also provided instructions for you to experiment and develop your telepathic abilities on your own and a Telepathic Journey is not an essential requirement for joining the Illuminati Order any longer.

* *

The Masonic-Illuminati Connection

We know that there are many (hundreds) of stories out there about the connection between the Illuminati Order and Freemasonry; therefore let's set the record straight. Reason being, there are many, even amongst the Worshipful Masters who know better yet still teach false origins of the Illuminati. First of all, The Illuminati is not about spiritual enlightenment, but rather the Enlightenment of man through the use of reason and mastery of the sciences.

The Illuminati Order was founded by a group of 13 friends in 1701, whom were all Atheists, Freethinkers and Deists. They wanted to find a way to establish a secret society that would establish a world government free from religion, racism and nationalism. The founders worked hard to infiltrate the Masonic Order which was at the time and time immemorial an Illuminist secret society and because within the Masonic brotherhood they could secretly recruit people whom were already in high positions and whom could be trusted, to certain degrees. There is absolutely no truth in connecting the Illuminati Order with any kind of mysticism what so ever.

The Enlightened Ones are men and women of reason whom revere the power of the human mind and the establishment of a purely secular society. Ayn Rand was our spoke person whom was charged with establishing our philosophy in an articulate fashion. This could not have been done early on, due to the religious nature of governments and society, and the most barbaric and savage minds of the majority of the population.

Now, let's touch on something, which is of out most importance. In ancient times, the Egyptians practiced what is known as telepathy. This was passed down through various secret fraternities, including Freemasonry. The Roman secret societies mastered this practice, and found that establishing a triad of master telepaths, they could transmit thoughts to any unsuspecting (persons whom did not know what telepathy was and how it works) subject, so powerful and disturbing, that the individual would think it is a mystical or godly/angel calling. By using this method, they were able to establish spiritual leaders whom would later do their biding and control the population via religions etc.

Telepathy is an ability all humans poses, but it takes a long time to master, but it is not a mystery. Many animals poses and use this ability, as well as birds and fish etc. Telepathy was used by Bishops, Jesuits and Nights whom joined the Masonic Brotherhood, to play around with other lower rank Masons, and they experimented with many of them causing them great harm. Telepathy is used by most Catholic priests to transmit thoughts to a congregation, to get them to donate money. The unsuspecting lay person thinks the thoughts are a communiqué from god or someone from the heavenly realms, and so they feel inclined to donate money. We mention this, so that all Illuminati are well aware of this and keep their minds on guard at all time.

I would recommend that you read "Fire In The Minds of Men" for a good understanding of this issue. But be warned that the book is not 100% accurate, in fact it is about 30% incorrect. Nevertheless, it is a worthy read. Furthermore, our agents have done a great job of spreading all kinds of conspiracy theories out there, that our organization is safer from persecution. The Church no longer has the power to harm us, and we have agents in most of the Church's secret organizations. Many of the Bishops and Nights are our agents, and help our cause

Now, as far as the Masonic-Illuminati connection is concerned, Masonry was originally an Illuminist secret order spanning thousands of years. The Jesuits infiltrated our society and turned it into a mixture of occultist and religious soup of mambo jumbo. Today, some 34% of all the highest ranking members of the Masonic order are in fact Illuminati, but do not expect to get any of our people to admit it since we are still fighting the Jesuits who seek world domination on behalf of the Vatican.

Many amongst the Illuminati consider most Masons 1St° Illuminati simply because we have yet to find any Masons who do not accept and agree with The Declaration of Individual Rights.

Furthermore, the goal of our Organization is the same as that of the Masonic Order; the main difference lies in how we reach it and the question of the supernatural. We also categorically reject the way Freemasonry treats the female gender.

The Jesuits, Masons and Illuminati share many secrets which we all agree not to make public knowledge because it is too dangerous to do so with the current state of the world.

All Masons are welcome to join us but due to your oath you will never be able to advance higher than a 2nd° unless one of our people within the Masonic order brings you up. There are many inner circles within the many realms of Freemasonry, which work to enlighten Masons who are active in the realm of politics and show a high degree of respect for individual rights, freedom and justice.

We absolutely reject irrationality of any sort, which means we reject any form of religion with the exception of Deism, which is not a religion at all in our opinion. We are Illuminists, the original Bavarian Illuminati and our organization was formed in 1701 and advanced by our beloved Adam, may he rest in peace.

All those who accept the Declaration of Individual Rights are recognized as 1st° Illuminati
Second degree Illuminati must accept the Illuminati Constitution as the guiding light for the establishment of The Golden Dawn.

To advance to the 3rd° you must accept the Prime Directives, which are set forth as a temporary measure in order to prepare the future for the formation and revelation of the Golden Dawn.

Much of the information about us found in the public realm is garbage, it is produced by fanatical Christians and especially the Jesuits who went to great lengths to invent all forms of occults in our name in order to discredit us.

Illuminati are Atheists, Agnostics, Deists and even some Pagans and Buddhists. Our main objection as far as religion is concerned is the need to eliminate all destructive forces and our focus is on Islam, Judaism and Christianity; these are religions, which represent the worst of evil in all of human history. Other New Age and Pagan religions is not of great concern to us as they do not get involved in politics nor are they necessarily evil for all intents and purposes. We will deal with them through education in the distant future.

Our policy is to never harm a Mason because we share the same vision and we never sought to destroy each other; in fact on many occasions we work together especially in the fight against the socialists and communists. This is all that needs to be said on this subject publicly.

****

The Illuminati 13 Degrees

The 13 °s of the Illuminati Order reformulated and re-instated in recently are mainly symbolic since initiation into the Order is by personal choice for the most part.

1st °　All who accept the Declaration of Individual Rights of the Illuminati Order.

2nd °　All who accept the Illuminati Constitution as the guiding light for the establishment of The Golden Dawn.

3rd °　All who accept the the Prime Directives, which are set forth as a temporary measure in order to prepare the future for the formation and revelation of the Golden Dawn.

4th °　All Grand Chancellors and Lodge Council members.

5th ° All activists and IRA fighters (Illuminati Republican Army cells and cell members).

6th ° Secret Invite only.

7th ° Secret Invite only.

8th ° Grandmasters. Initiators and Insinuators and Masters of the Craft. Invite only.

9th ° Secret Invite only.

10th ° Secret Invite only.

11th ° Secret Specially appointed by the Circle of Light.

12th ° Secret Invite only.

13th° Secret Specially Appointed by the Illuminati Council.

Notes

✳✳

Special Notes

Essential reading list.

1.   The Fountainhead
2.   "The Illuminati Manifesto" by Solomon Tulbure

      2. Atlas Shrugged

      3. "Philosophy: Who Needs It" in Philosophy: Who Needs It

      4. "Philosophy and Sense of Life" in The Romantic Manifesto

3.   "Lord Satan" by Solomon Tulbure

      5. "For the New Intellectual" in For the New Intellectual

4.   5.5 "Christianity Exposed" by Solomon Tulbure

      6. "Introduction" and "The Objectivist Ethics" in The Virtue of Selfishness

      7. "The Metaphysical Versus the Man-Made" in Philosophy: Who Needs It

      8. "Causality Versus Duty" in Philosophy: Who Needs It

5.   8.8 "Islam" By Solomon Tulbure

      9. "The Ethics of Emergencies" in The Virtue of Selfishness

      10. "The 'Conflicts' of Men's Interests" in The Virtue of Selfishness

      11. "Doesn't Life Require Compromise?" in The Virtue of Selfishness

12. "How does One Lead a Rational Life in an Irrational Society?" in The Virtue of Selfishness

13. "The Cult of Moral Grayness" in The Virtue of Selfishness

14. "Man's Rights" in The Virtue of Selfishness

15. "The Nature of Government" in The Virtue of Selfishness

16. "What is Capitalism?" in Capitalism: The Unknown Ideal

17. "'Extremism,' or The Art of Smearing" in Capitalism: The Unknown Ideal

18. "The Roots of War" in Capitalism: The Unknown Ideal

19. "Conservatism: An Obituary" in Capitalism: The Unknown Ideal

20. "Racism" in The Virtue of Selfishness

21. "The Cashing-in: The Student 'Rebellion'" in Capitalism: The Unknown Ideal

22. "The Anti-Industrial Revolution" in Return of the Primitive:The Anti-Industrial Revolution

23. "The Psycho-Epistemology of Art" in The Romantic Manifesto

24. "Art and Sense of Life" in The Romantic Manifesto

25. Objectivism: The Philosophy of Ayn Rand by Leonard Peikoff

6.   Other Articles and Essays published on www.AuthorsDen.Com by Solomon Tulbure and other Illuminati.

Essential Websites

www.ObjectivistCenter.Org
www.libertarian.org
www.DumbLaws.Com
www.OneWorldOrder.Org
www.ChristianityExposed.Com
www.IlluminatiMatchmaker.Com For those of you seeking lovers and friends to play with.
www.TheIlluminatiOrder.Com
www.infidels.org
www.FFRF.Org
www.Swingers.com for those of you seeking lovers and friends to play with.
www.AuthorsDen.Com for those of you wishing to publish Essays, Articles and other materials.
www.iUniverse.Com for those who wish to self-publish books and Essays.

Those of you who establish Illuminati websites for your countries or regions should publish them on Yahoo Groups and also start a Yahoo Group for the Illuminati Order in your city or Country.

＊＊＊

The following is an insert of my own which has nothing to do with the manifesto.

The Law of Language

By Solomon Tulbure

Every so many years men and women of the mind come onto the arena of human existence, which improve the facts of life by innovating and inventing. Such people are profound thinkers, analytical persons whom often times become famous for their inventions or contributions to humanity. Sadly enough, such people are hardly ever appreciated for their innovations, for the product of their minds, while they are still alive. Nevertheless, I too feel that I have something to contribute to the future of humanity, and even if I do not get credit for my work while I am still alive, I have decided to publish my work, the work of my reason, my mind's intellect, not because people like me seek to be admired or adored, unlike most people, but because thinking, for people of the mind, is pleasurable; using our minds is fun; educating ourselves is entertainment. My contribution to our future is The Law of Language. In introducing this law, I shall, in this document, concentrate on the Law of Language, as it should be applied to the English language, or rather the English language re-designed scientifically. By applying the scientific method to any endeavor we are able to advance our knowledge or improve our life and existence; this, however, simply means that we are conquering nature itself. Like Einstein, I have thought a great deal about the nature of language, linguistics and its inner workings. Having been born in Romania, into a society whose language is somewhat superior to the English, I feel I have a lot to contribute to this subject. I have lived in the US since the age of 12, and even now, no matter how hard I try, the English language, while it is one of the best languages in the world in terms of integrity and power to convey meanings and thoughts, it is also one of the worst, in that it is poorly designed; wait, no it is not designed at all, it has no fundamental structure nor any linguistic standard. English is not the only one suffering from such, as most if not all languages are still in their barbaric states. Language, being one of the most important tools of our existence, should be simple and easy to learn and use. I find it utterly ridiculous that children in the US have "spelling" contests, and most people here never master their own language. The reason the English language is so ridiculously hard, is because the American and English educational system, like many others, suffer from a lack of intellectual integrity on the part of the educators. Simply taking some word someone else has invented and teaching it to our young is not an act of intellectual integrity. Scientific methods must be applied to all aspects of life, if humanity is to advance. The way current English is causes the minds of children to waste a large amount of their memory on a language, which is ridiculously and needlessly complex. But to apply a scientific method to anything, we need to establish laws to the method, not laws that are contrived through our whims, but objective, and logical laws and these laws can only be realized through the use of reason. No god or spirit is going to appear to us and hand these laws to us. It is our duty and obligation, therefore, to utilize our minds fully, at all times no exceptions. Here are the Laws of Language.

The Laws of Language

1. A letter of the alphabet must have only one sound.
2. A word may not contain redundant letters.
3. No letter may be substituted for another.
4. A word may only have one single and absolute meaning and may only convey one concept.
5. All words, therefore, are (and must be) pronounced exactly as they are written, and/or written exactly as they are pronounced.

The Benefits of a Scientifically Designed Language

Before I continue with a demonstration of applied language law, let me try to give you a glimpse at the benefits of such a perfected linguistic system. First, I shall make a blank statement; that is that the benefits are unlimited and priceless. Communications is the most fundamental need of existence for our species and as such, all miscommunications amongst humans will disappear. Say, for example, we were to place a book of American laws in front of a 12 year old, or even a 18 year old, he/she would have no idea what the laws mean, simply because the language used is like another language entirely. There is this so called "intellectual English" language, which acts like another language entirely. The idea that two or more words, with the same meaning, but completely different spelling and pronunciation are accepted in any society, is ridiculous in that it is intellectual robbery. It is intellectual depravation. No college level English or language should exist. College should be a place of advanced learning. Language is a basic tool and all should be able to learn it all in the early education years. Here is a short listing of benefits to be enjoyed from the adaptation of the Law of Language and the redesigning of the English language.

1. Communications among people would be perfected.
2. The human ability to store knowledge would increase at least 50%, because words would be unique, and concepts simple and easy to grasp, due to the fact that all words would be pronounced as written and written as pronounced.
3. Humans would have a greater ability to be more intelligent and advanced because there would be much more extra space in memory. More space means more room for storing knowledge, which in turn gives our brain more information to work with.

4. Less trees would have to be cut, since the Laws of Language forces words to occupy less space on paper, as well as reduce the need for saying in 20 words what can be said in 3.
5. Energy would be conserved, because computers and electronics would not need to write redundant letters and words.
6. Computer storage space would increase.
7. All children who can speak and knows the alphabet automatically know how to spell the words as well, because each letter in every word would be pronounced the same as in the alphabet.
8. There are many more to list, but I don't have time to write volumes on the subject...

The Meaning of Words

Addressing the issue of the meaning of words is beyond the scope of my introduction to the Law of Language. This is an issue which the educators need to deal with, a problem they need to fix. All words with the same meaning should be filtered and only one of them is to remain in the language and dictionary. It is essential, to a civilized society, to have a clear and concise language. I shall hope educators will undertake this task.

0-595-21055-4

Printed in the United States
3974

9 780595 210558